the Science of Surfing

A SURFSIDE GIRLS GUIDE TO THE OCEAN

KIM DWINELL

Top Shelf PRODUCTIONS

"In the end,

we will conserve only what we love,

we will love only what we understand, and we

will understand only what we are taught."

– Baba Dioum,

Senegalese environmentalist

Thanks so much to my editor Chris Staros for understanding what I wanted to do in this book and supporting it. Also, big thanks to Dr. Chris Lowe of the California State University, Long Beach Shark Lab for checking my science.

THE SCIENCE OF SURFING: A SURFSIDE GIRLS GUIDE TO THE OCEAN © 2021 Kim Dwinell.

Editor-in-Chief: Chris Staros.
Edited by Chris Staros & Zac Boone.
Designed by Nate Widick.
Typeface design by Dakota Swanson.
Surfside Girls logo design by Chris Ross.

Published by Top Shelf Productions, an imprint of IDW Publishing, a division of Idea and Design Works, LLC. Offices: Top Shelf Productions, c/o Idea & Design Works, LLC, 2765 Truxtun Road, San Diego, CA 92106. Top Shelf Productions®, the Top Shelf logo, Idea and Design Works®, and the IDW logo are registered trademarks of Idea and Design Works, LLC. All Rights Reserved. With the exception of small excerpts of artwork used for review purposes, none of the contents of this publication may be reprinted without the permission of IDW Publishing. IDW Publishing does not read or accept unsolicited submissions of ideas, stories, or artwork.

Visit our online catalog at www.topshelfcomix.com.

ISBN 978-1-60309-494-8

Printed in Korea.

25 24 23 22 21   1 2 3 4 5

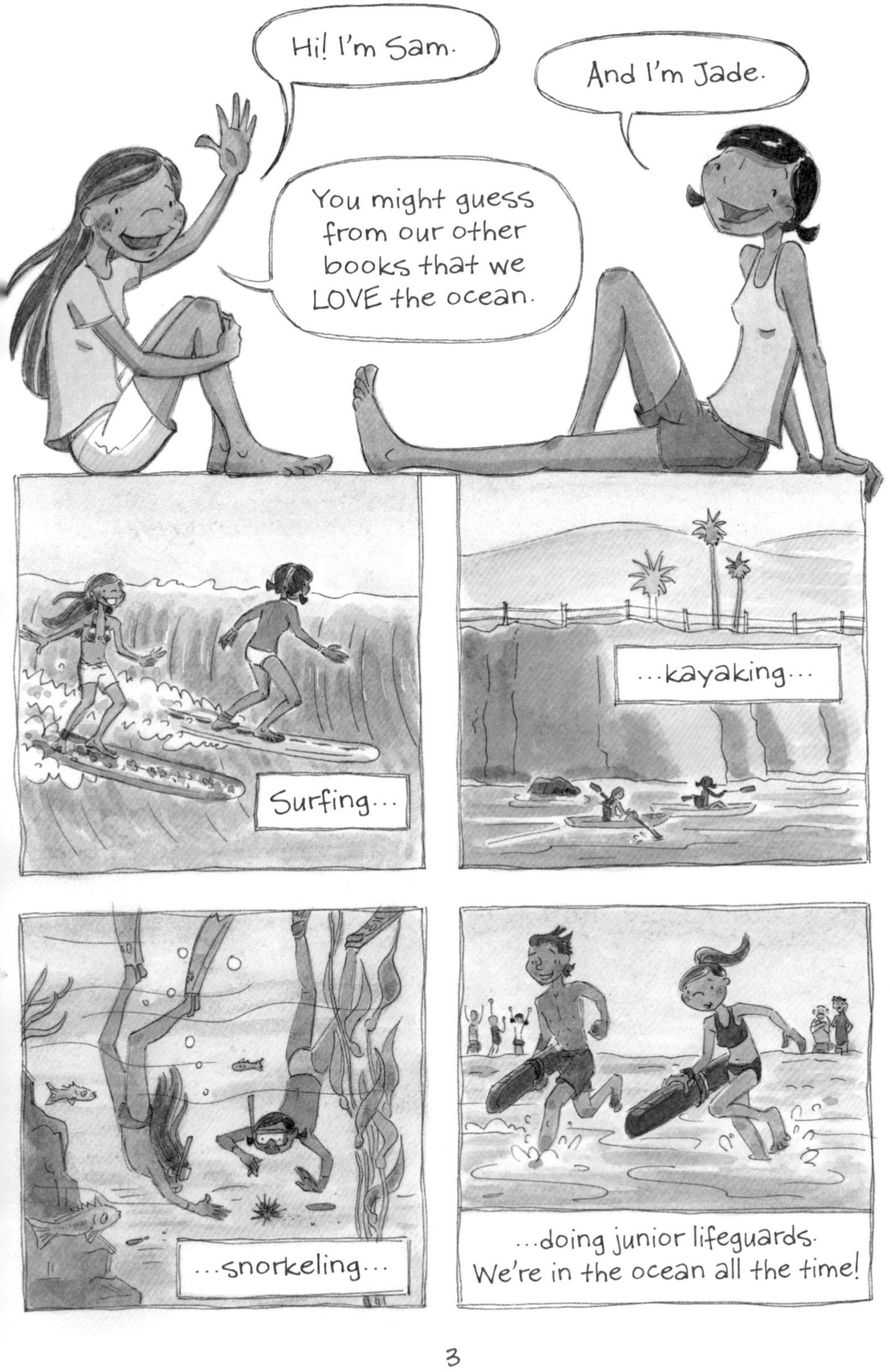
Hi! I'm Sam.
And I'm Jade.
You might guess from our other books that we LOVE the ocean.
Surfing...
...kayaking...
...snorkeling...
...doing junior lifeguards. We're in the ocean all the time!

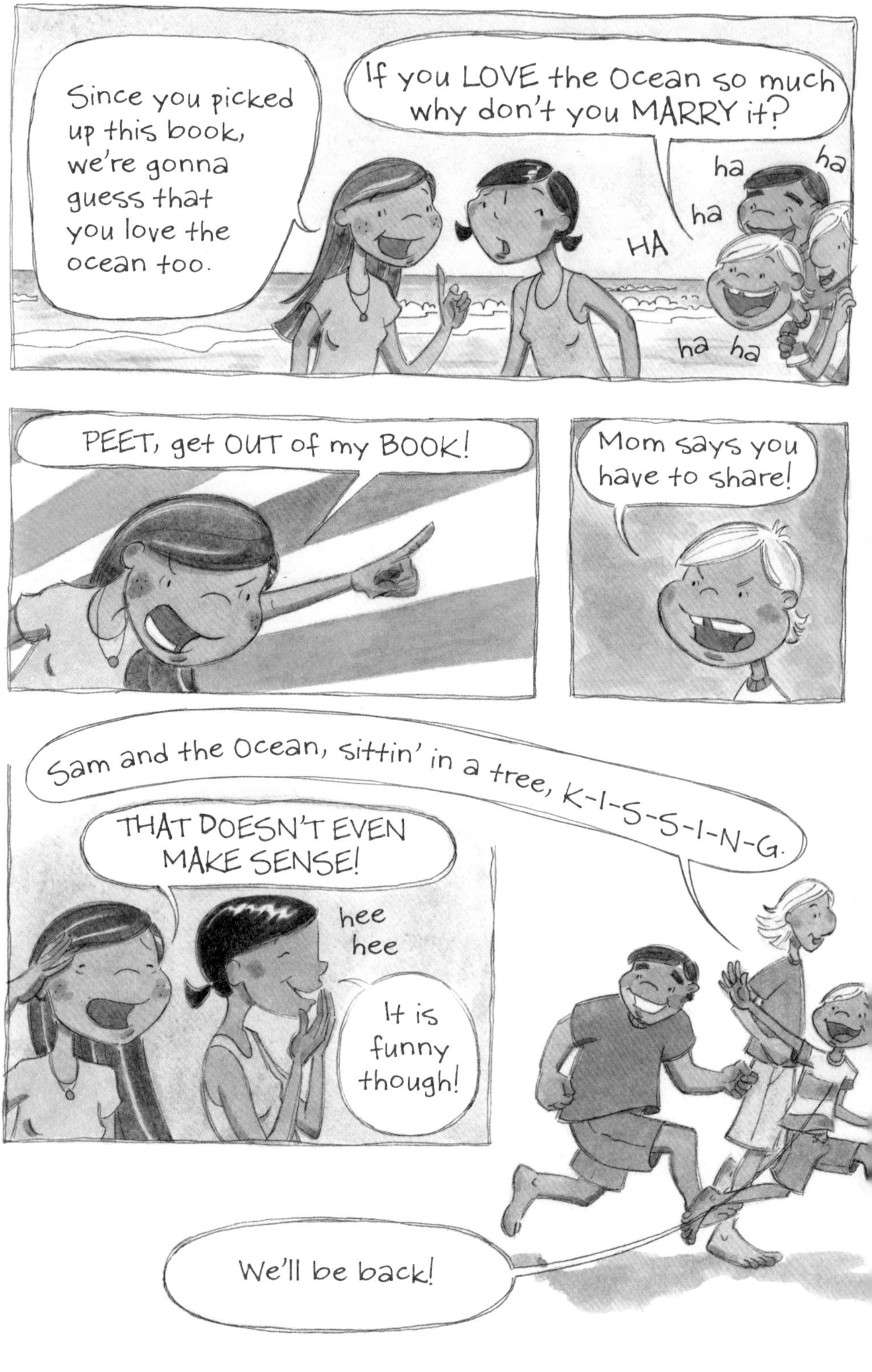
Since you picked up this book, we're gonna guess that you love the ocean too.
If you LOVE the Ocean so much why don't you MARRY it?
ha ha ha HA ha ha
PEET, get OUT of my BOOK!
Mom says you have to share!
Sam and the Ocean, sittin' in a tree, K-I-S-S-I-N-G.
THAT DOESN'T EVEN MAKE SENSE!
hee hee
It is funny though!
We'll be back!

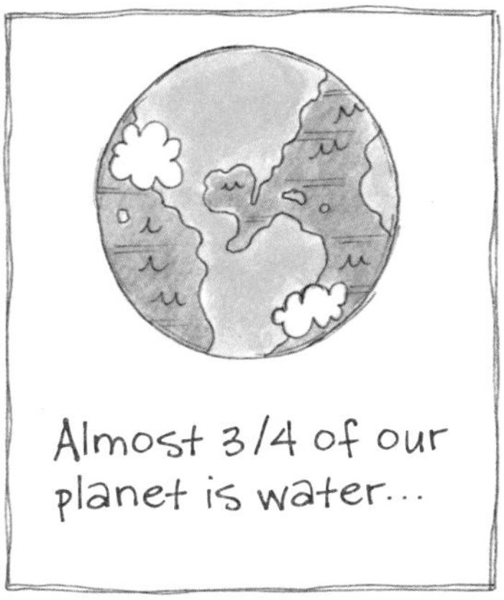
Almost 3/4 of our planet is water...

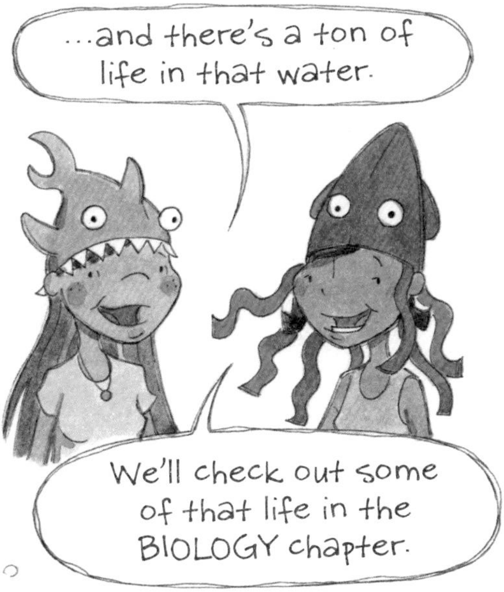
...and there's a ton of life in that water.
We'll check out some of that life in the BIOLOGY chapter.

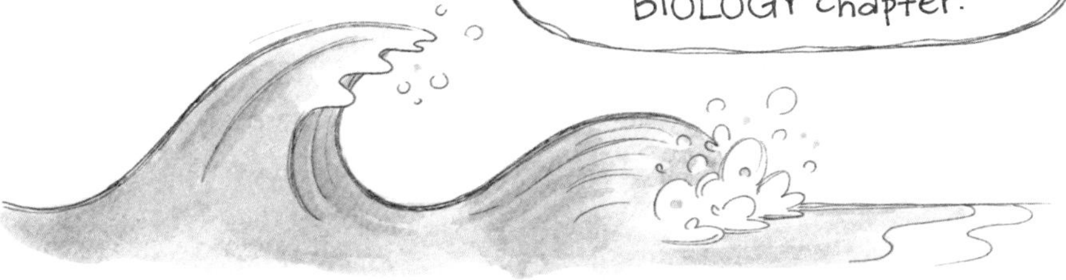

Did you ever wonder why there are waves?
Find out what makes a wave in the PHYSICS chapter.

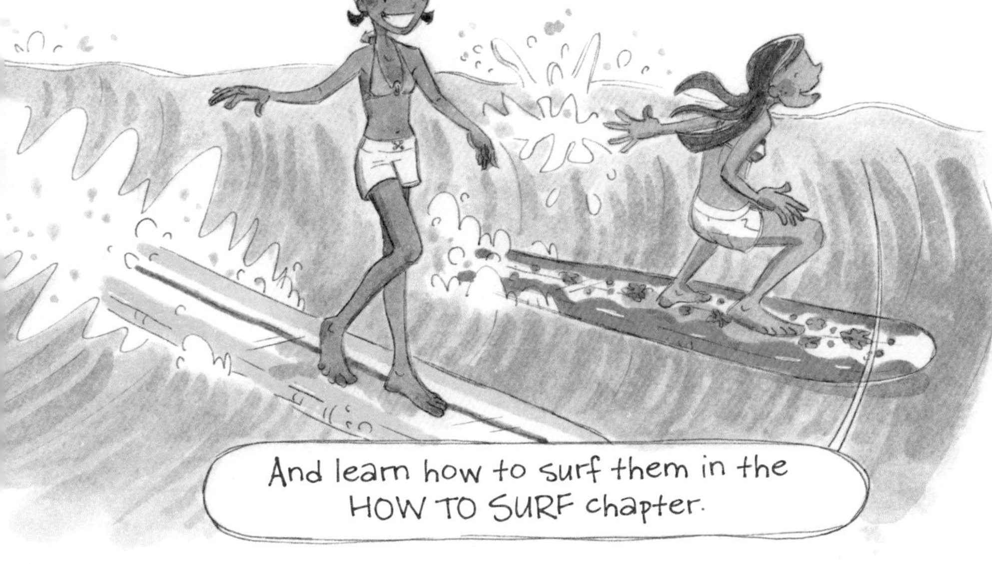
And learn how to surf them in the HOW TO SURF chapter.

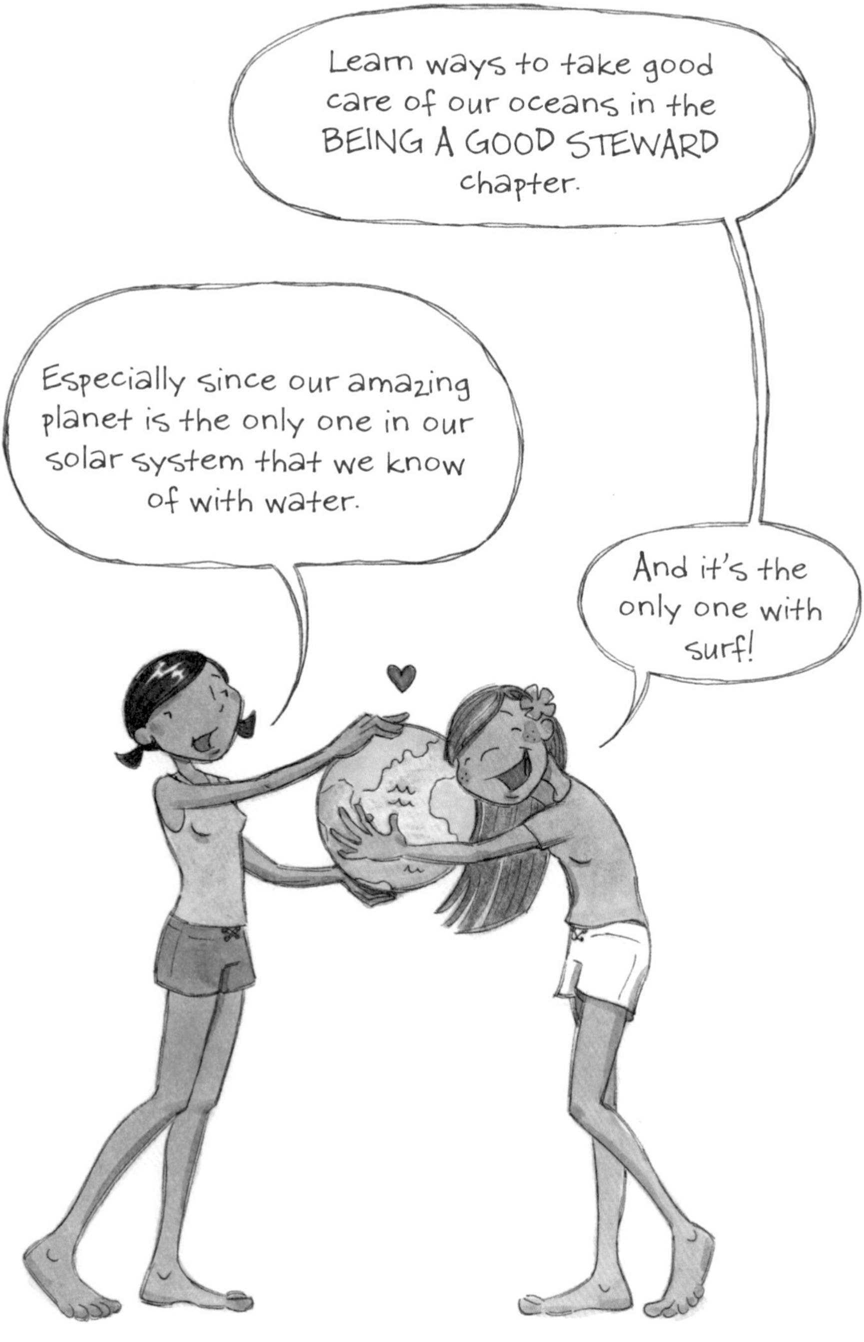
Learn ways to take good care of our oceans in the BEING A GOOD STEWARD chapter.
Especially since our amazing planet is the only one in our solar system that we know of with water.
And it's the only one with surf!

TABLE of CONTENTS

INTRODUCTION 3

1. PHYSICS 9

    Tides 10

    Moon Cycles 17

    Waves 25

    Weather 35

2. BIOLOGY 43

    On the Beach 44

    In Between – The Intertidal Zone 54

    In the Water – Subtidal 59

3. STRANGE OCEAN PHENOMENA 75

4. HOW TO SURF 81

5. BEING A GOOD STEWARD 107

Chapter 1

PHYSICS

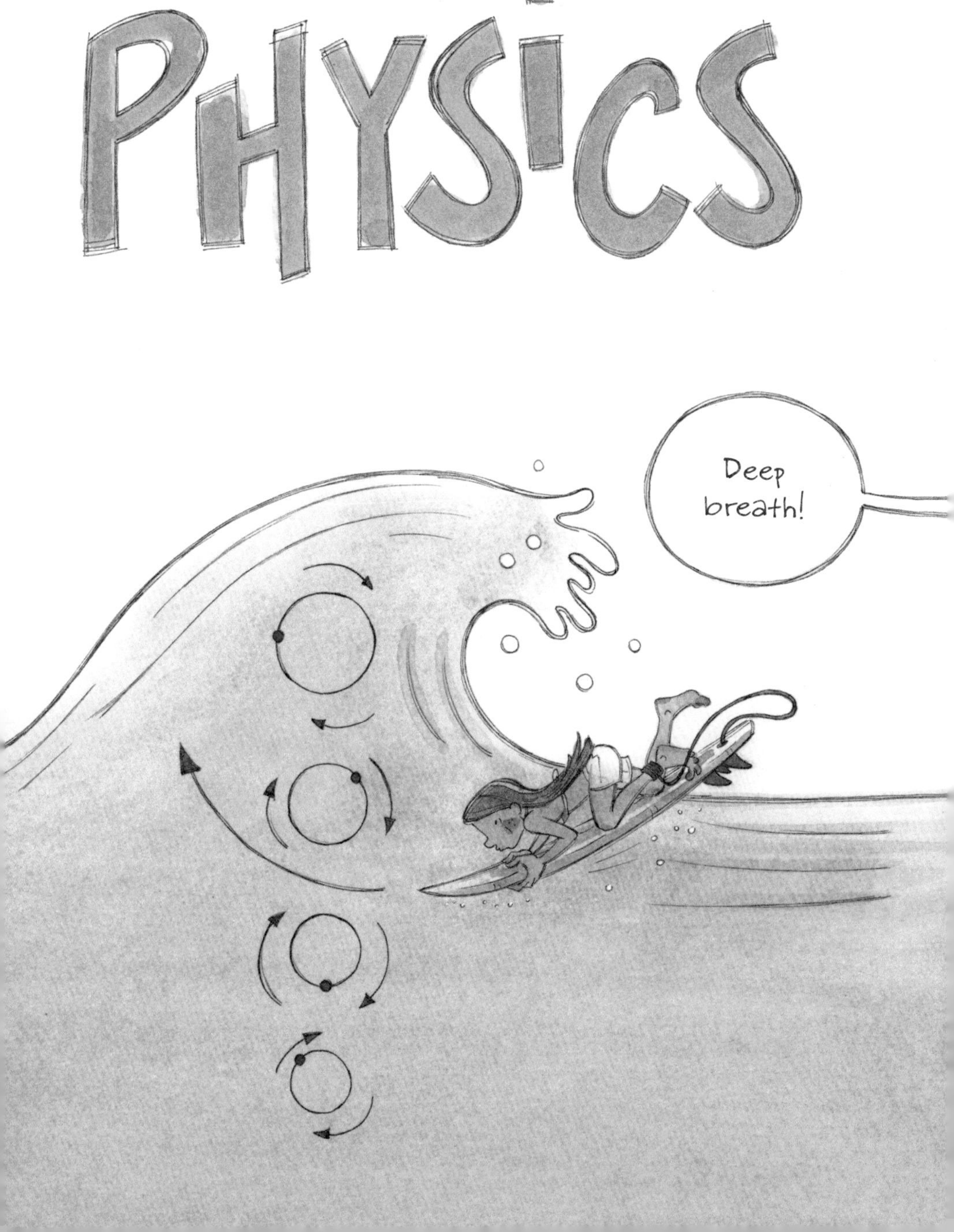
Deep breath!

Tides

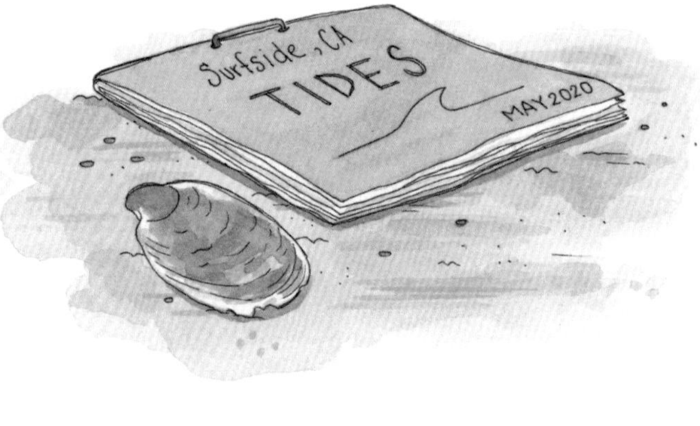
Surfside, CA
TIDES
MAY 2020

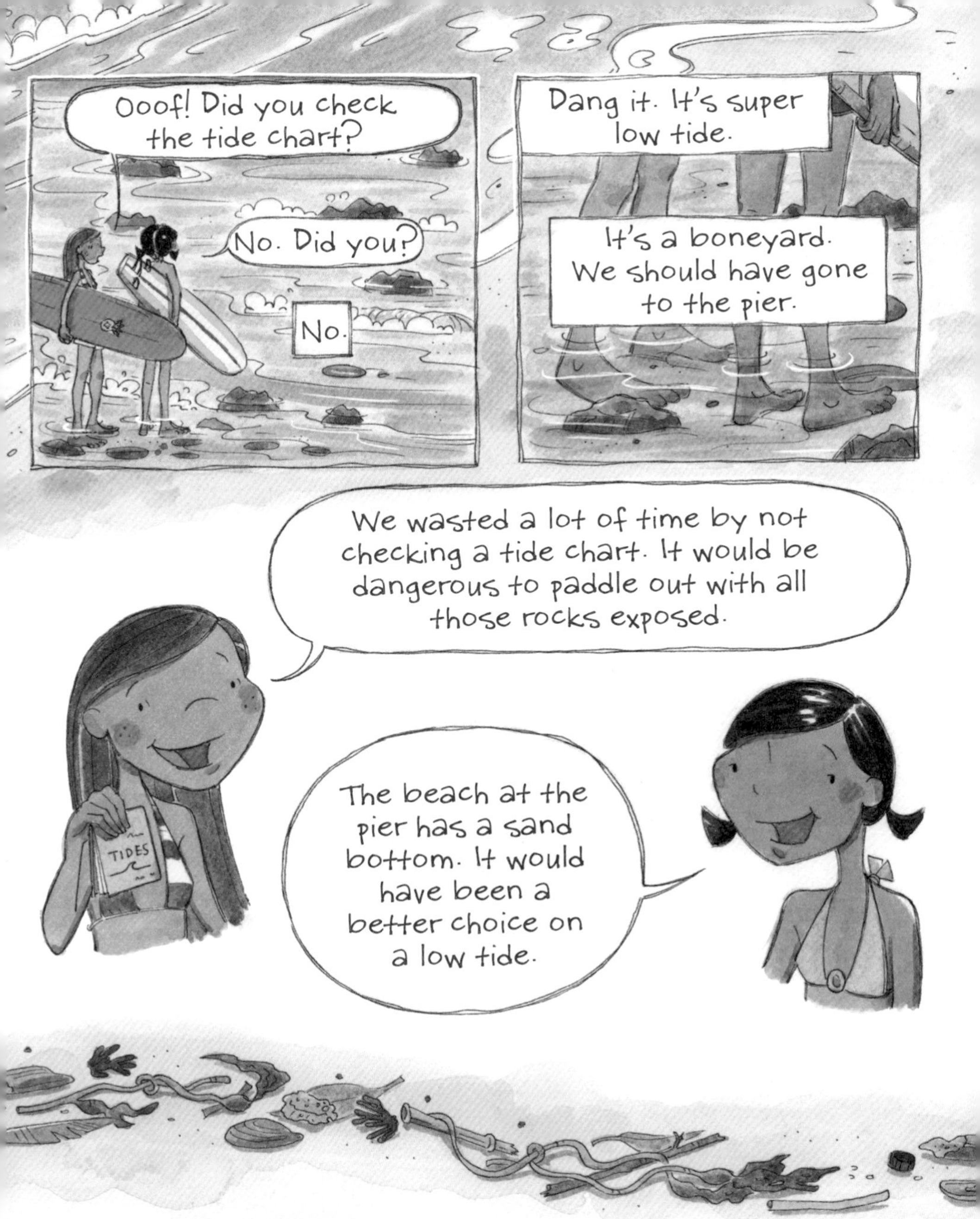
Ooof! Did you check the tide chart?
No. Did you?
No.
Dang it. It's super low tide.
It's a boneyard. We should have gone to the pier.
We wasted a lot of time by not checking a tide chart. It would be dangerous to paddle out with all those rocks exposed.
TIDES
The beach at the pier has a sand bottom. It would have been a better choice on a low tide.

So what is a TIDE CHART? And why is it so important to a surfer?

Most beaches have

two high tides

and

two low tides

per day.

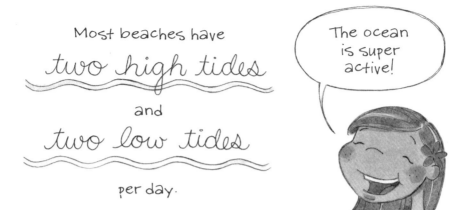

The ocean is super active!

Someone was smart enough to organize the times for these tides into a chart!

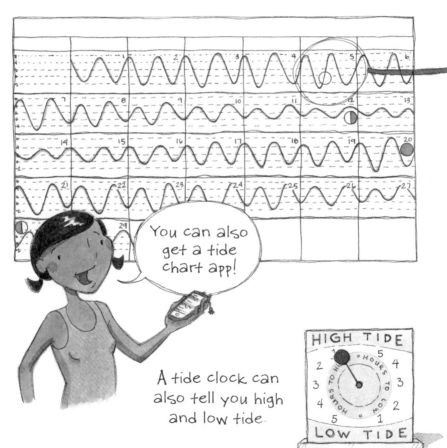

You can also get a tide chart app!

A tide clock can also tell you high and low tide.

HIGH TIDE

HOURS TO HIGH • HOURS TO LOW

LOW TIDE

HERE'S HOW A TIDE CHART WORKS:

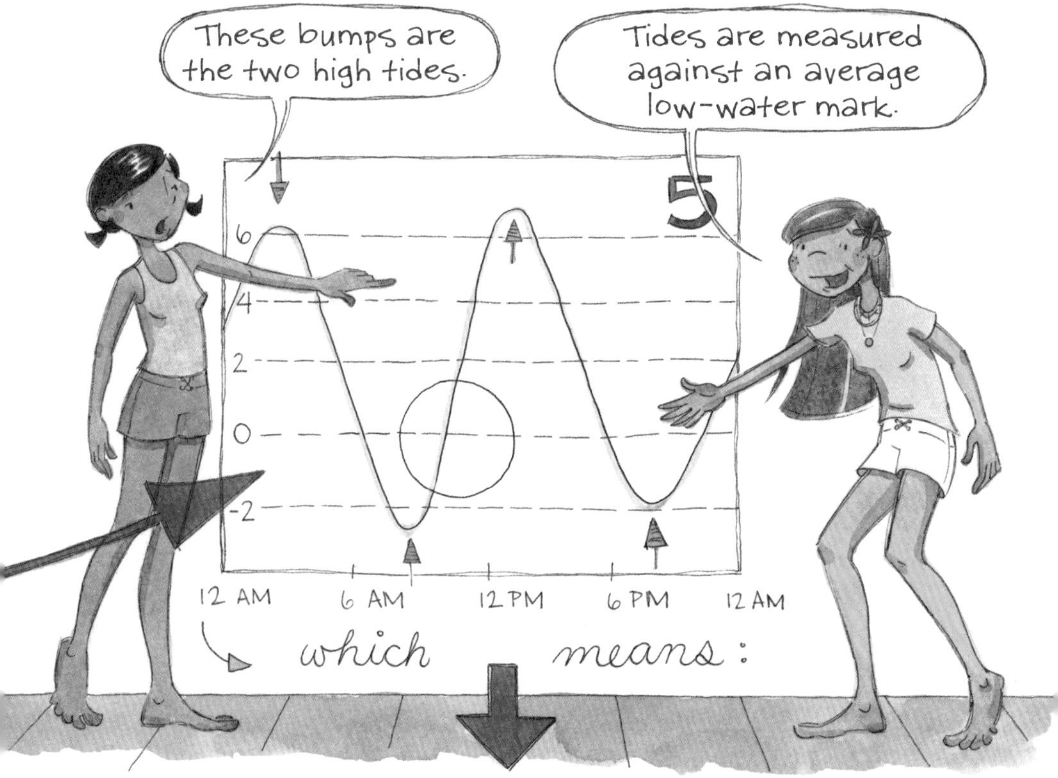
These bumps are the two high tides.
Tides are measured against an average low-water mark.
5
6
4
2
0
-2
12 AM
6 AM
12 PM
6 PM
12 AM
which means:

HIGH:	1:00 AM,	6 feet
LOW:	7:00 AM,	-2.5 feet
HIGH:	1:02 PM,	7 feet
LOW:	7:05 PM,	-2 feet

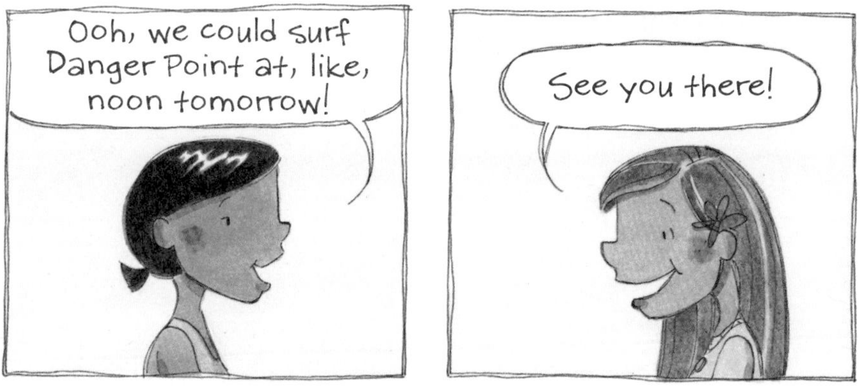
Ooh, we could surf Danger Point at, like, noon tomorrow!
See you there!

Tide charts are *local* to each area. Every beach works best on a specific tide. Surfers talk about tides all the time, because tides really affect the surf!

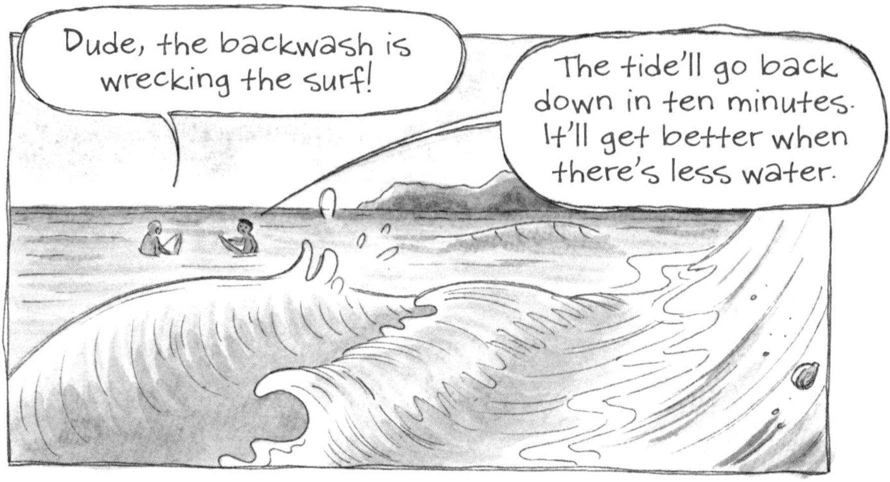
Dude, the backwash is wrecking the surf!
The tide'll go back down in ten minutes. It'll get better when there's less water.

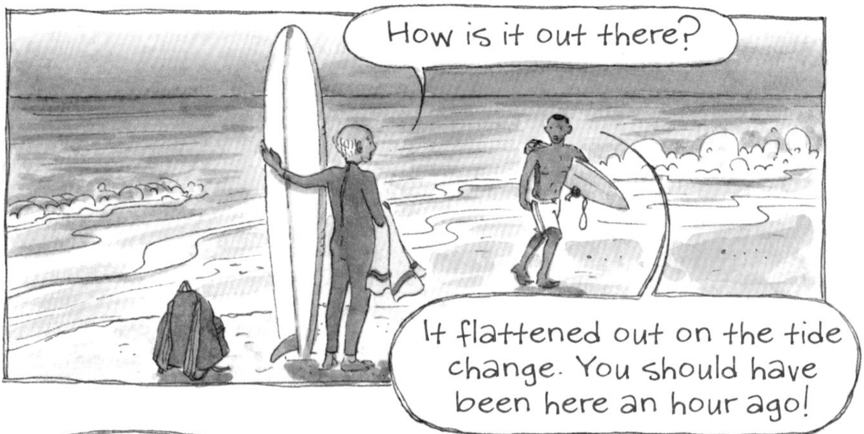
How is it out there?
It flattened out on the tide change. You should have been here an hour ago!

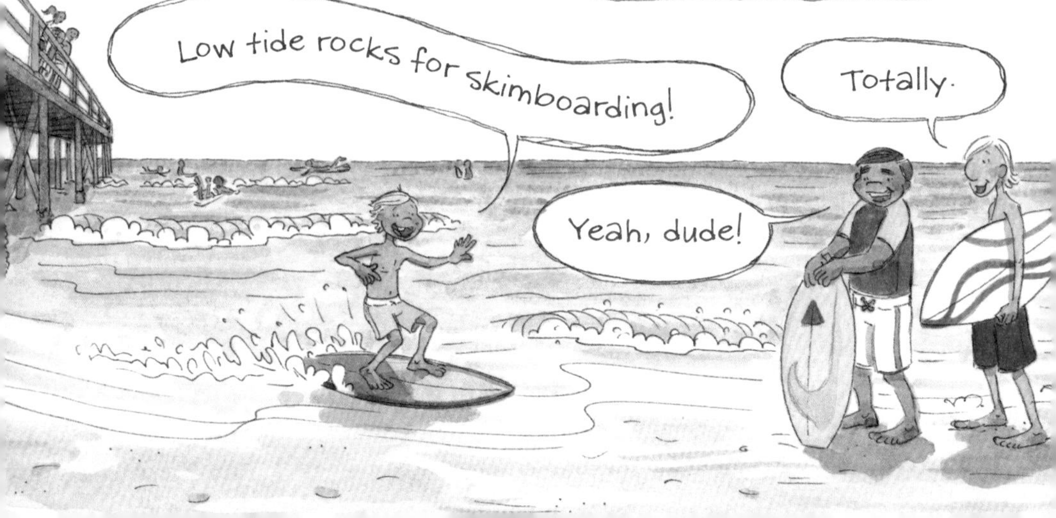
Low tide rocks for skimboarding!
Yeah, dude!
Totally.

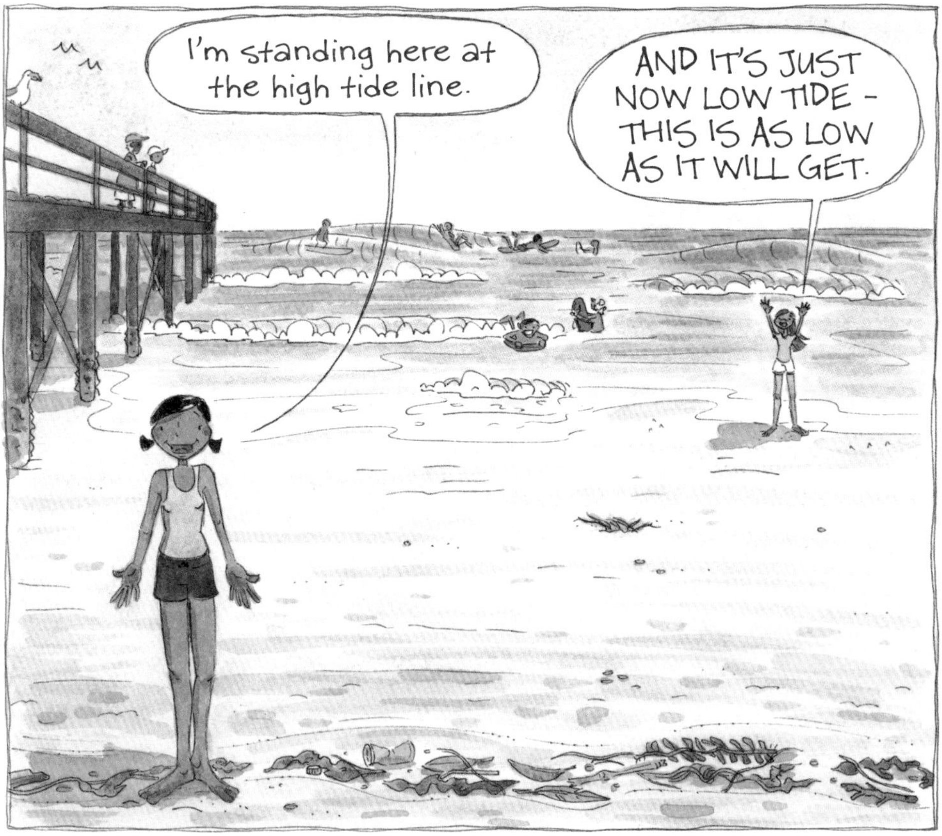
I'm standing here at the high tide line.
AND IT'S JUST NOW LOW TIDE - THIS IS AS LOW AS IT WILL GET.

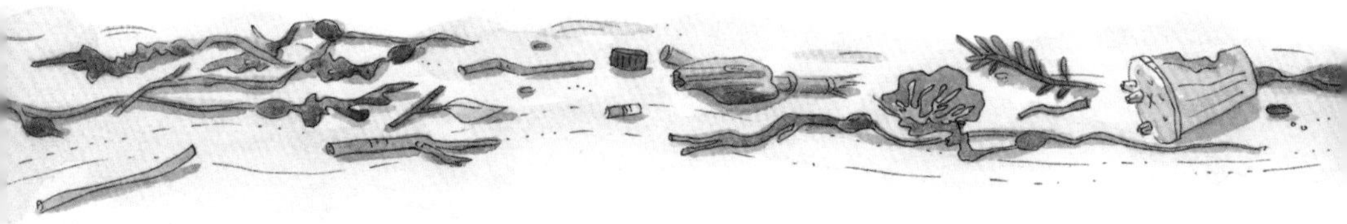

THE HIGH TIDE LINE is easy to spot -

it's a line on the sand where all the seaweed and bits of wood and - sadly - sometimes trash gets pushed up, and then the tide turns and the ocean starts going back down.

TRY THIS! Find the high tide line at your beach.

There's a cool surfing beach in County Clare, Ireland, in a town called Lahinch. Lahinch has two high tides and two low tides a day, like most places, but the difference between high and low tide is

15 FEET!

FACT: The difference between high and low tide is called TIDAL RANGE.

At low tide this is a long, flat beach with a seawall and steps up to the road.

At high tide, the ocean is halfway up the seawall and there's no beach at all! And a storm will push waves right up onto the street, and sometimes onto the shops!

Here, don't leave yer towel on the sand!

Moon Cycles

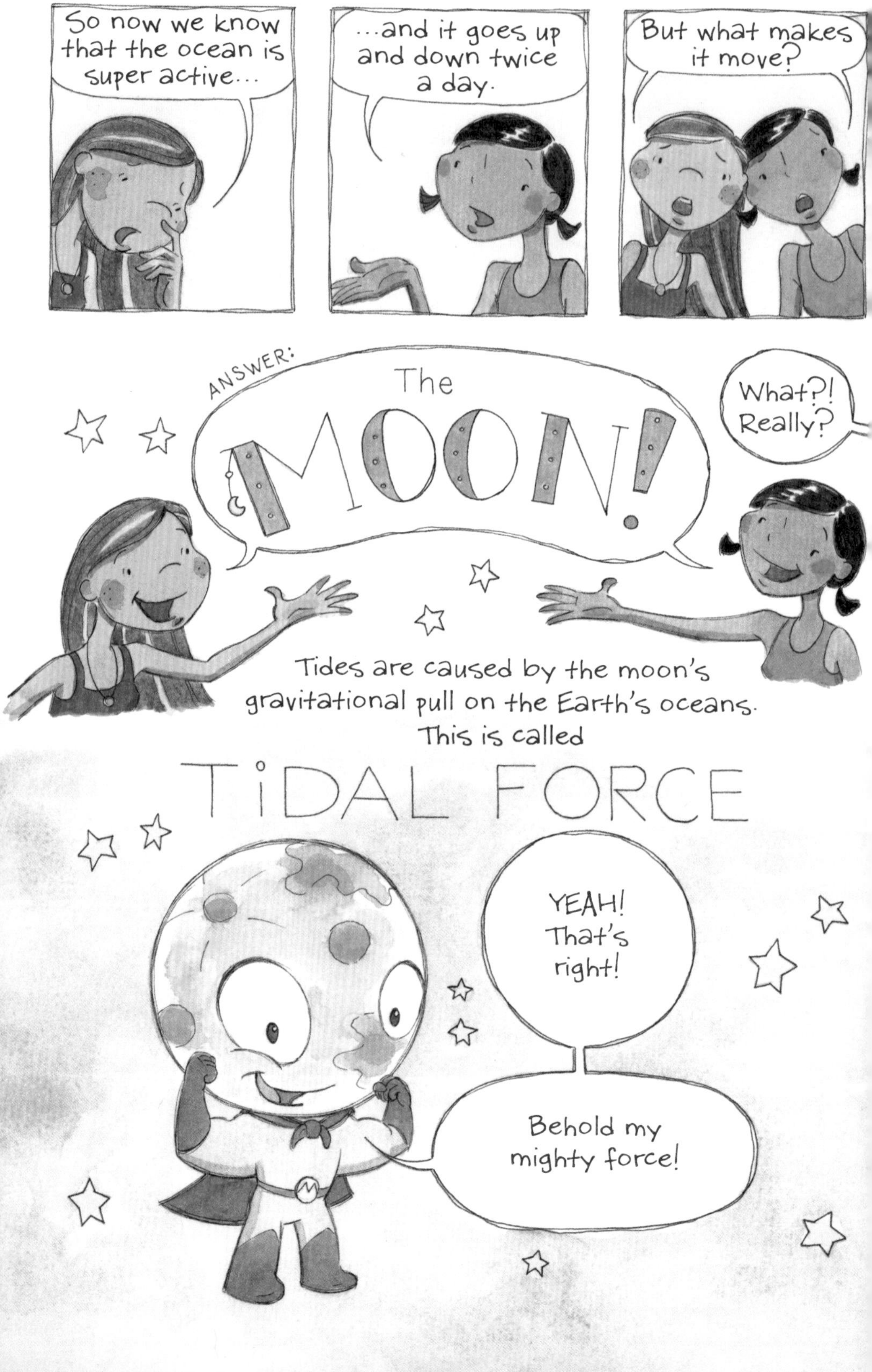
So now we know that the ocean is super active...
...and it goes up and down twice a day.
But what makes it move?
ANSWER:
The MOON!
What?! Really?
Tides are caused by the moon's gravitational pull on the Earth's oceans. This is called
TiDAL FORCE
YEAH! That's right!
Behold my mighty force!

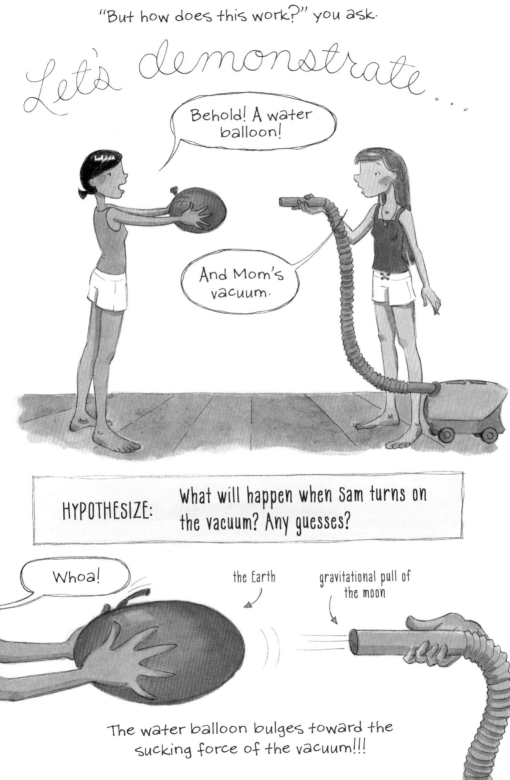

"But how does this work?" you ask.

Let's demonstrate . . .

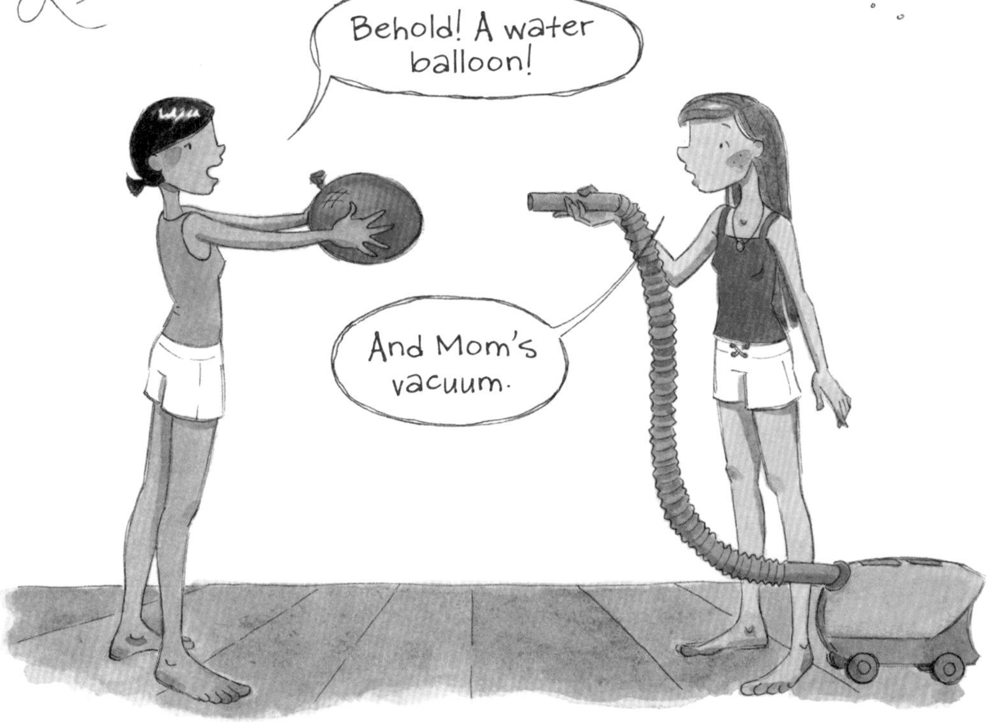

Behold! A water balloon!
And Mom's vacuum.

HYPOTHESIZE: What will happen when Sam turns on the vacuum? Any guesses?

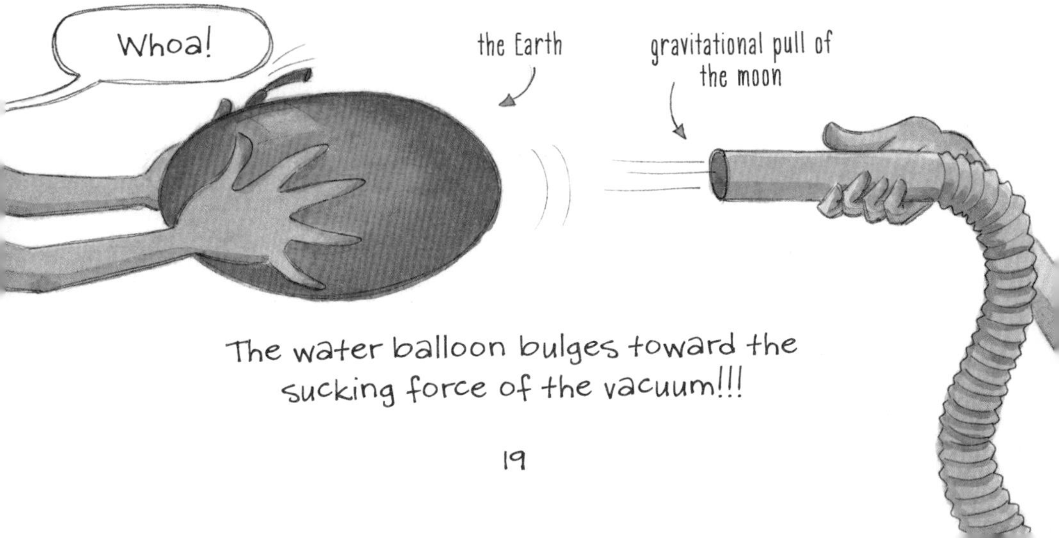

Whoa!
the Earth
gravitational pull of the moon

The water balloon bulges toward the sucking force of the vacuum!!!

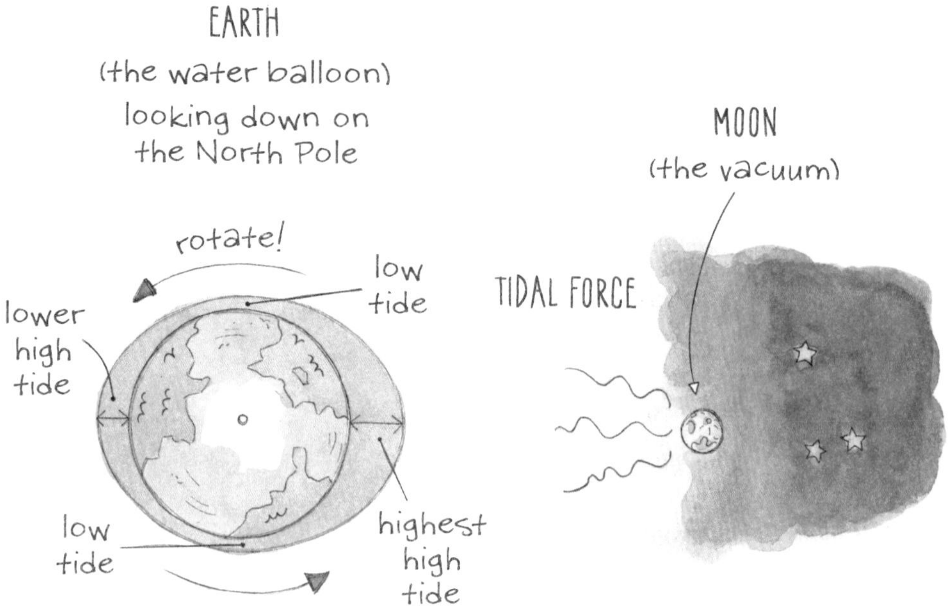
EARTH
(the water balloon)
looking down on the North Pole
rotate!
low tide
lower high tide
low tide
highest high tide
MOON
(the vacuum)
TIDAL FORCE

NOW... remember that the Earth rotates one full rotation in 24 hours - we call this a DAY. Just like that water balloon and vacuum, the moon's pull distorts the oceans into bulges. The one closer to the moon is bigger (the higher high tide) and the one on the far side is smaller (the lower high tide).

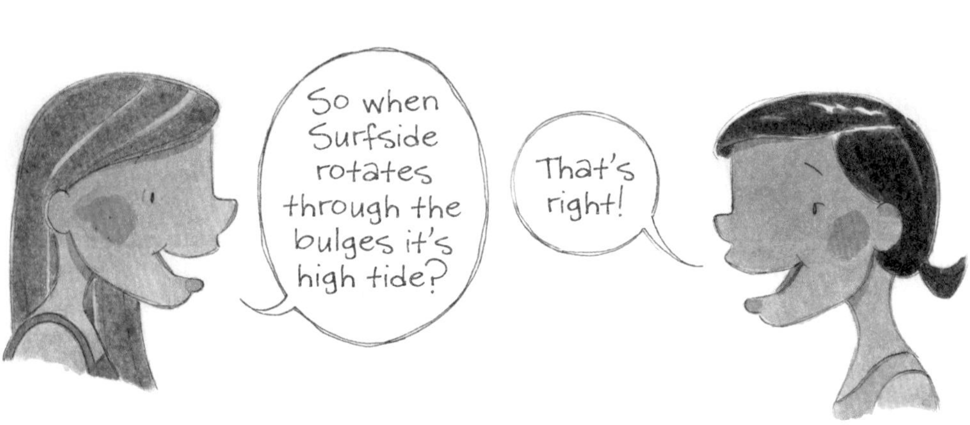
So when Surfside rotates through the bulges it's high tide?
That's right!

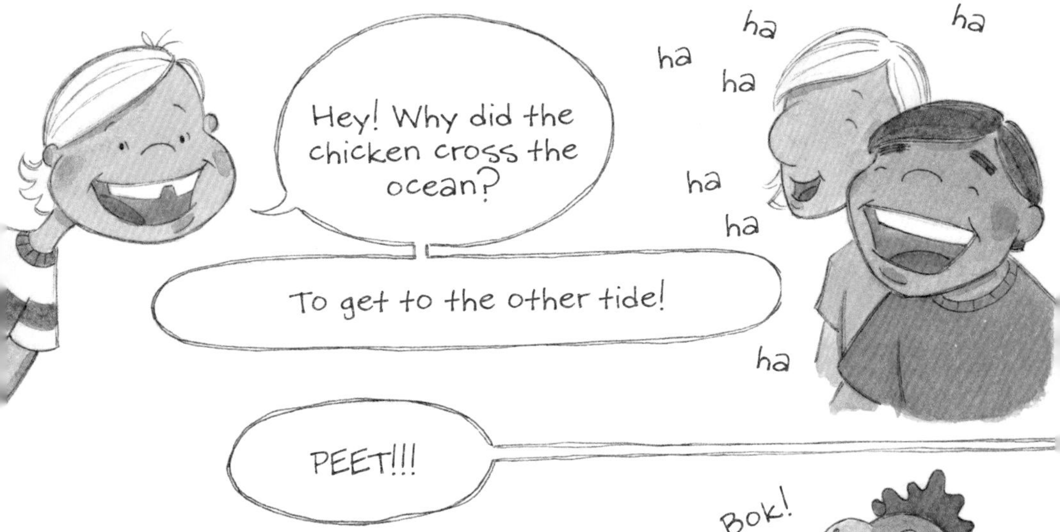
Hey! Why did the chicken cross the ocean?
To get to the other tide!
ha
ha
ha
ha
ha
ha
ha
PEET!!!

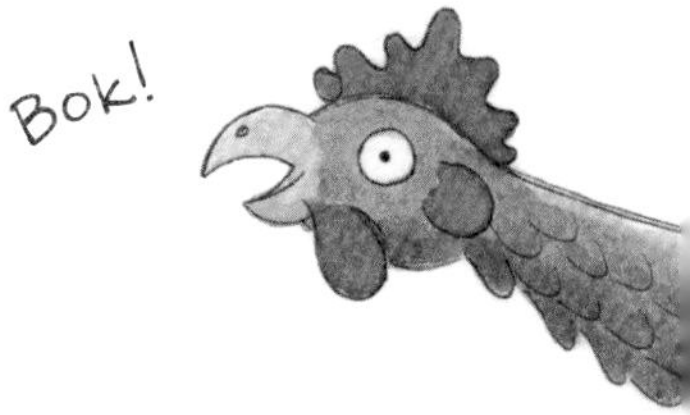
Bok!

Okay, so we just learned that the moon's gravitational pull – TIDAL FORCE – is what makes tides. BUT DID YOU KNOW that the cycle of the moon affects how strongly that pull is felt?

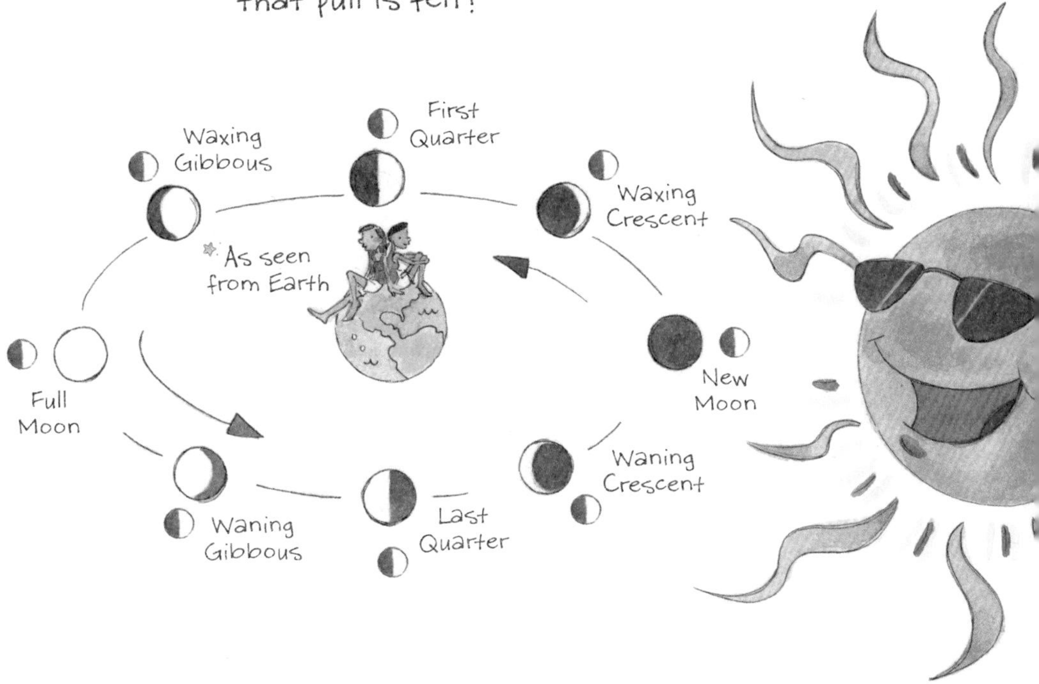
First Quarter
Waxing Gibbous
Waxing Crescent
As seen from Earth
Full Moon
New Moon
Waning Crescent
Waning Gibbous
Last Quarter

It takes 28 days for the moon to travel around the Earth.

Depending on where you live on Planet Earth, the moon will look different throughout that cycle.

moon

the sun

shadow

When the moon is closest to the sun, what we see is the shadow. That's called a NEW MOON.

When the moon is on the far side of the Earth, it is all lit up and round – a FULL MOON.

Both a *New Moon* and a *Full Moon* have **POWER!**

Did you notice the moon symbols in the tide chart?

IN ALIGNMENT...

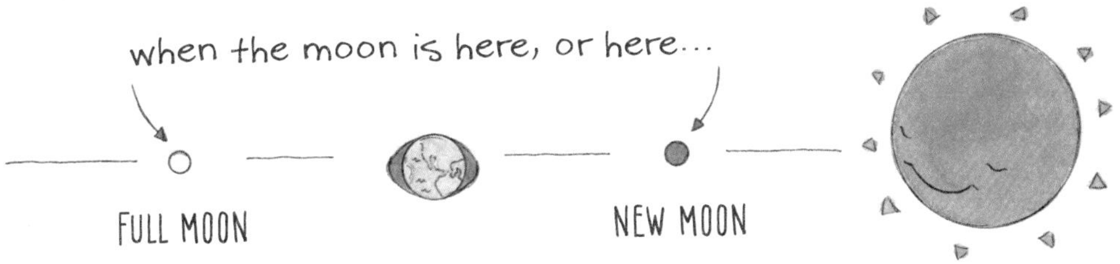

when the moon is here, or here...
FULL MOON
NEW MOON

...you get two times the power of pull.

So FULL MOON or NEW MOON alignments are powerful!

SOLAR TIDE (sun) + LUNAR TIDE (moon) = SPRING TIDE.

Get your sandbags!

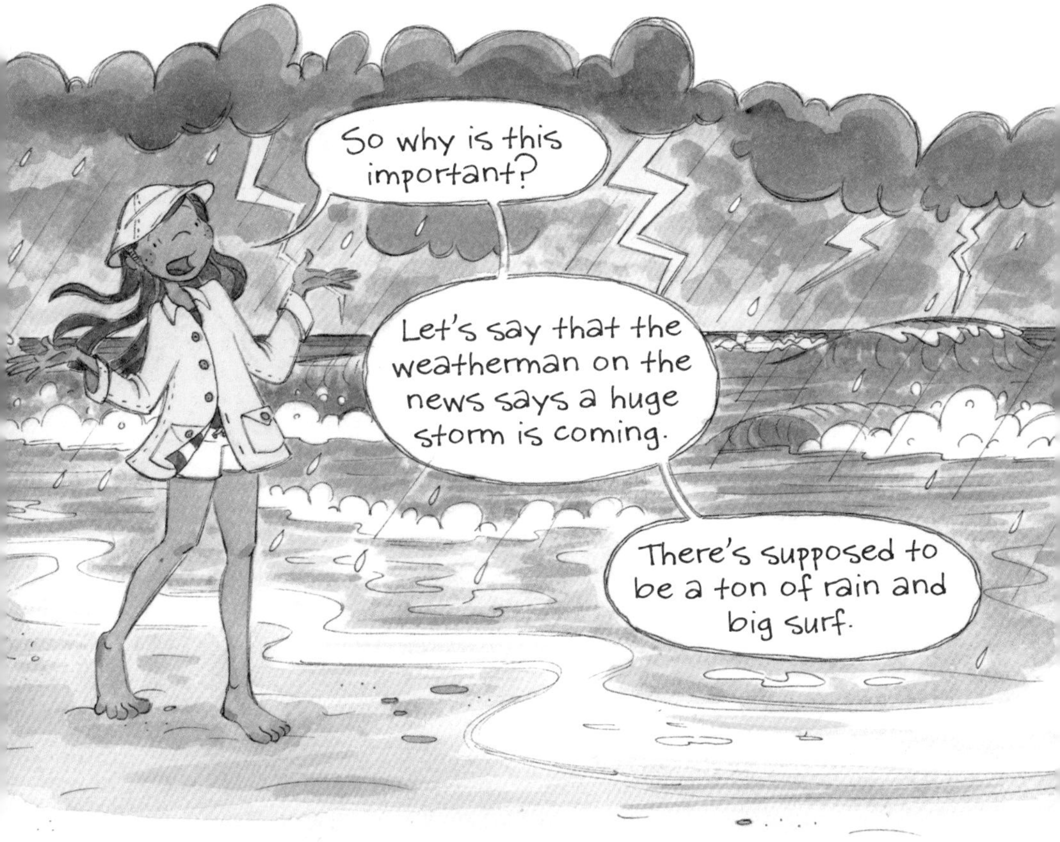

So why is this important?
Let's say that the weatherman on the news says a huge storm is coming.
There's supposed to be a ton of rain and big surf.

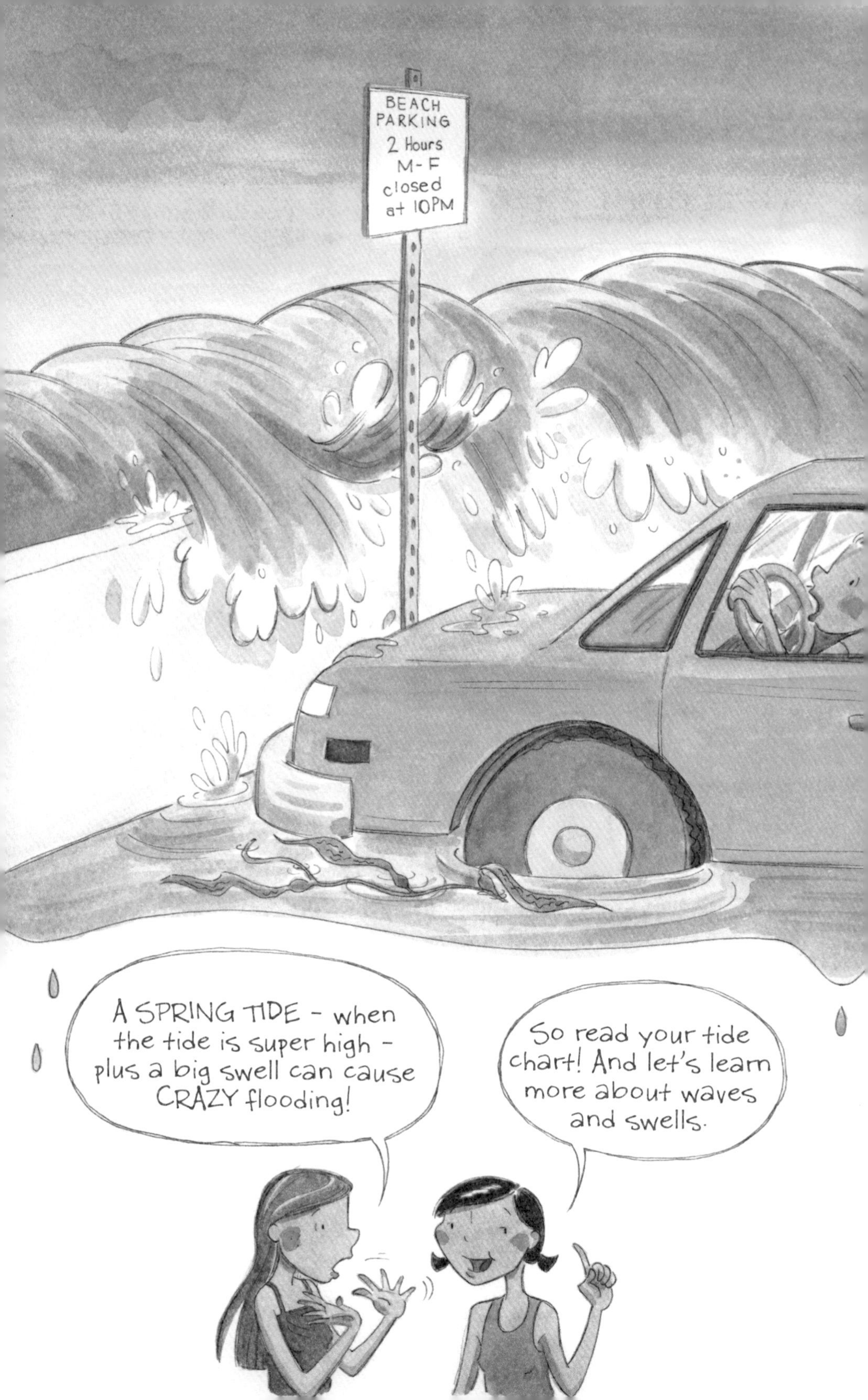
BEACH PARKING 2 Hours M-F closed at 10PM
A SPRING TIDE - when the tide is super high - plus a big swell can cause CRAZY flooding!
So read your tide chart! And let's learn more about waves and swells.

Waves

I dream about waves.
Me too.

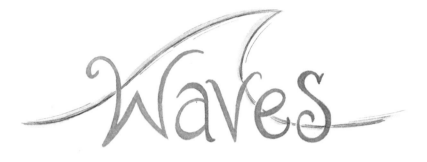

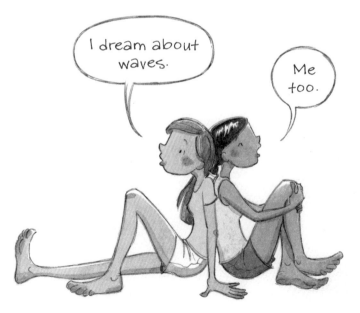

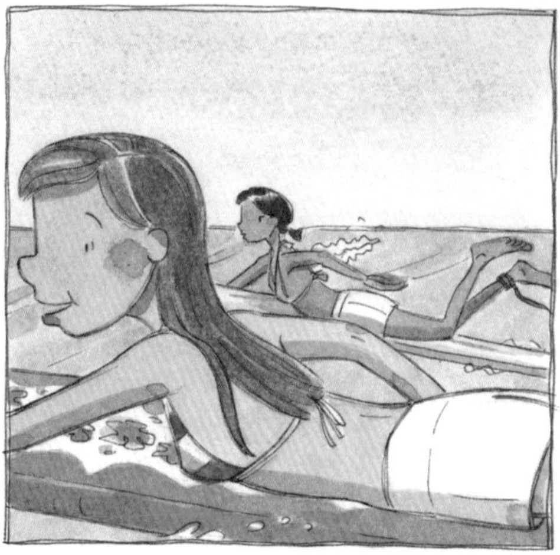
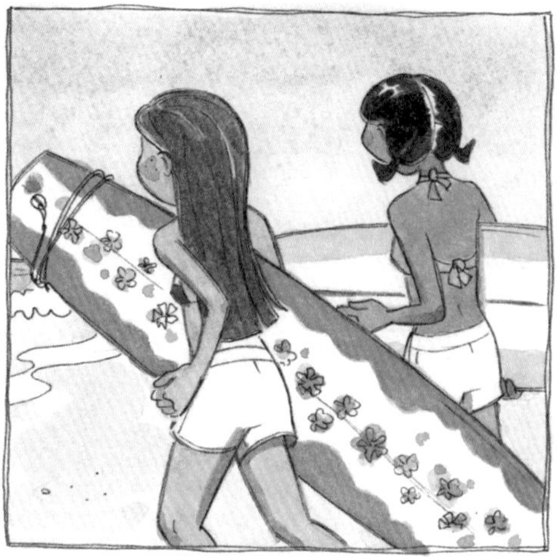
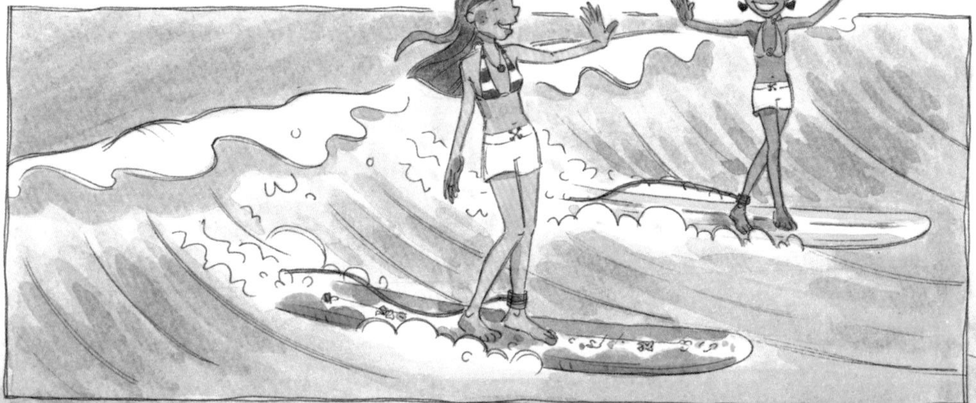
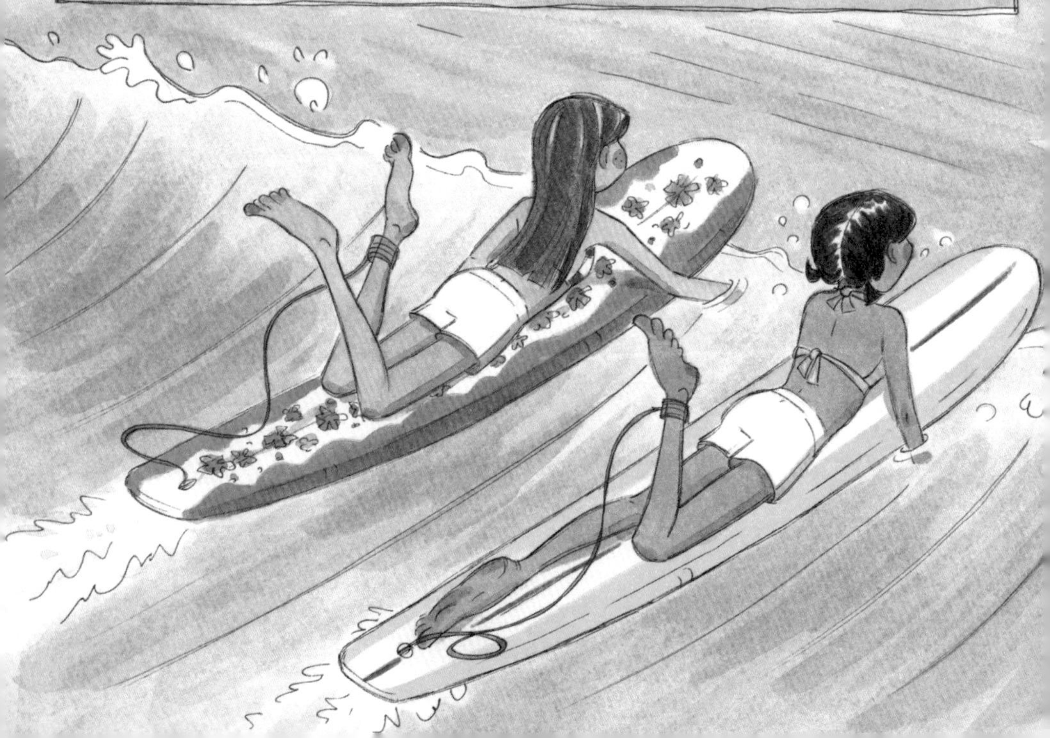

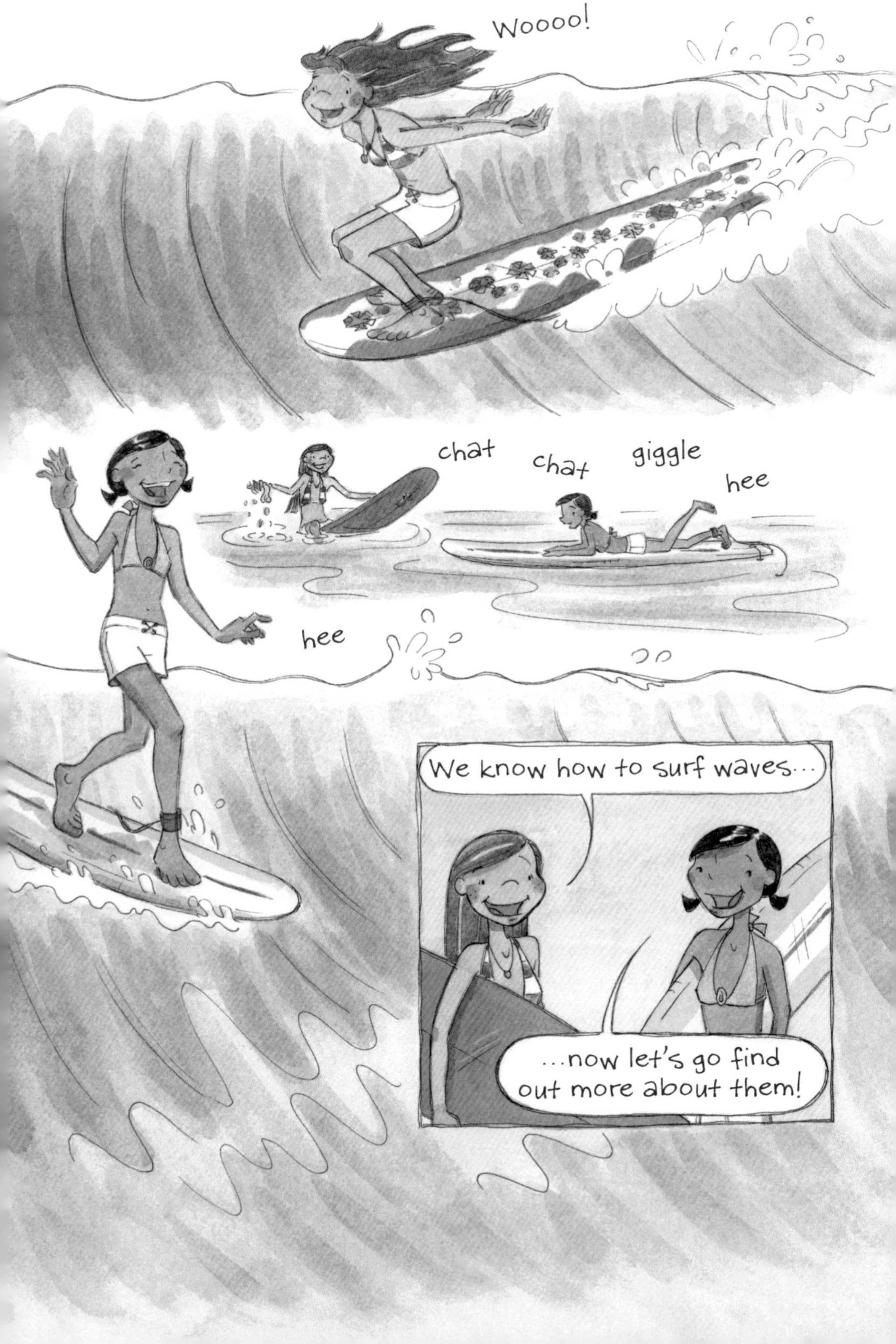
Woooo!
chat
chat
giggle
hee
hee
We know how to surf waves...
...now let's go find out more about them!

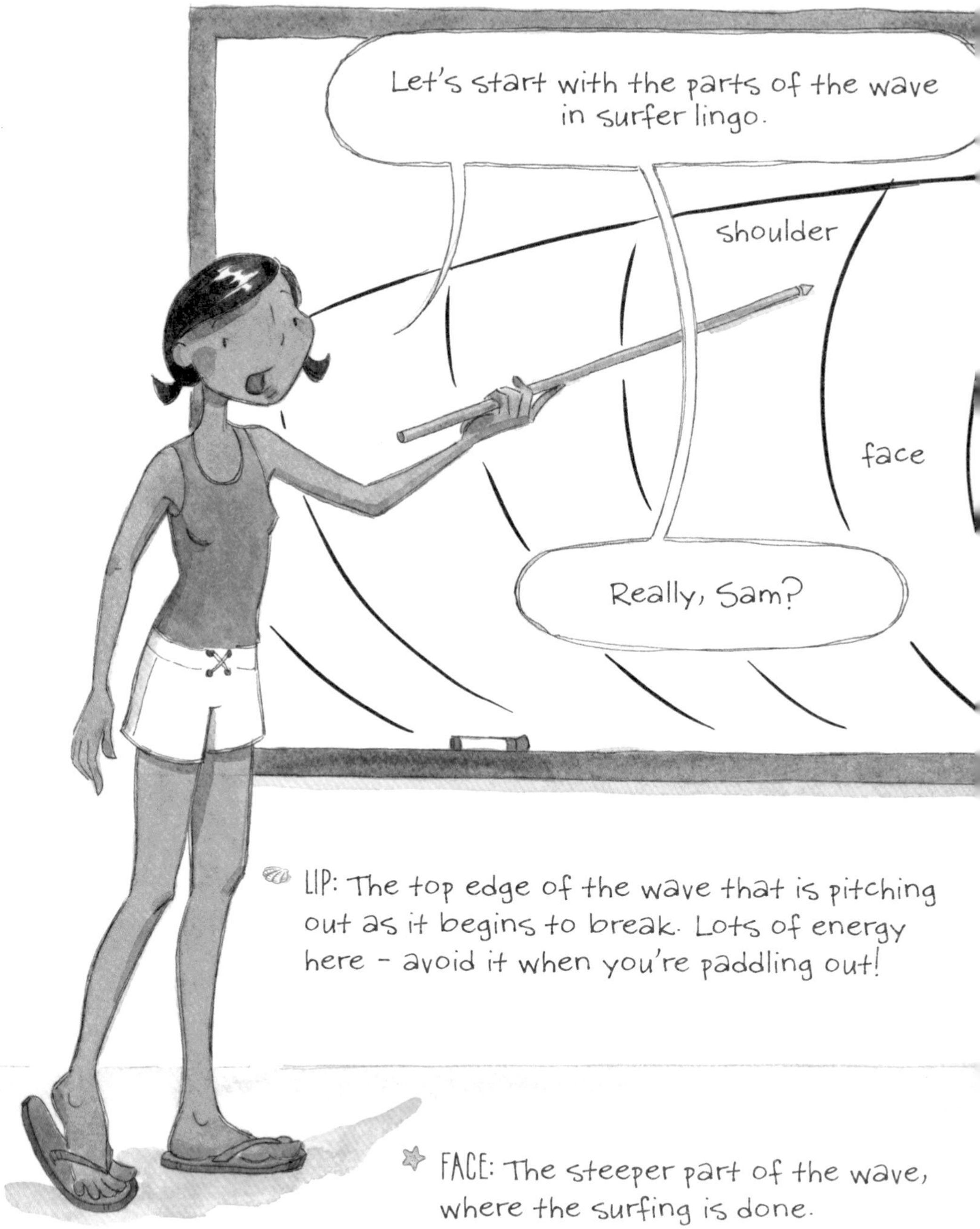
Let's start with the parts of the wave in surfer lingo.
shoulder
face
Really, Sam?

LIP: The top edge of the wave that is pitching out as it begins to break. Lots of energy here - avoid it when you're paddling out!

FACE: The steeper part of the wave, where the surfing is done.

WHITE WATER: The white foamy part of the wave that has all the breaking bubbles.

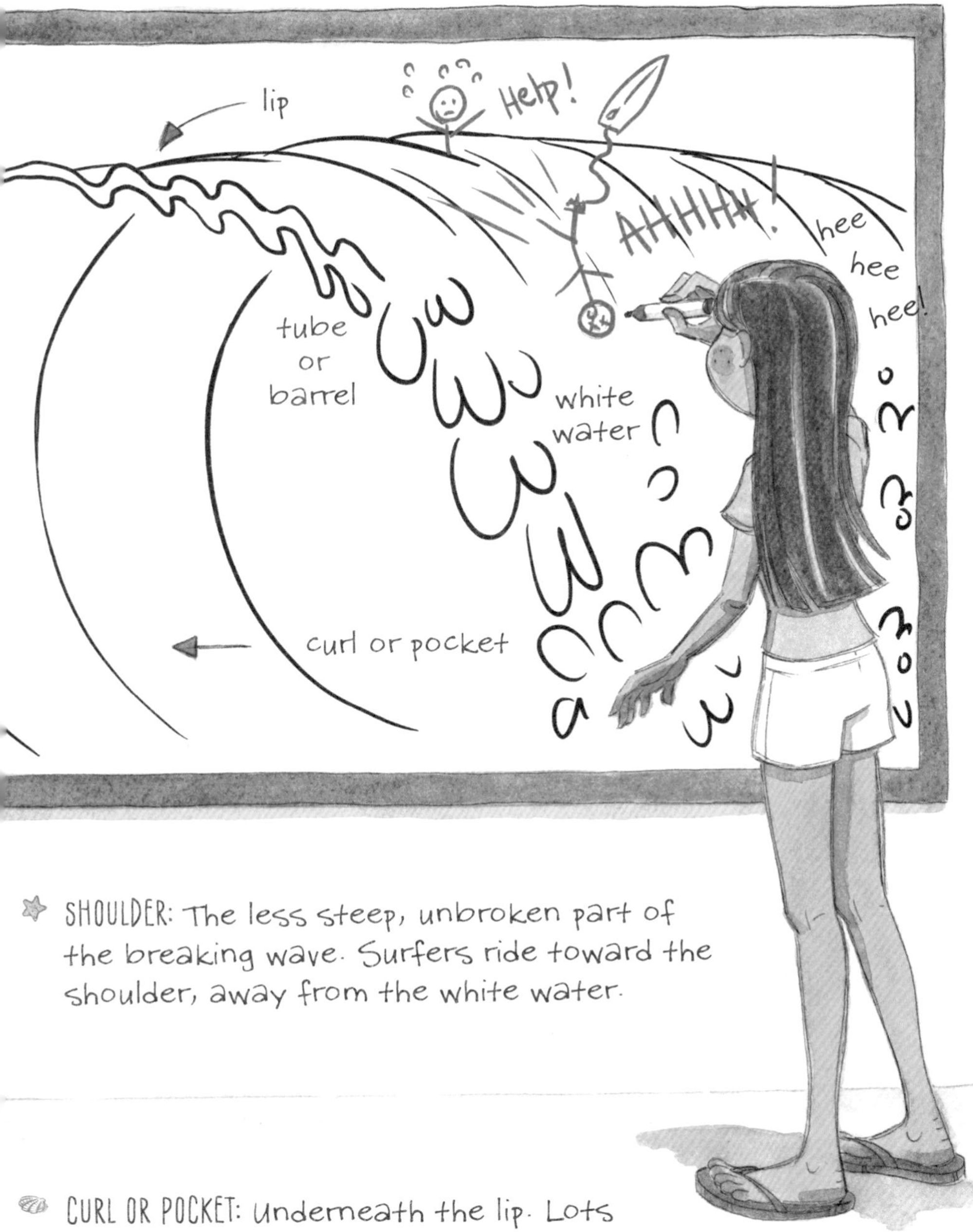
lip
Help!
AHHHH!
hee
hee
hee!
tube
or
barrel
white
water
curl or pocket

SHOULDER: The less steep, unbroken part of the breaking wave. Surfers ride toward the shoulder, away from the white water.

CURL OR POCKET: Underneath the lip. Lots of power here too.

TUBE OR BARREL: The hollow part of the wave. When you're in here, it's called "getting tubed" or "getting barreled." Also known as the Green Room.

WAVES are ENERGY

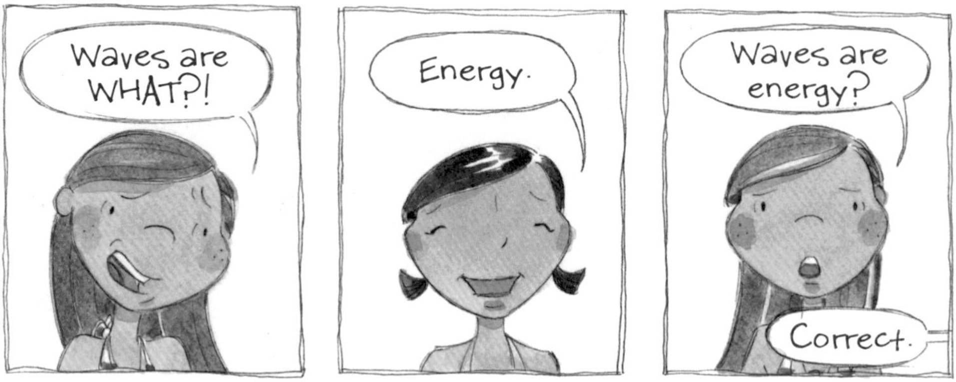
Waves are WHAT?!
Energy.
Waves are energy?
Correct.

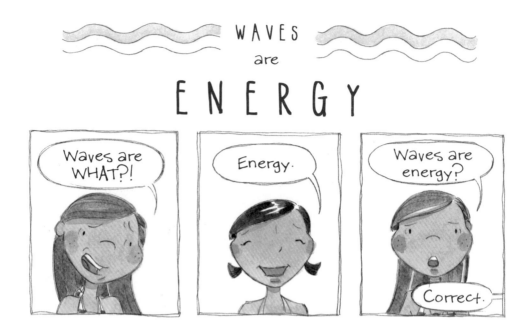

This might sound totally confusing. I mean, that wet, foamy thing that just landed you on your butt on the beach seems like a lot more than just energy!

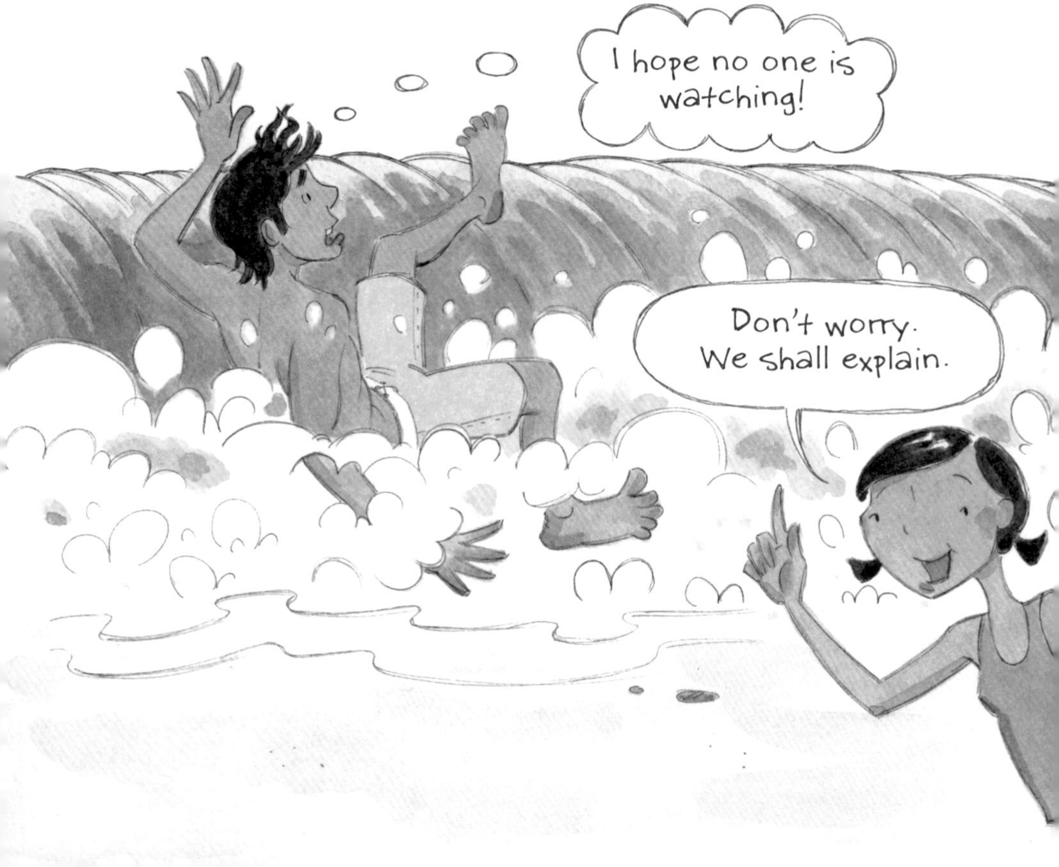
I hope no one is watching!
Don't worry. We shall explain.

Waves are
ENERGY
that moves
through
water.

Try dropping a
rock into a pond!

bloop!

All of those circles that run out from the middle?
That is ENERGY moving outward from the impact.

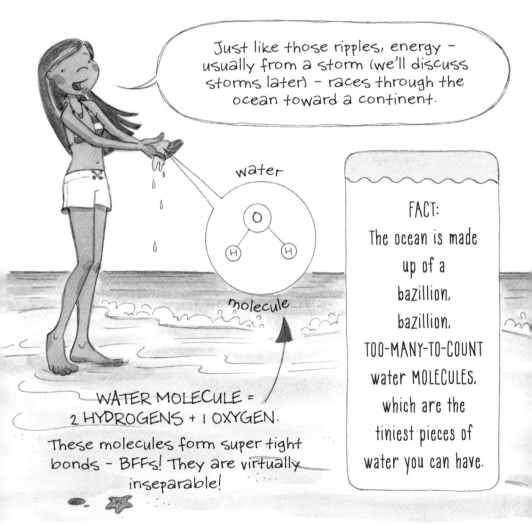

Just like those ripples, energy –
usually from a storm (we'll discuss
storms later) – races through the
ocean toward a continent.

water

O

H   H

molecule

WATER MOLECULE =
2 HYDROGENS + 1 OXYGEN.

These molecules form super tight
bonds – BFFs! They are virtually
inseparable!

FACT:
The ocean is made
up of a
bazillion,
bazillion,
TOO-MANY-TO-COUNT
water MOLECULES,
which are the
tiniest pieces of
water you can have.

When these water molecules are hit with energy, they move - but not how you might think. They ROTATE around in an orbit!

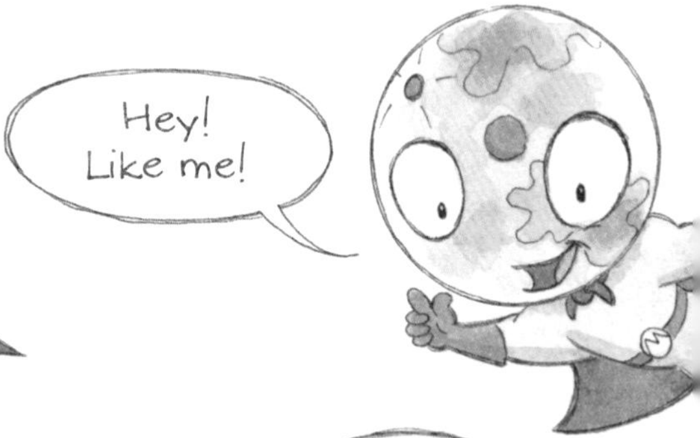
Hey! Like me!

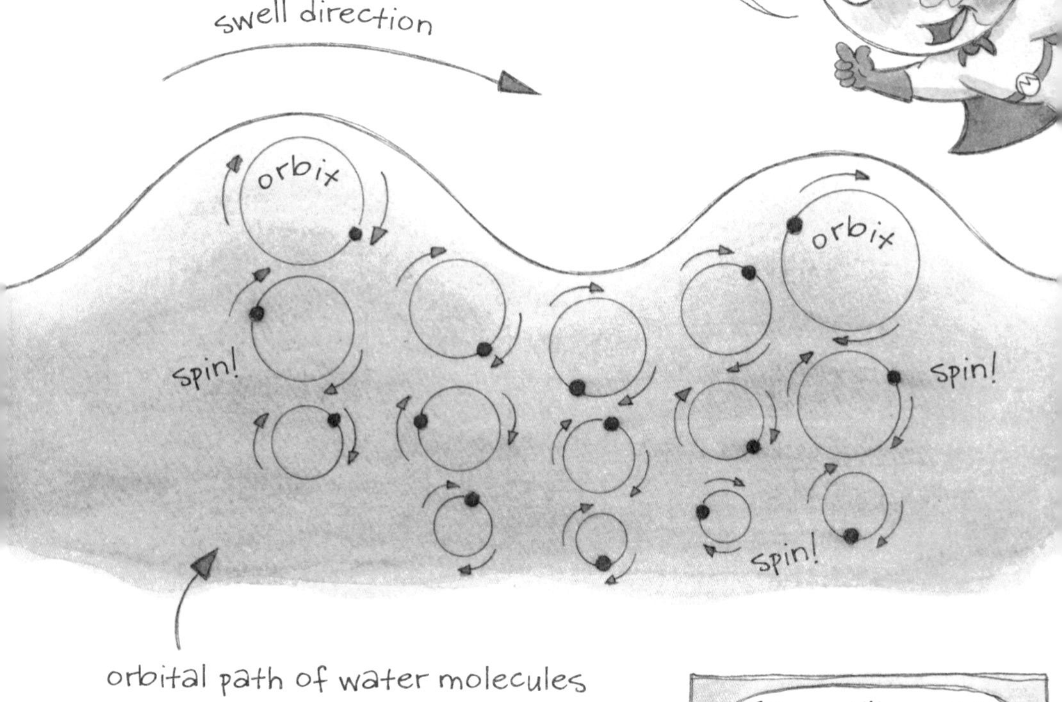
swell direction
orbit
orbit
spin!
spin!
spin!
orbital path of water molecules

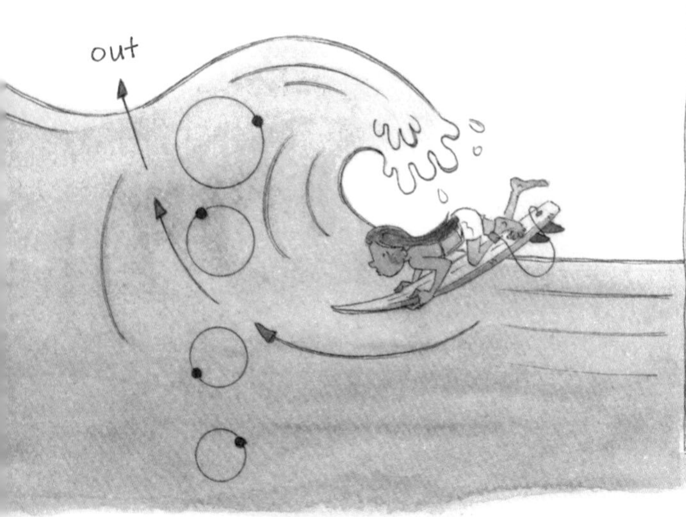
out

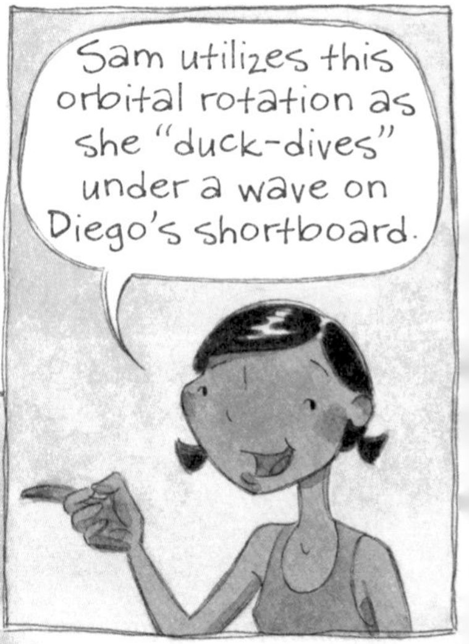
Sam utilizes this orbital rotation as she "duck-dives" under a wave on Diego's shortboard.

Here are some

SCIENTIFIC

wave words . . .

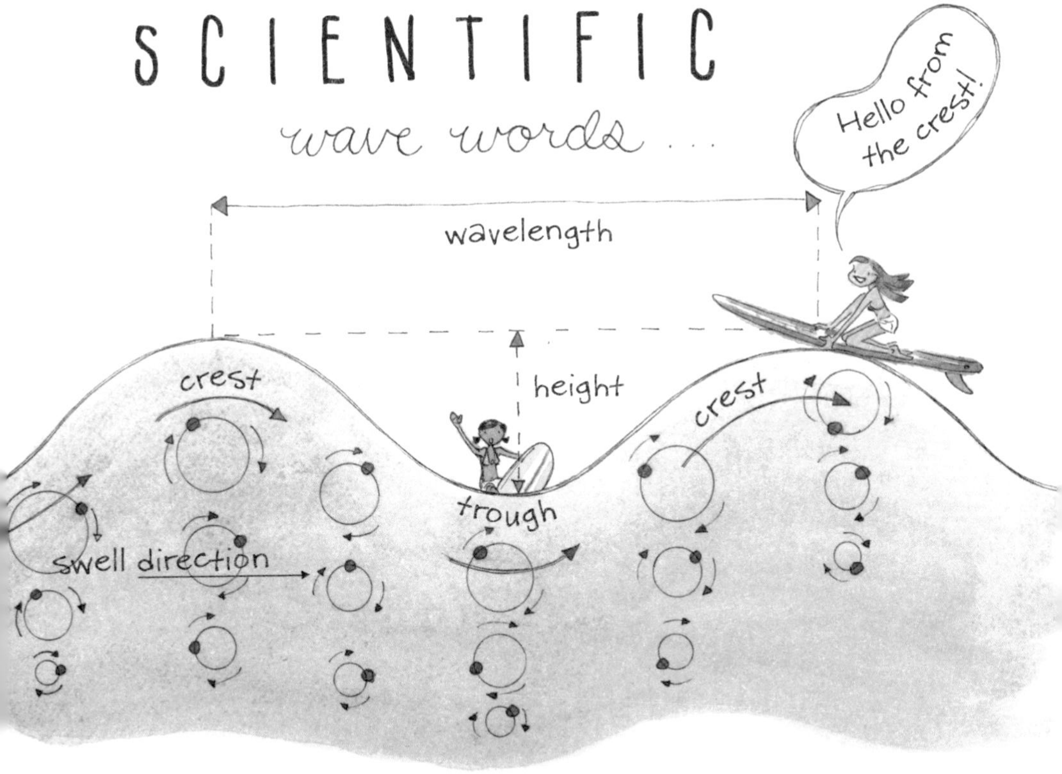

Hello from the crest!
wavelength
height
crest
crest
trough
swell direction

In totally scientific terms, a WAVE is actually "a disturbance that travels through SPACE and MATTER transferring energy from one place to another." Here are some more scientific definitions:

- CREST - The highest point of a wave.
- TROUGH - The lowest point of the wave.
- WAVELENGTH - The distance from CREST to CREST.
- WAVE HEIGHT - The distance from TROUGH to CREST.

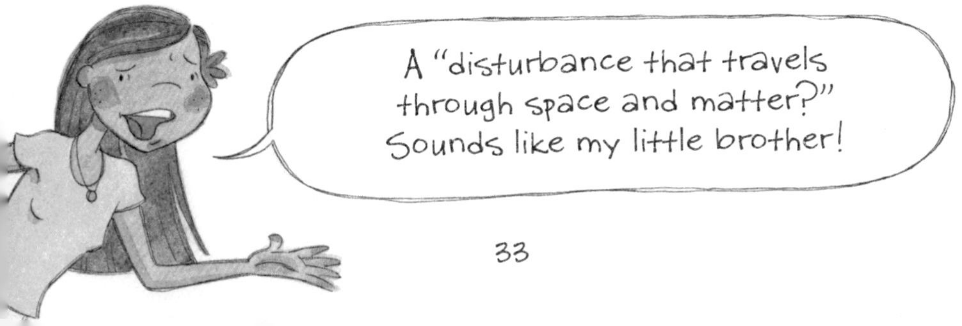

A "disturbance that travels through space and matter?" Sounds like my little brother!

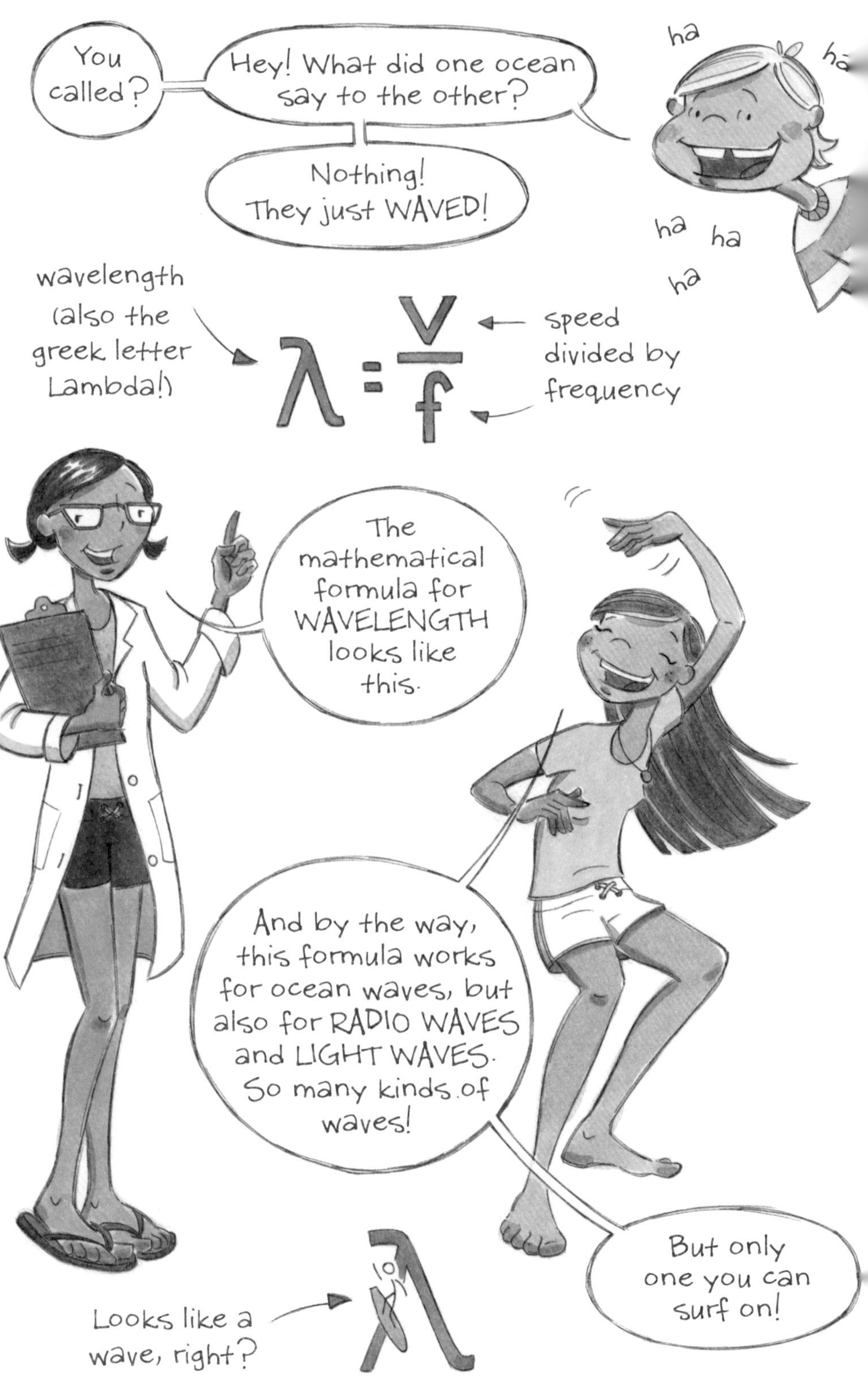
You called?
Hey! What did one ocean say to the other?
Nothing! They just WAVED!
ha ha ha ha ha
wavelength (also the greek letter Lambda!)
λ = v/f
speed divided by frequency
The mathematical formula for WAVELENGTH looks like this.
And by the way, this formula works for ocean waves, but also for RADIO WAVES and LIGHT WAVES. So many kinds of waves!
But only one you can surf on!
Looks like a wave, right?

Weather

and its effects on your beach!

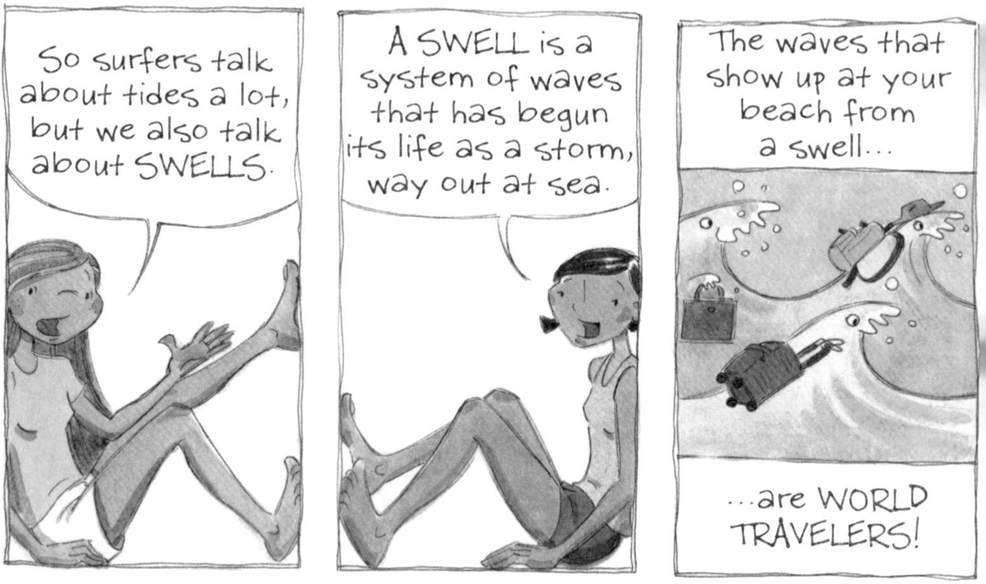
So surfers talk about tides a lot, but we also talk about SWELLS.
A SWELL is a system of waves that has begun its life as a storm, way out at sea.
The waves that show up at your beach from a swell...
...are WORLD TRAVELERS!

You can usually tell that a SWELL has hit because of all of the cars with surfboards on them that are headed for the beach.

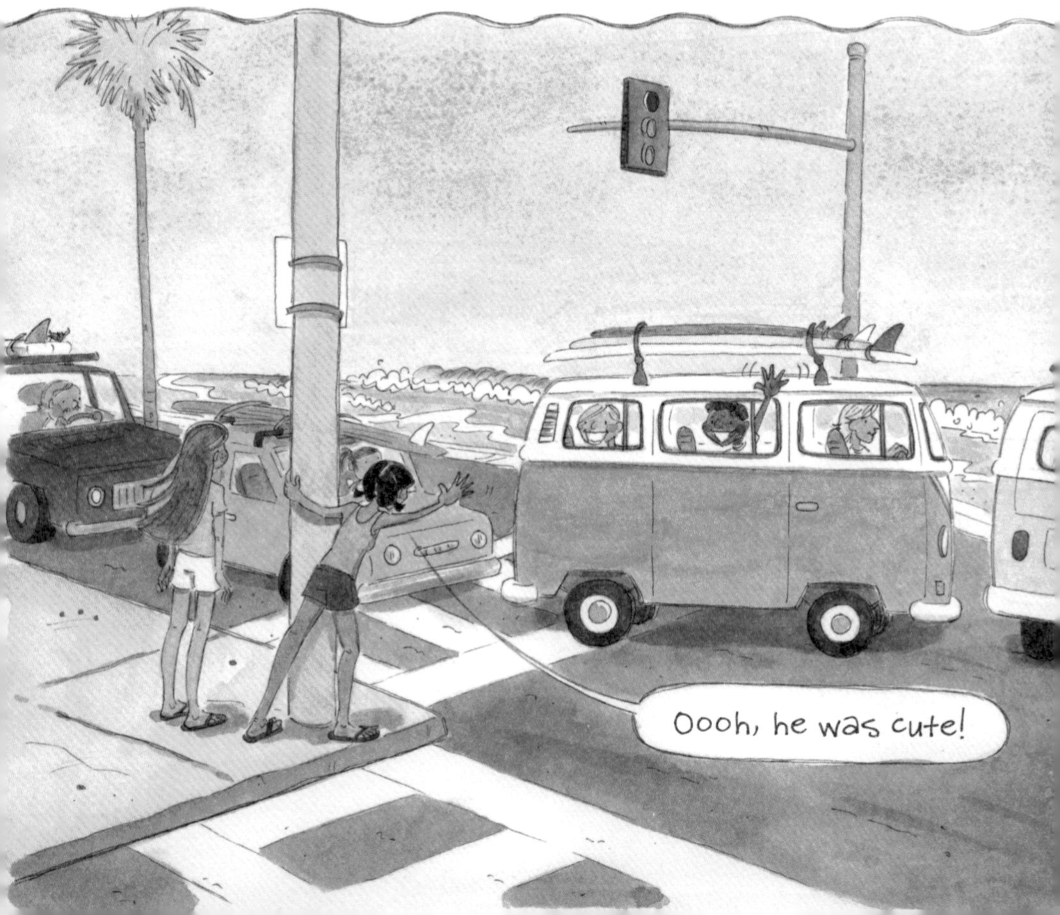
Oooh, he was cute!

A SWELL starts as a breeze, far out in the middle of the ocean - the beginning of a storm!

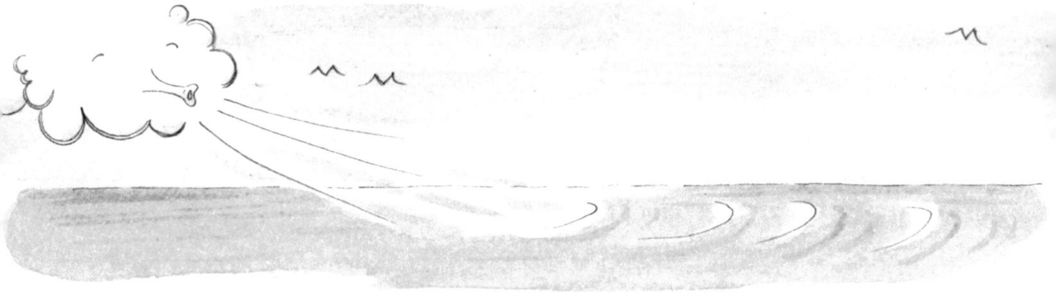

The breeze blows over the top of the flat ocean, causing little waves called CAPILLARY WAVES.

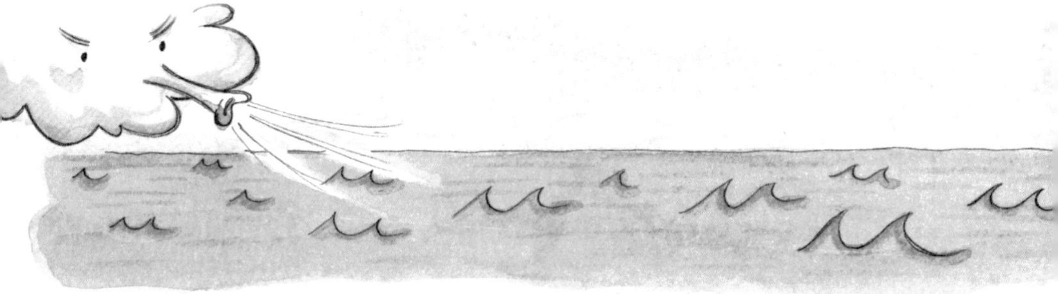

Now that the surface of the ocean isn't flat anymore, it gets all crazy! The wind blowing over these little waves starts to roll, and this makes them bigger.

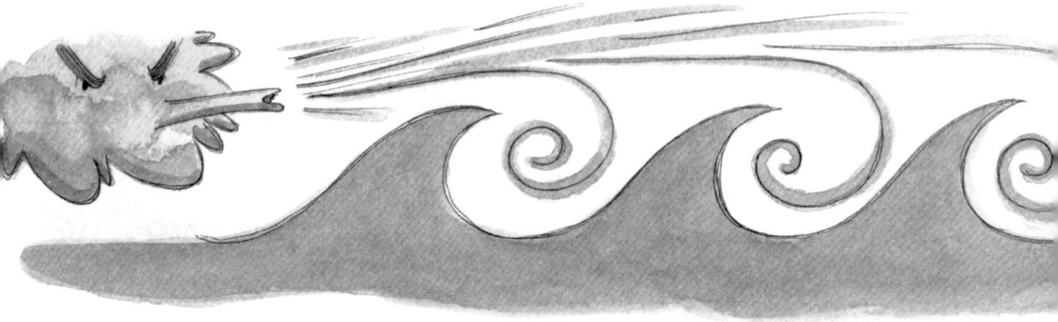

The harder the wind blows, the bigger it rolls in the troughs, and the bigger the waves get. These waves go racing away, traveling for days across miles of open ocean. A TON of swell energy is now racing toward a continent, and then...

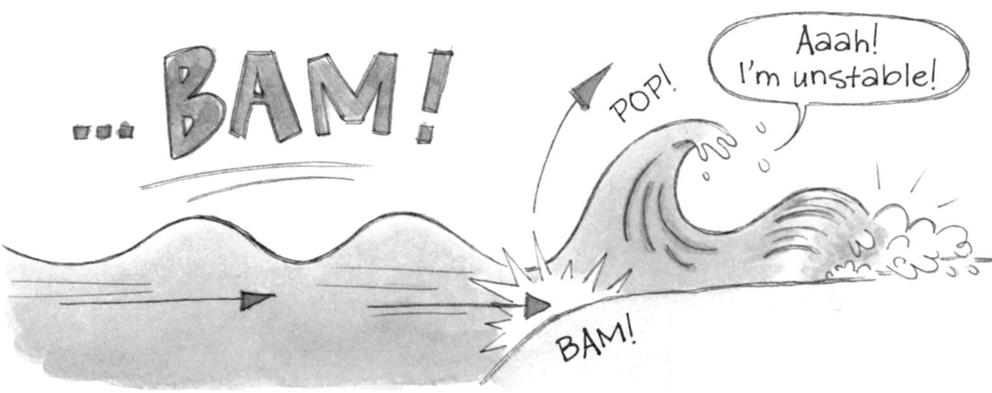
...BAM!
POP!
Aaah!
I'm unstable!
BAM!

SO MUCH ENERGY hits the shallow bottom!!!

All of that energy has to go somewhere, and the friction that happens when the bottom edge of the wave hits the shallow ocean floor of your beach POPS the wave up to where it becomes unstable and breaks. This is called SHOALING, and it's where the surfing is done.

Every beach faces a different direction.

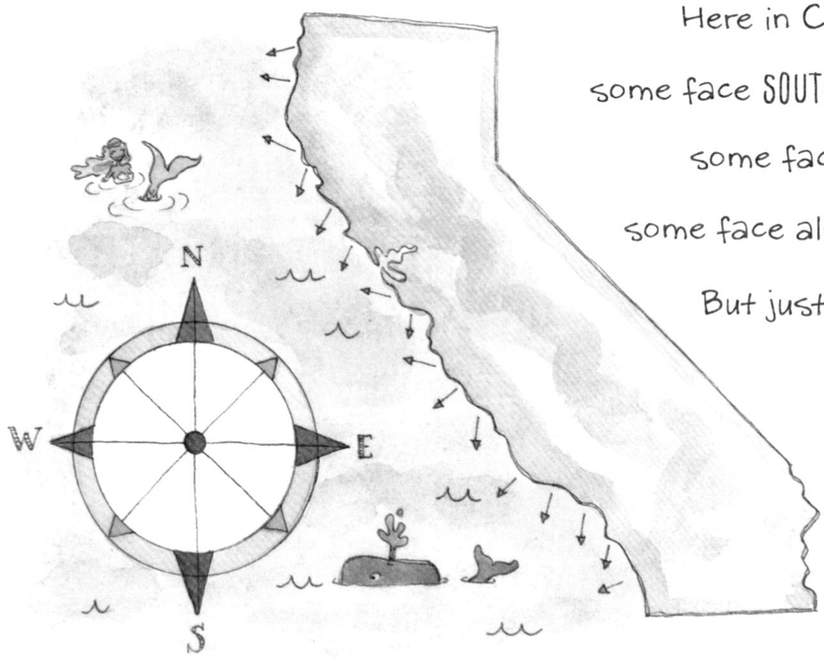
N
W
E
S

Here in California,

some face SOUTH,

some face WEST,

some face almost NORT

But just not EAST!

Each beach breaks best on a specific direction of swell.

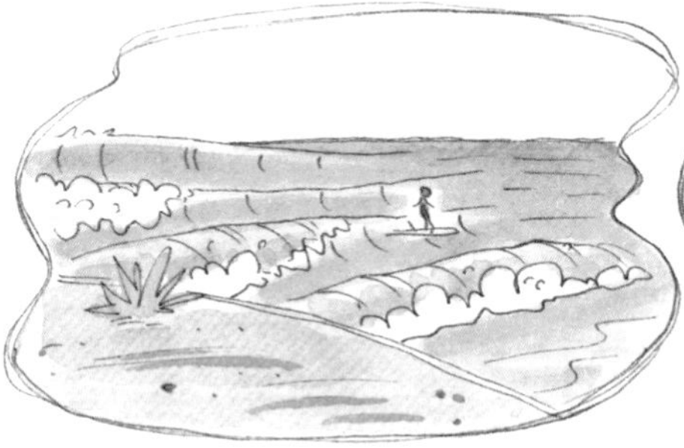

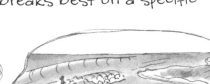

Some beaches work best on a south swell - a storm down south that has sent waves.

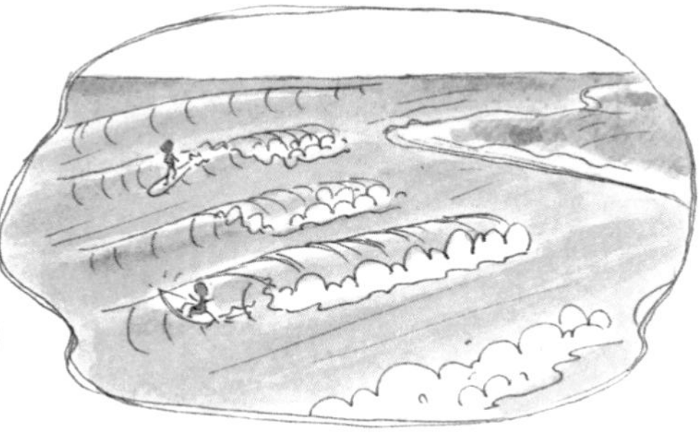

Some like a northwest swell, where perhaps a storm out to sea up by Alaska has sent waves.

TRY THIS!
Ask the lifeguard which swell direction works best at your local beach.

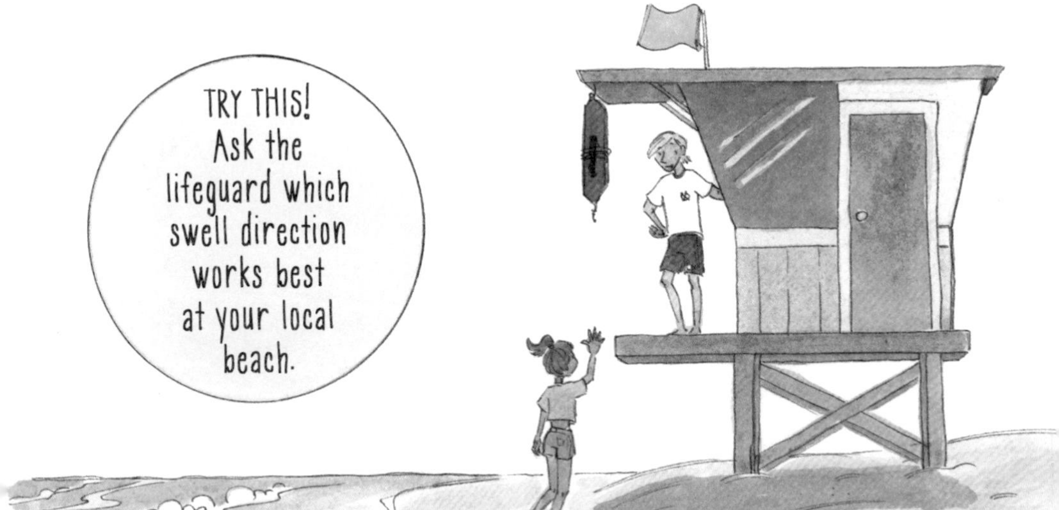

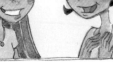

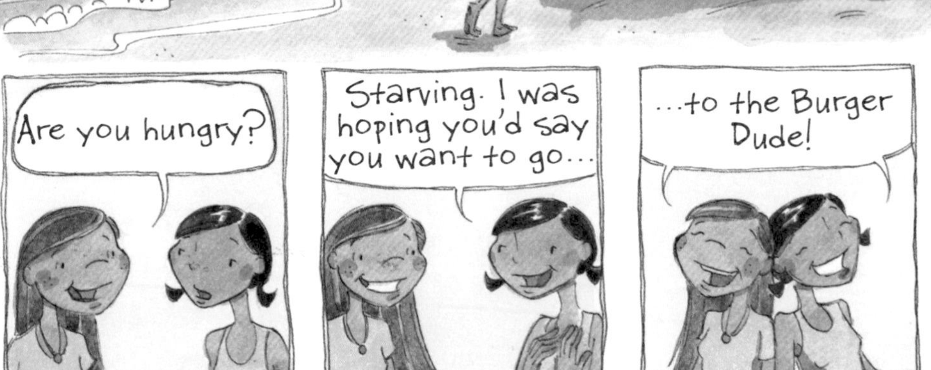
Are you hungry?
Starving. I was hoping you'd say you want to go...
...to the Burger Dude!

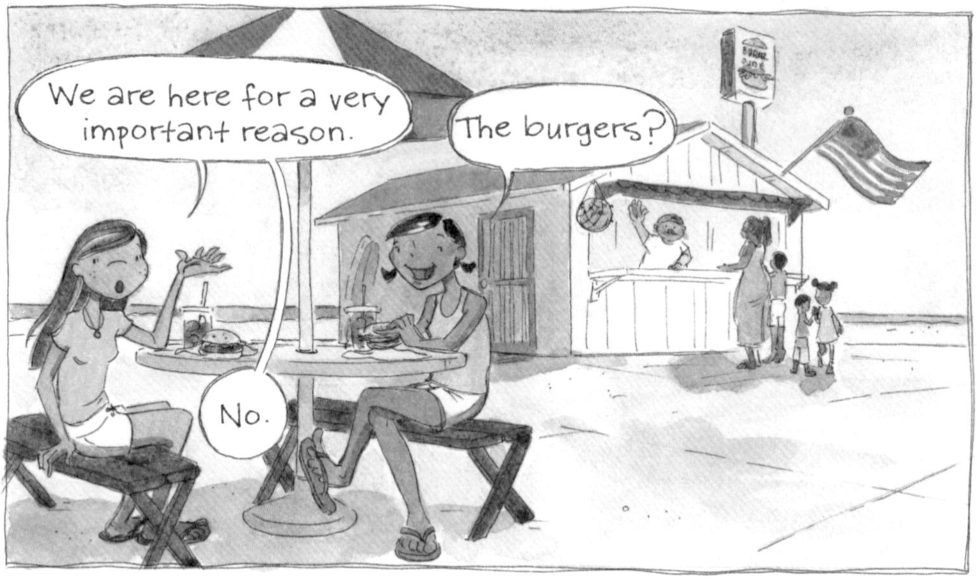
We are here for a very important reason.
The burgers?
No.

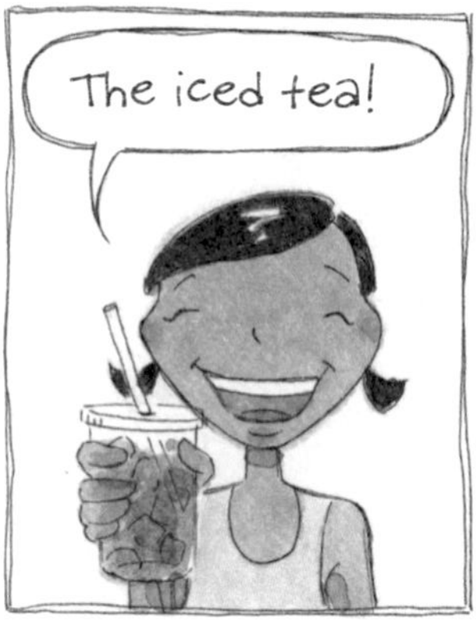
The iced tea!

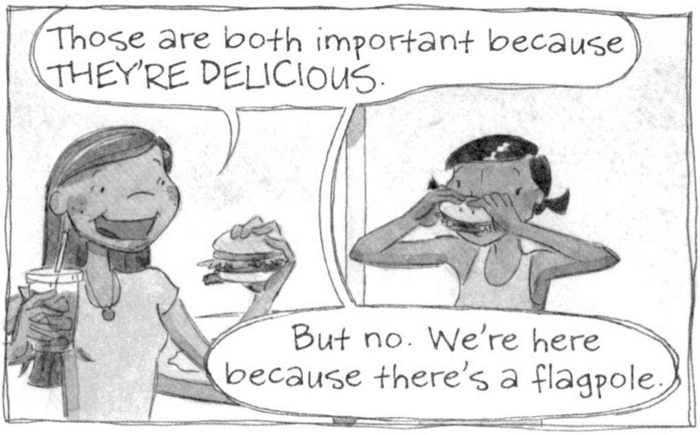
Those are both important because THEY'RE DELICIOUS.
But no. We're here because there's a flagpole.

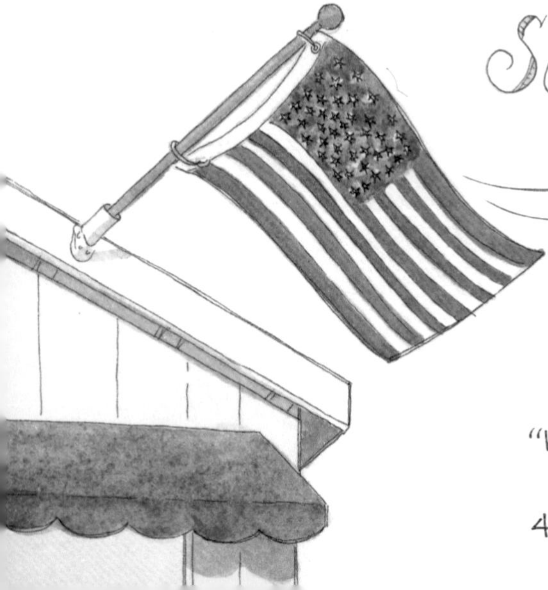

Surfers watch flagpoles.

Flagpoles tell you a lot. They tell you which direction the wind is coming from, and that can tell you a lot about what the surf is like. "How is this possible?" you ask.

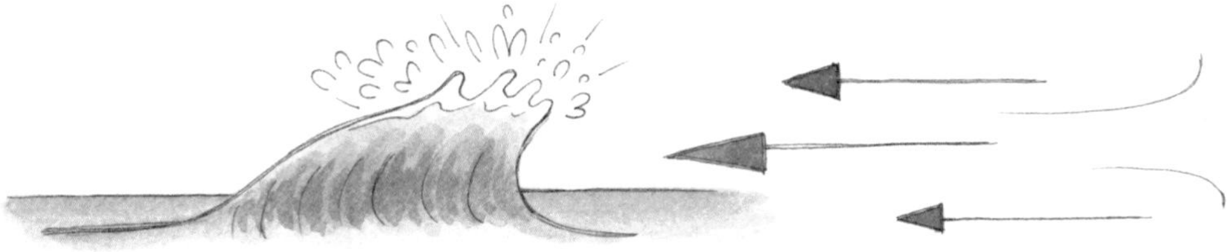

OFFSHORE WIND comes from the LAND onto the ocean.

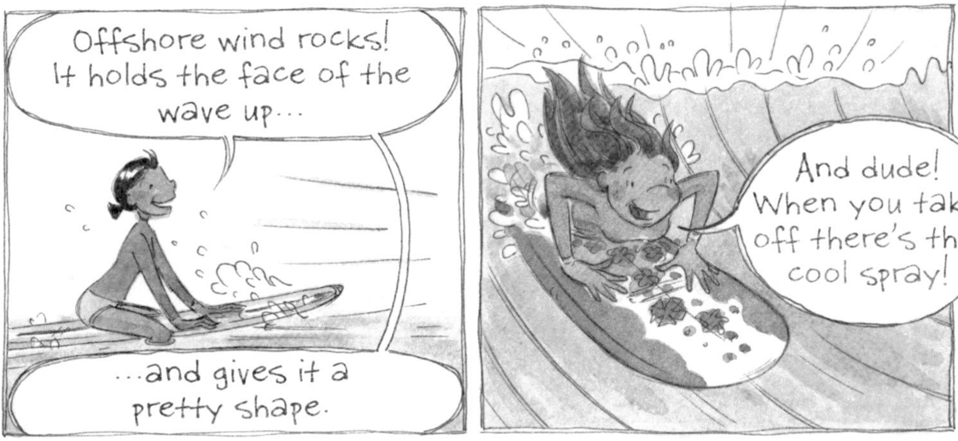
Offshore wind rocks! It holds the face of the wave up...
...and gives it a pretty shape.
And dude! When you take off there's this cool spray!

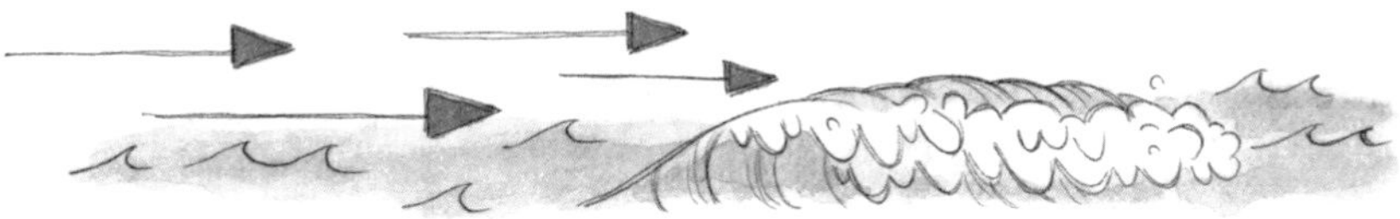

ONSHORE WIND comes from out in the ocean, toward the shore. It pushes the back of the wave over. This is not ideal. This can cause it to be what surfers call mushy, dumpy, or blown out. And it makes whitecaps.

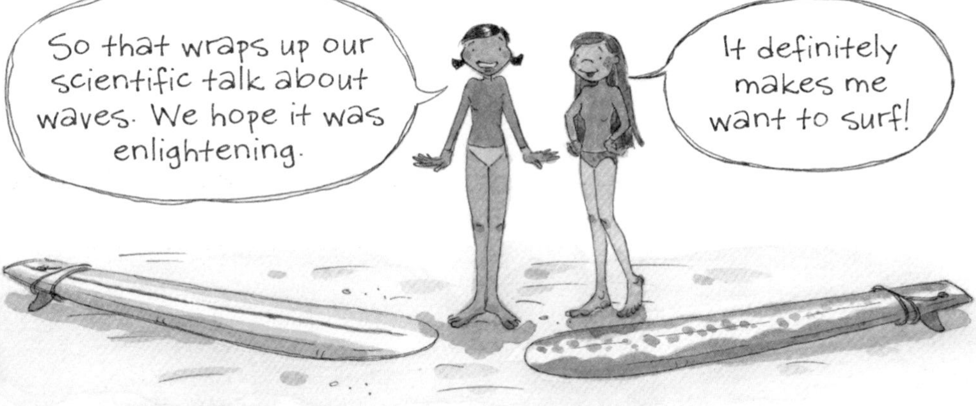
So that wraps up our scientific talk about waves. We hope it was enlightening.
It definitely makes me want to surf!

Chapter 2

BIOLOGY

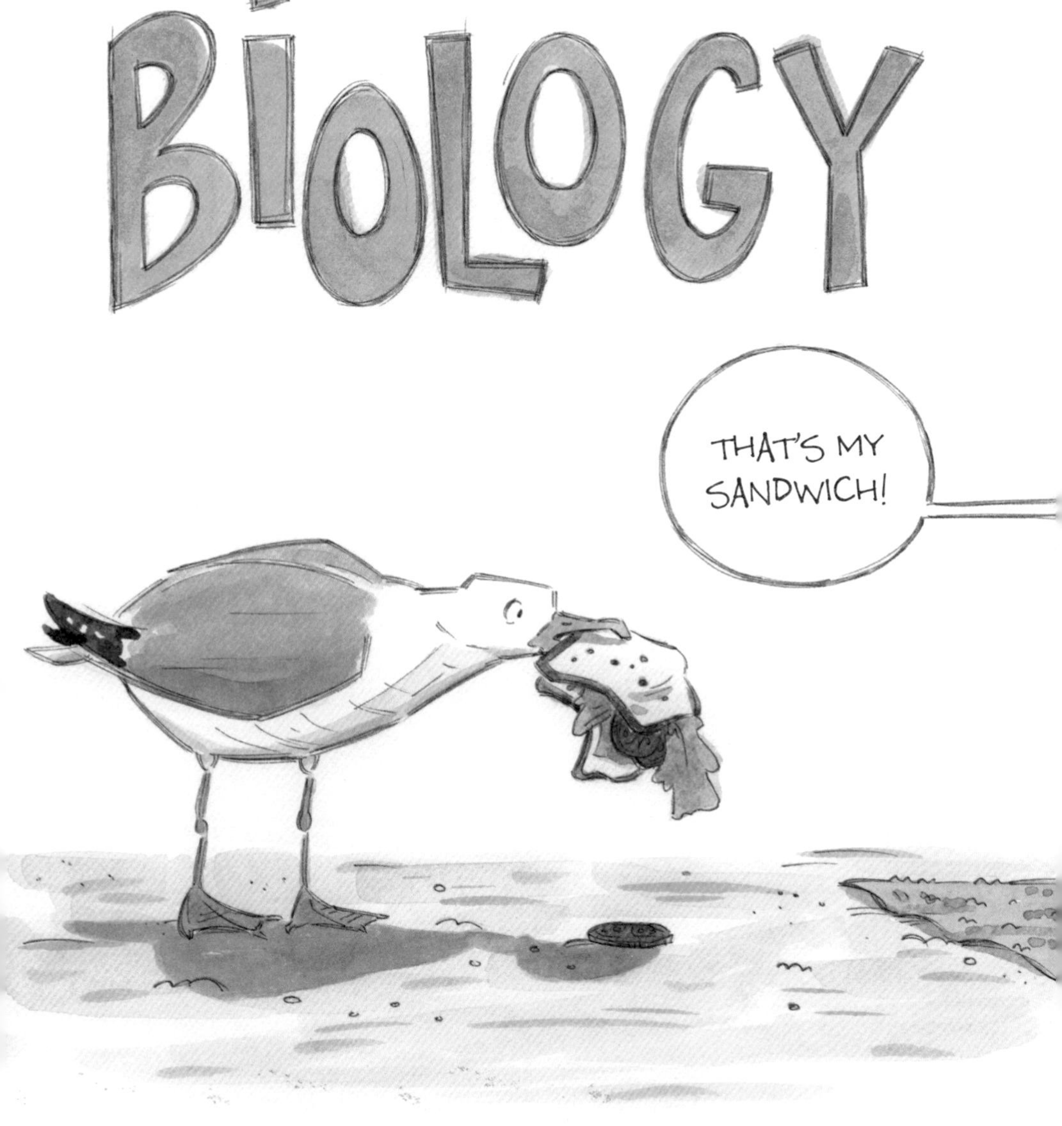
THAT'S MY SANDWICH!

on the beach

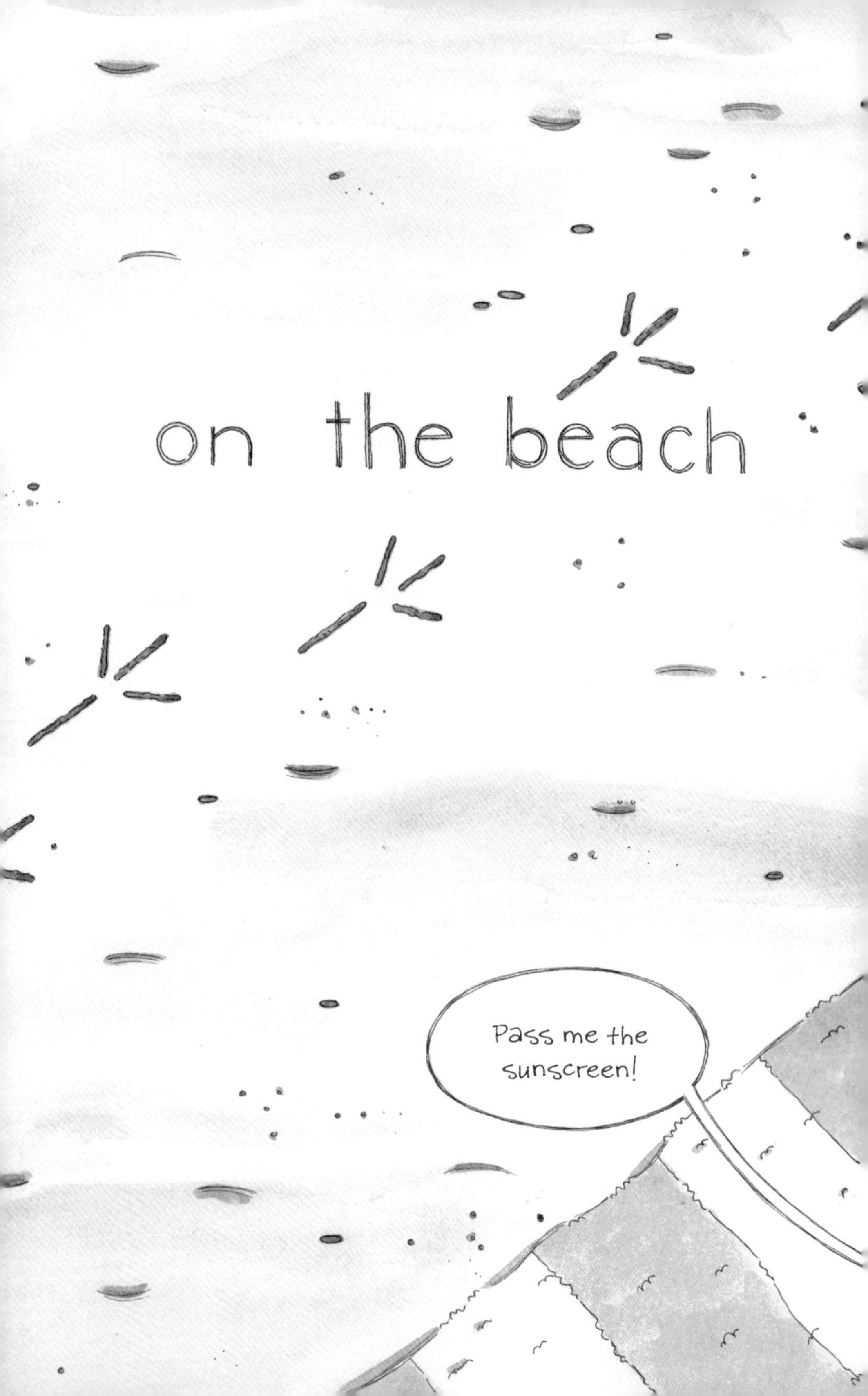
Pass me the sunscreen!

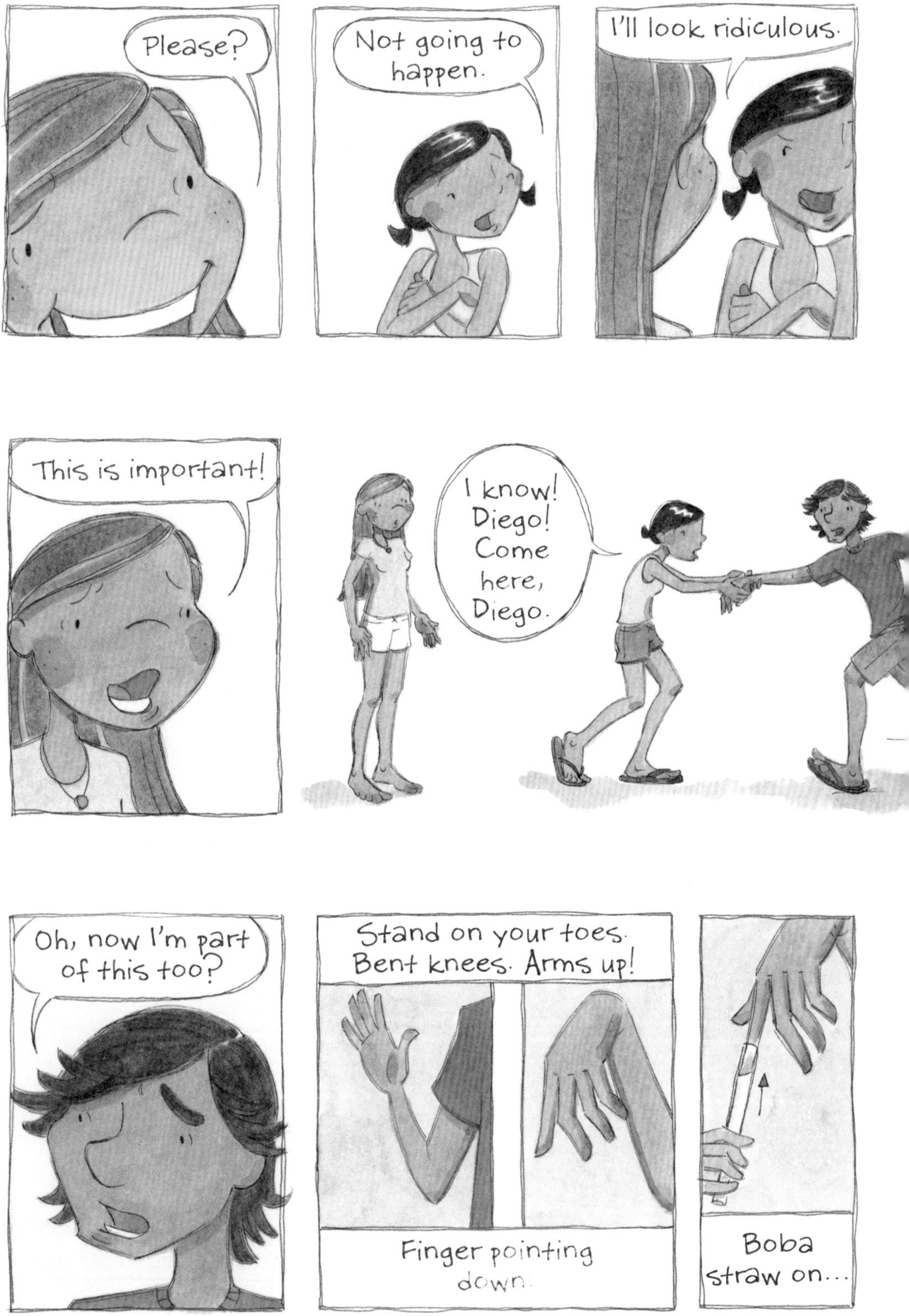
Please?
Not going to happen.
I'll look ridiculous.
This is important!
I know! Diego! Come here, Diego.
Oh, now I'm part of this too?
Stand on your toes. Bent knees. Arms up!
Finger pointing down.
Boba straw on...

Can you see the resemblance?

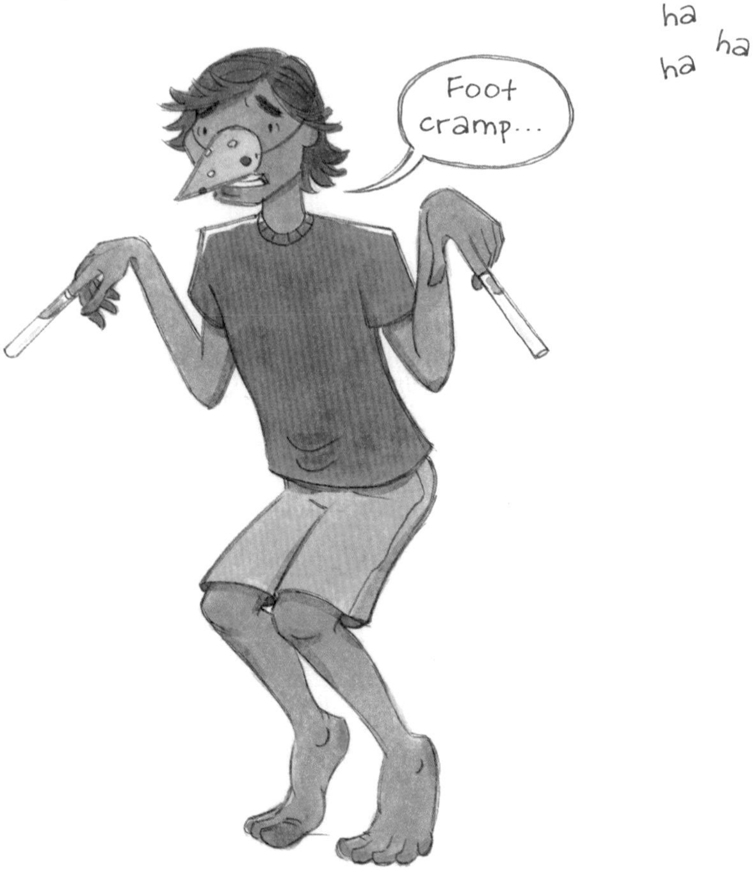
ha
ha
ha
Foot cramp...

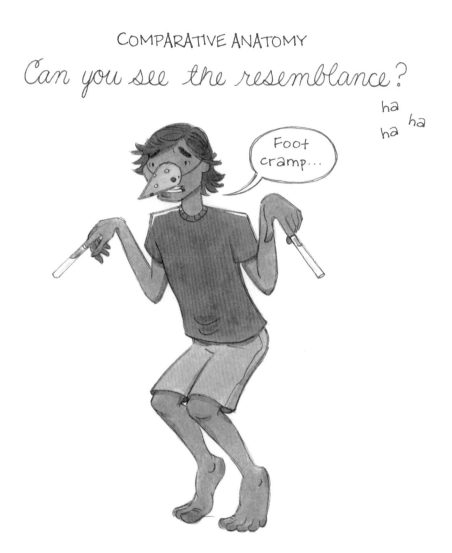

Comparative anatomy compares the body structures of different species of creatures. We're going to compare HUMAN ANATOMY (Diego!) to bird anatomy. Did you ever wonder why it seems like birds' knees bend backward? We've got you covered! Read on!

TRY THIS! Pose like Diego and feel how a bird stands!

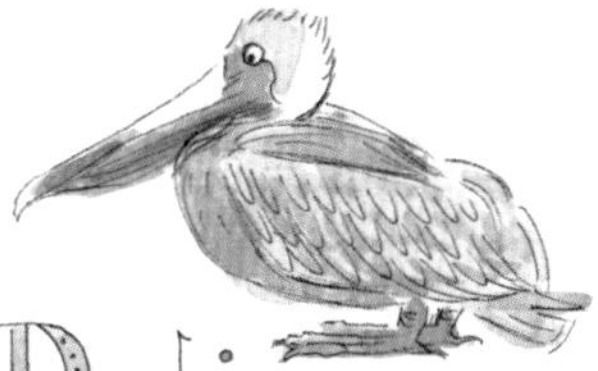

Pelican

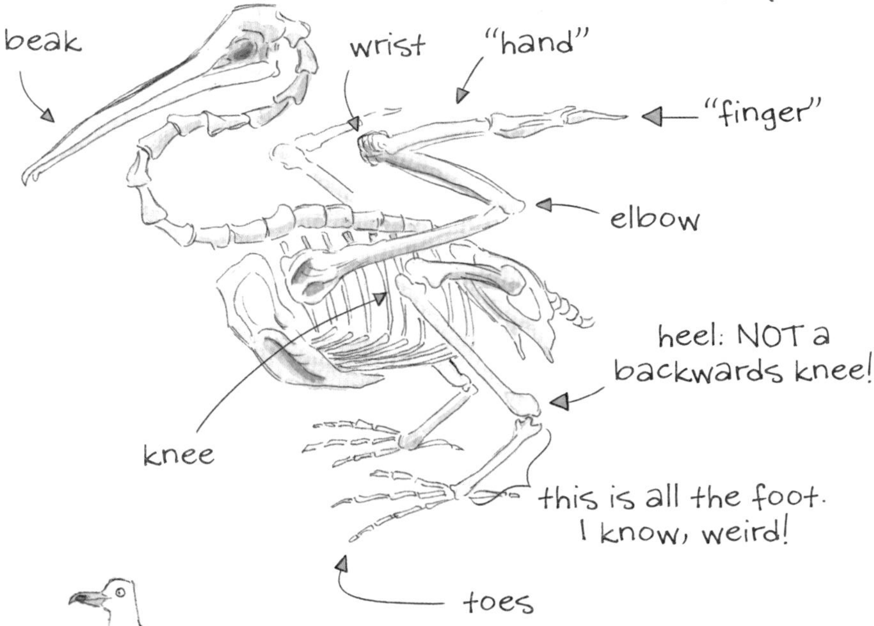
beak
wrist
"hand"
"finger"
elbow
heel: NOT a backwards knee!
knee
this is all the foot. I know, weird!
toes

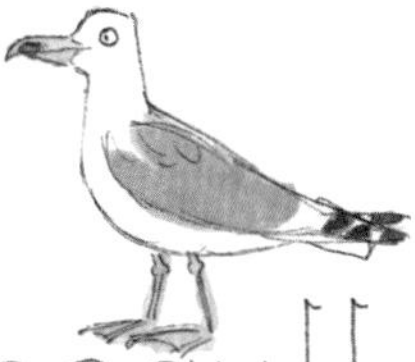

Seagull

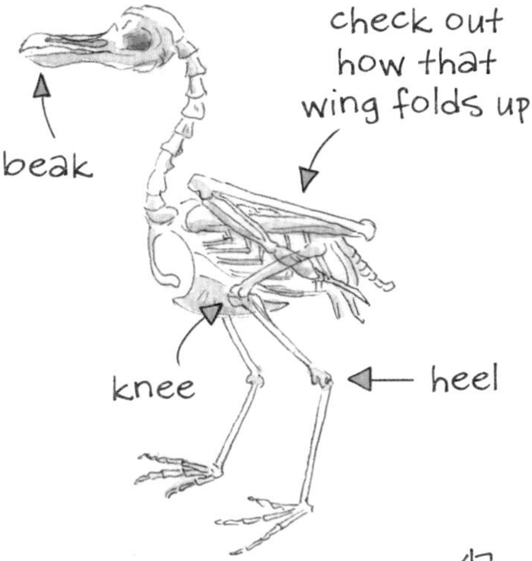
check out how that wing folds up
beak
knee
heel

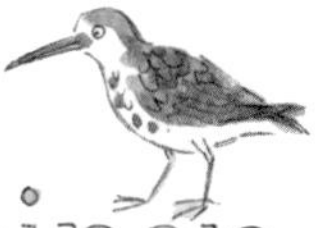

Sandpiper

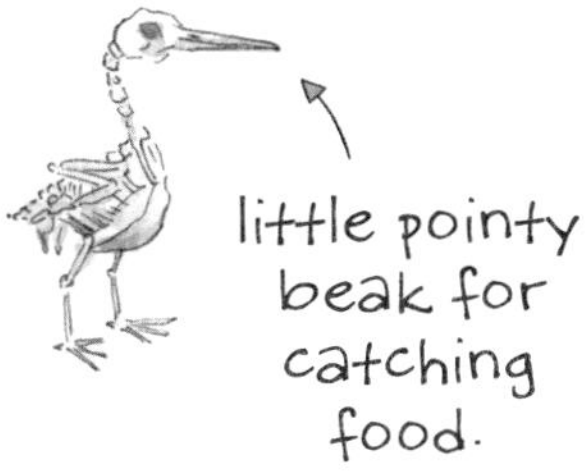
little pointy beak for catching food.

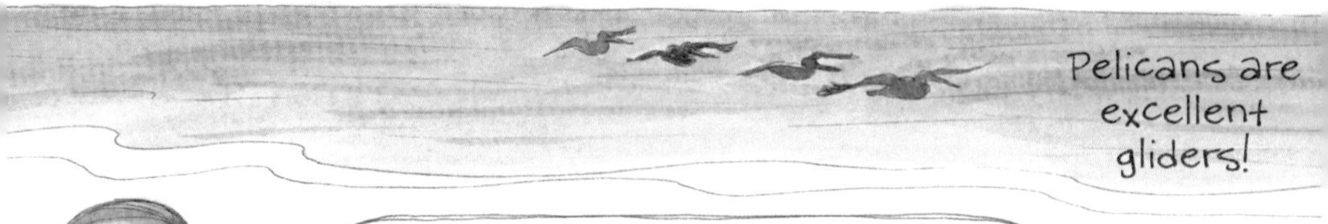
Pelicans are excellent gliders!

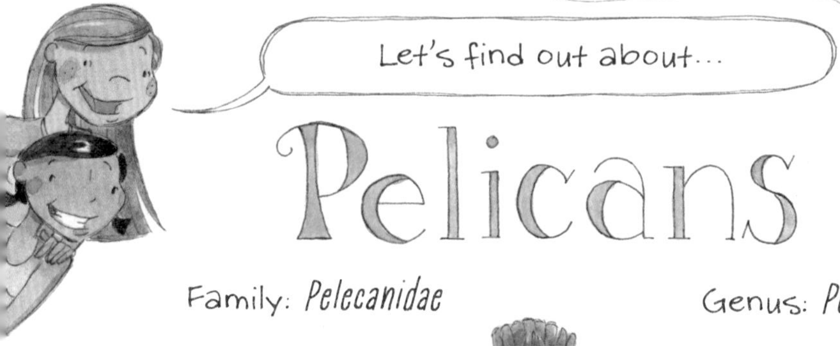
Let's find out about...

Pelicans

Family: *Pelecanidae*

Genus: *Pelecanus*

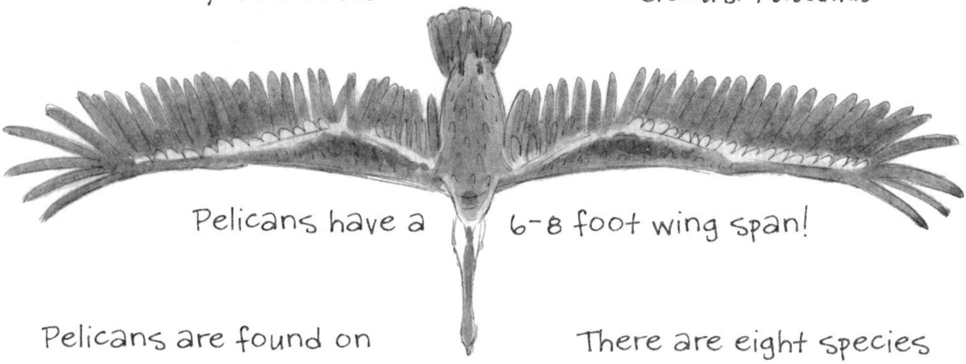

Pelicans have a 6-8 foot wing span!

Pelicans are found on every continent except Antarctica.

There are eight species of pelicans, including all-white ones!

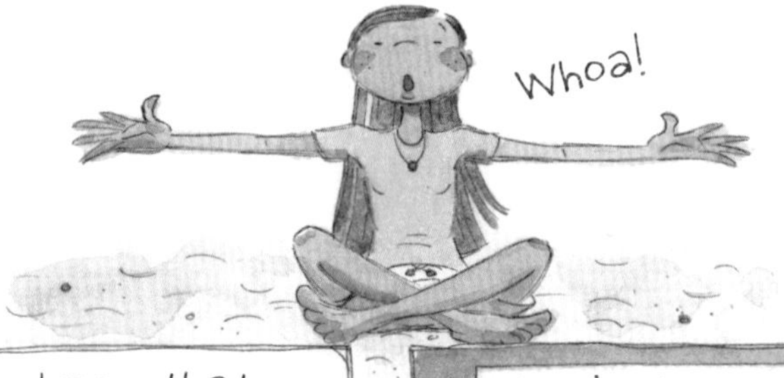
Whoa!

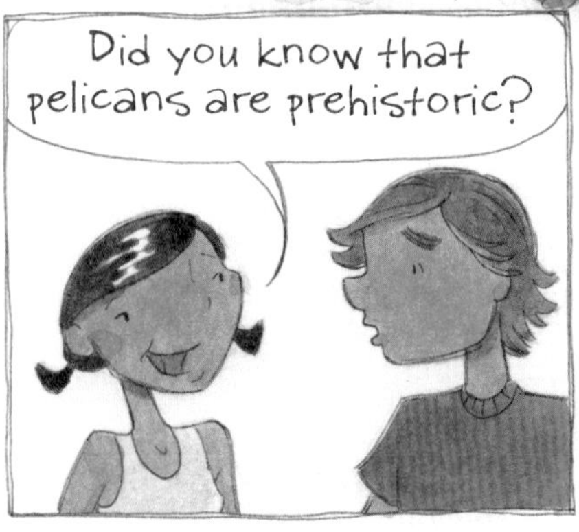
Did you know that pelicans are prehistoric?

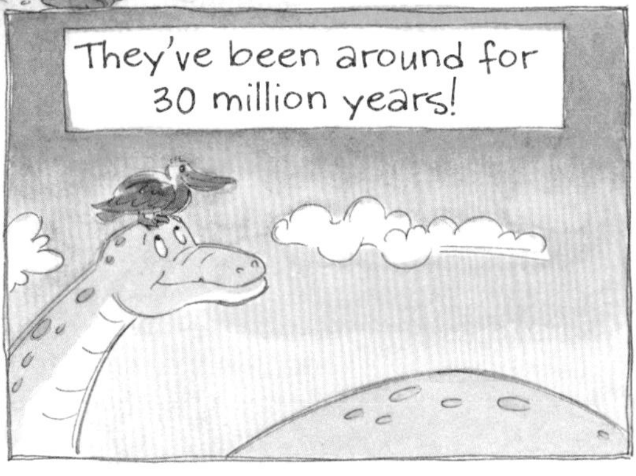
They've been around for 30 million years!

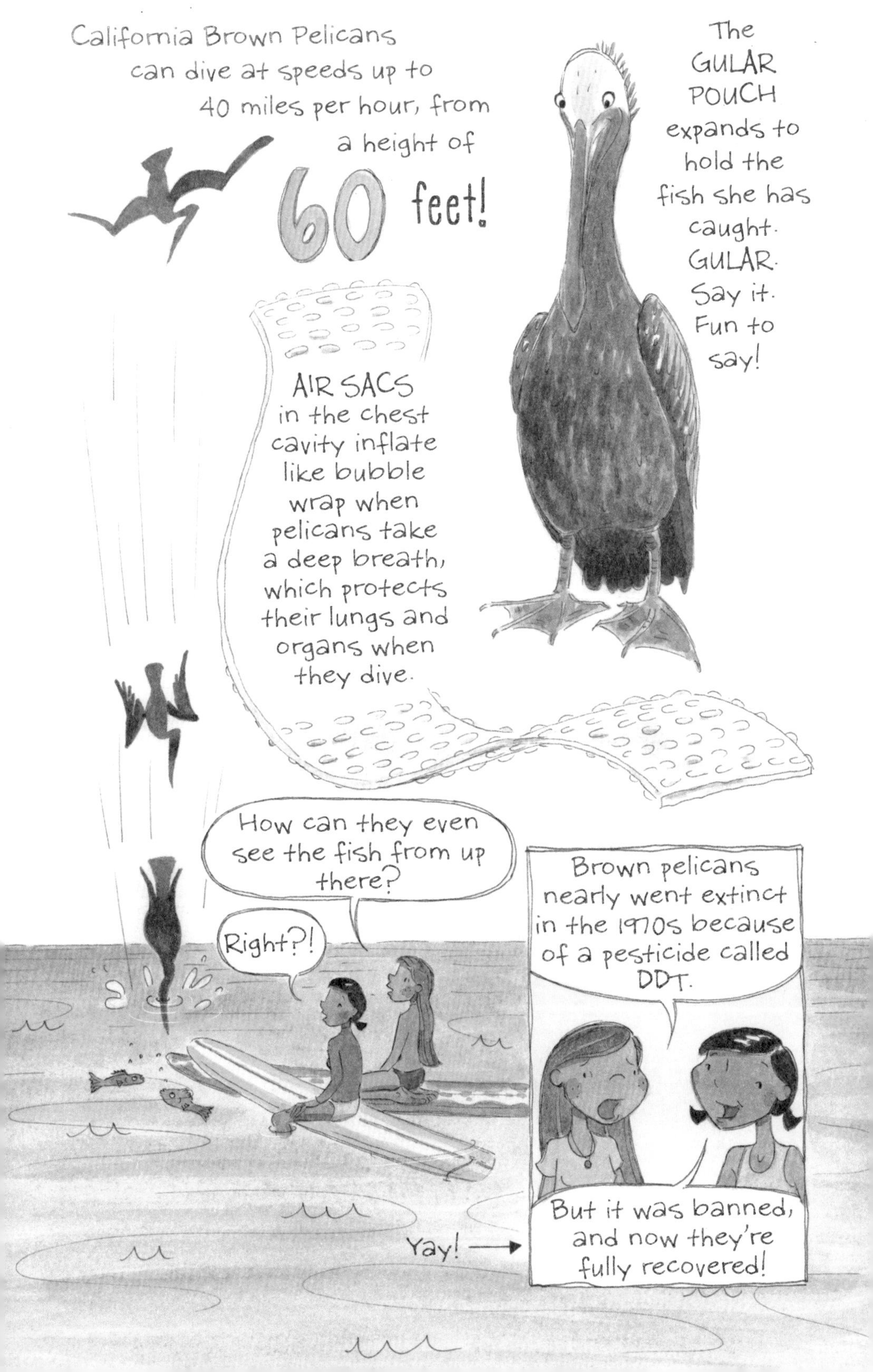
California Brown Pelicans can dive at speeds up to 40 miles per hour, from a height of
60 feet!
The GULAR POUCH expands to hold the fish she has caught. GULAR. Say it. Fun to say!
AIR SACS in the chest cavity inflate like bubble wrap when pelicans take a deep breath, which protects their lungs and organs when they dive.
How can they even see the fish from up there?
Right?!
Brown pelicans nearly went extinct in the 1970s because of a pesticide called DDT.
But it was banned, and now they're fully recovered!
Yay!

Lots of things you didn't know about

SEAGULLS!

Larus occidentalis

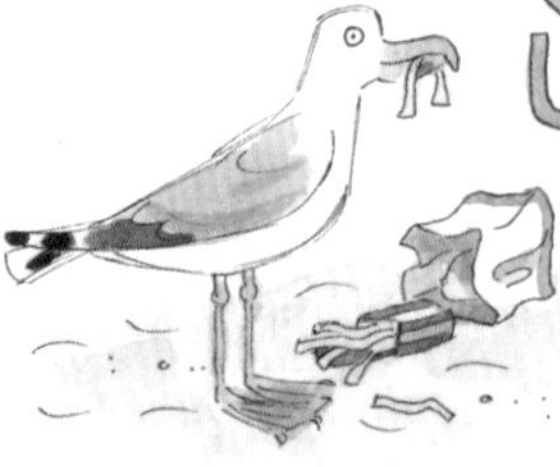

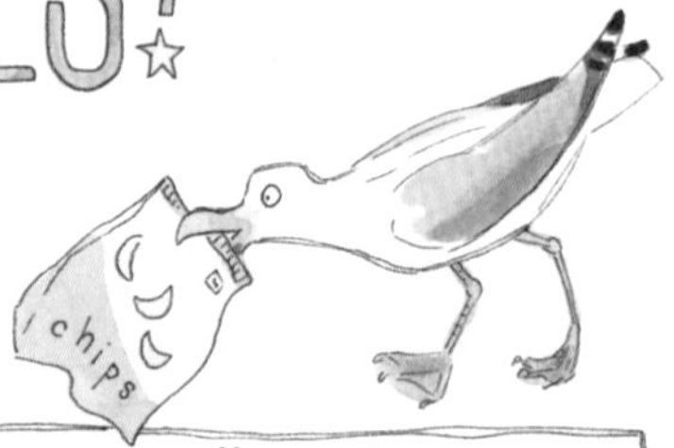
chips

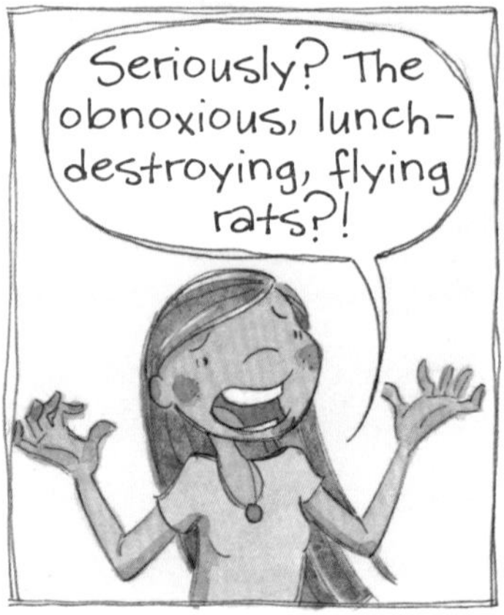
Seriously? The obnoxious, lunch-destroying, flying rats?!

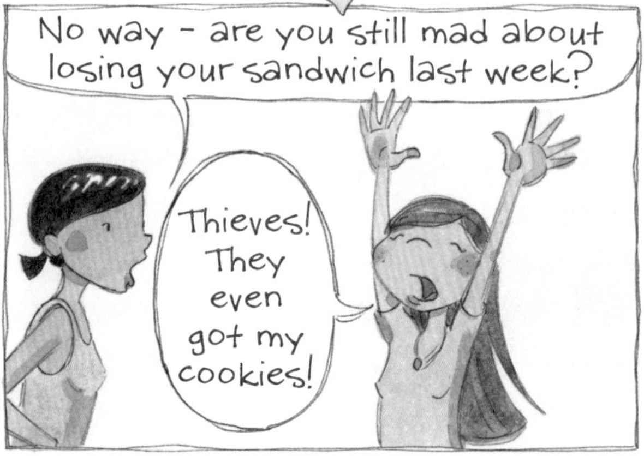
No way - are you still mad about losing your sandwich last week?
Thieves! They even got my cookies!

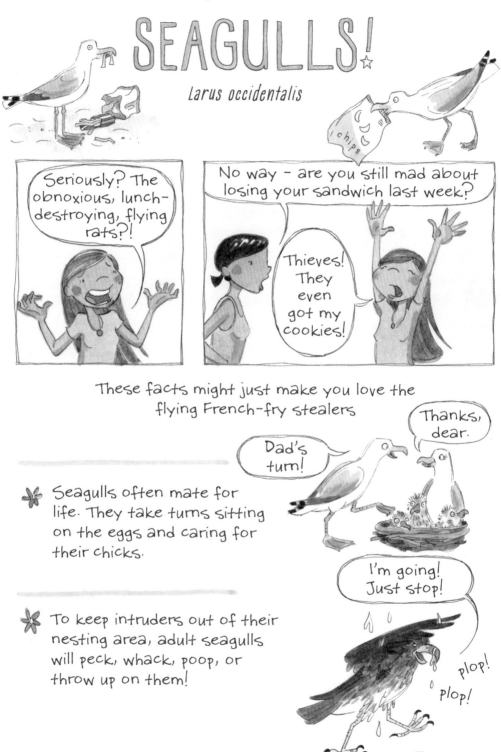

These facts might just make you love the flying French-fry stealers

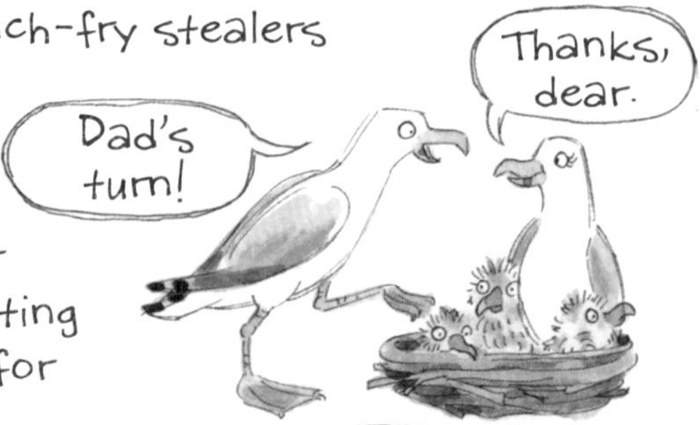
Dad's turn!
Thanks, dear.

- Seagulls often mate for life. They take turns sitting on the eggs and caring for their chicks.

- To keep intruders out of their nesting area, adult seagulls will peck, whack, poop, or throw up on them!

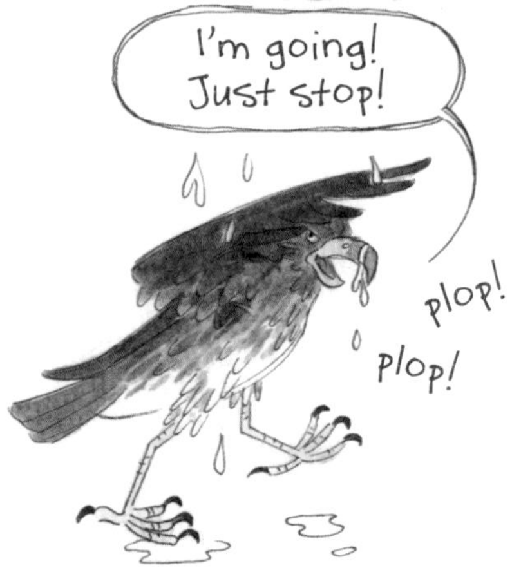
I'm going! Just stop!
plop!
plop!

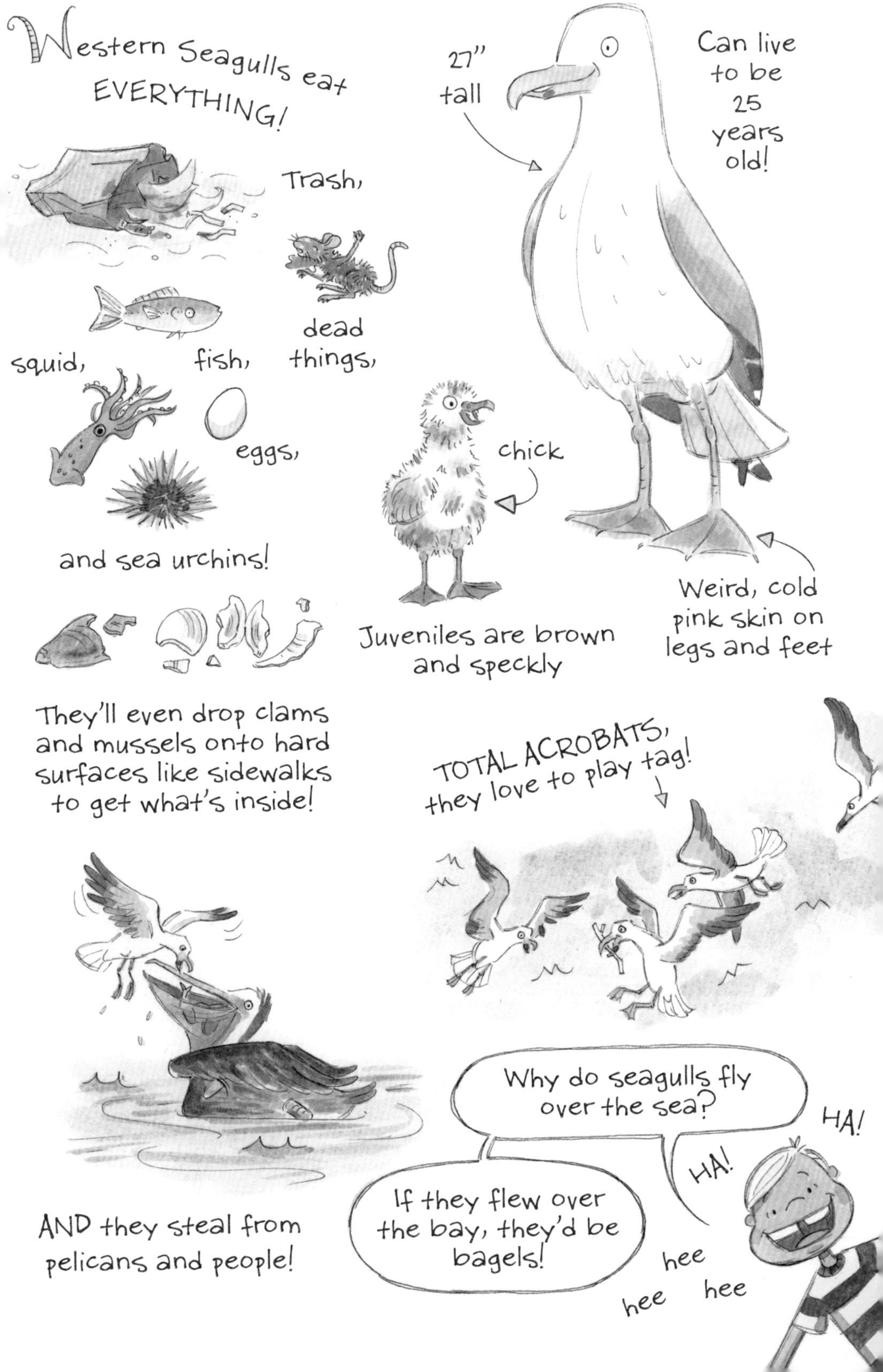
Western Seagulls eat EVERYTHING!
Trash,
dead things,
fish,
squid,
eggs,
and sea urchins!
They'll even drop clams and mussels onto hard surfaces like sidewalks to get what's inside!
27" tall
Can live to be 25 years old!
chick
Juveniles are brown and speckly
Weird, cold pink skin on legs and feet
TOTAL ACROBATS, they love to play tag!
AND they steal from pelicans and people!
Why do seagulls fly over the sea?
If they flew over the bay, they'd be bagels!
HA!
HA!
hee
hee
hee

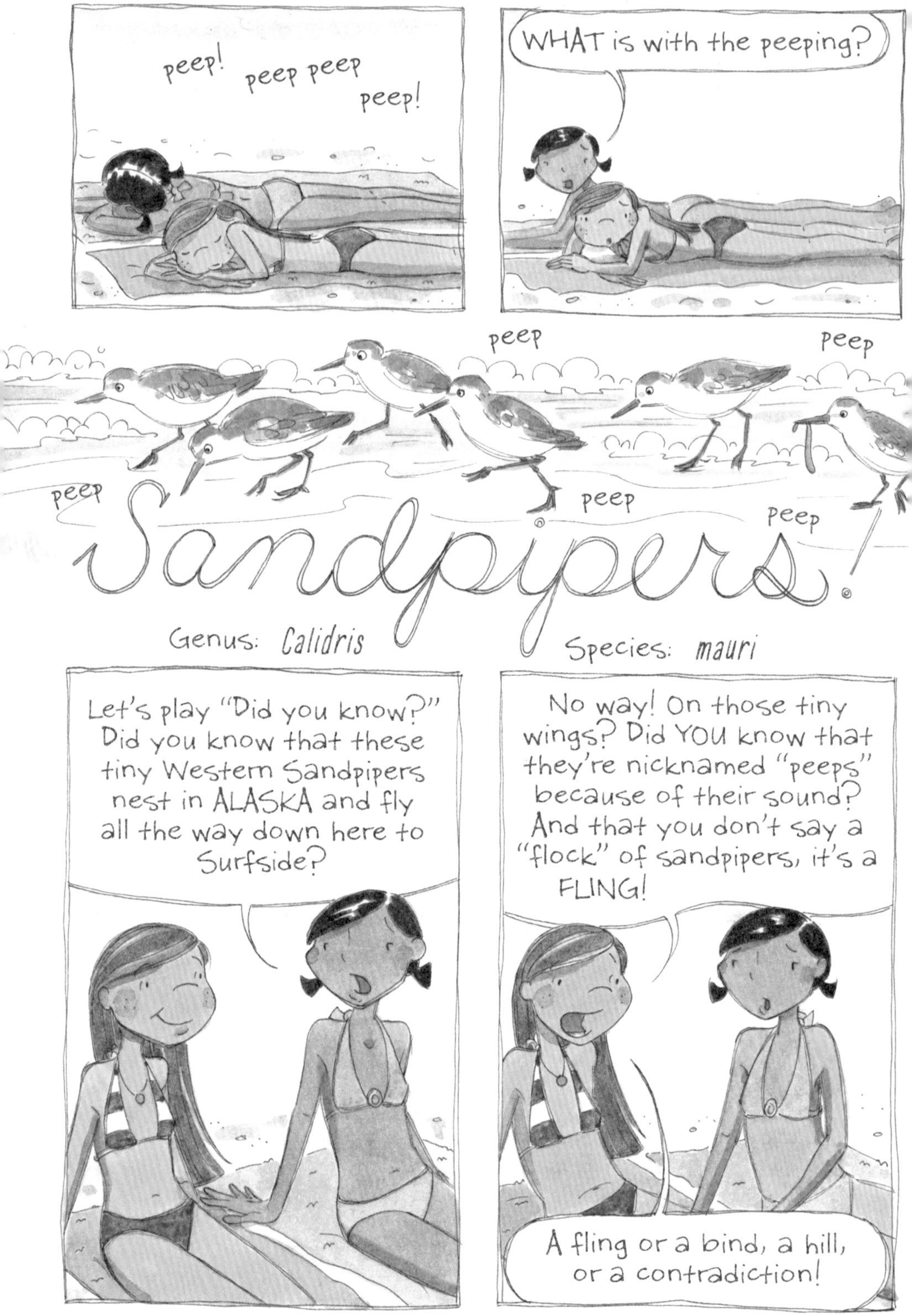

peep! peep peep peep!
WHAT is with the peeping?
peep peep peep peep peep
Sandpipers!
Genus: Calidris
Species: mauri
Let's play "Did you know?" Did you know that these tiny Western Sandpipers nest in ALASKA and fly all the way down here to Surfside?
No way! On those tiny wings? Did YOU know that they're nicknamed "peeps" because of their sound? And that you don't say a "flock" of sandpipers, it's a FLING!
A fling or a bind, a hill, or a contradiction!

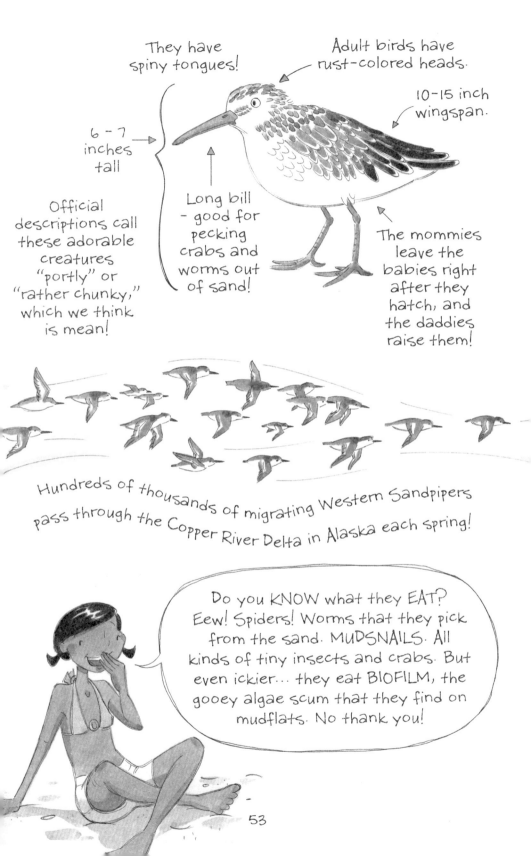

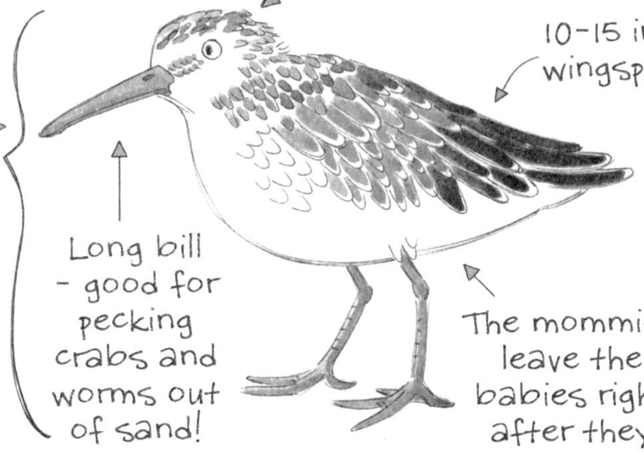
They have spiny tongues!
Adult birds have rust-colored heads.
10-15 inch wingspan.
6 - 7 inches tall
Long bill - good for pecking crabs and worms out of sand!
Official descriptions call these adorable creatures "portly" or "rather chunky," which we think is mean!
The mommies leave the babies right after they hatch, and the daddies raise them!

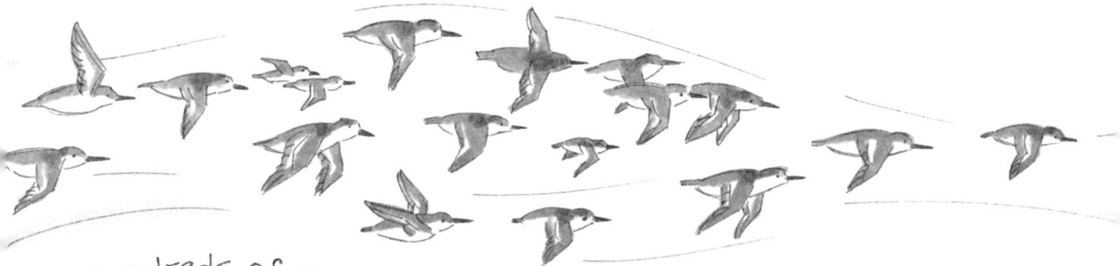

Hundreds of thousands of migrating Western Sandpipers pass through the Copper River Delta in Alaska each spring!

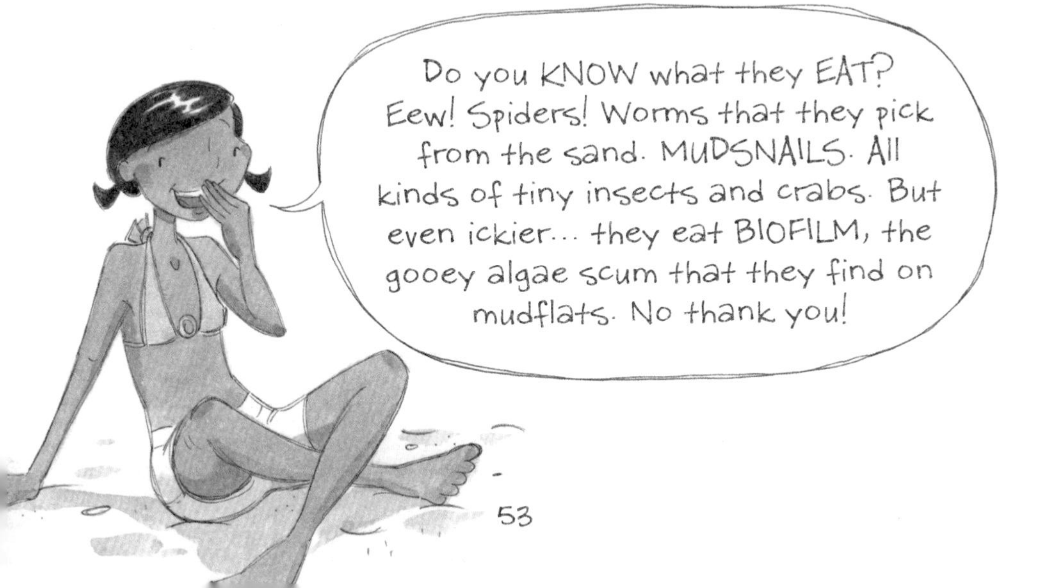
Do you KNOW what they EAT? Eew! Spiders! Worms that they pick from the sand. MUDSNAILS. All kinds of tiny insects and crabs. But even ickier... they eat BIOFILM, the gooey algae scum that they find on mudflats. No thank you!

in between...
THE
INTERTIDAL
ZONE

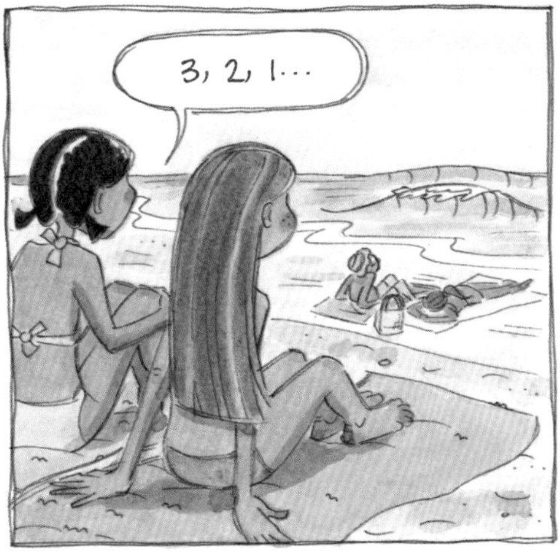
3, 2, 1...

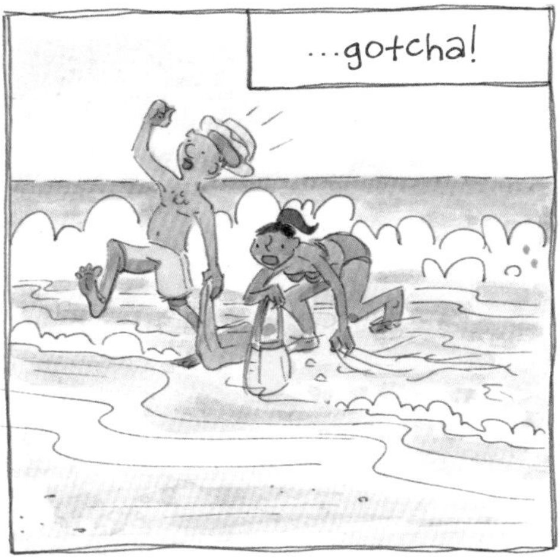
...gotcha!

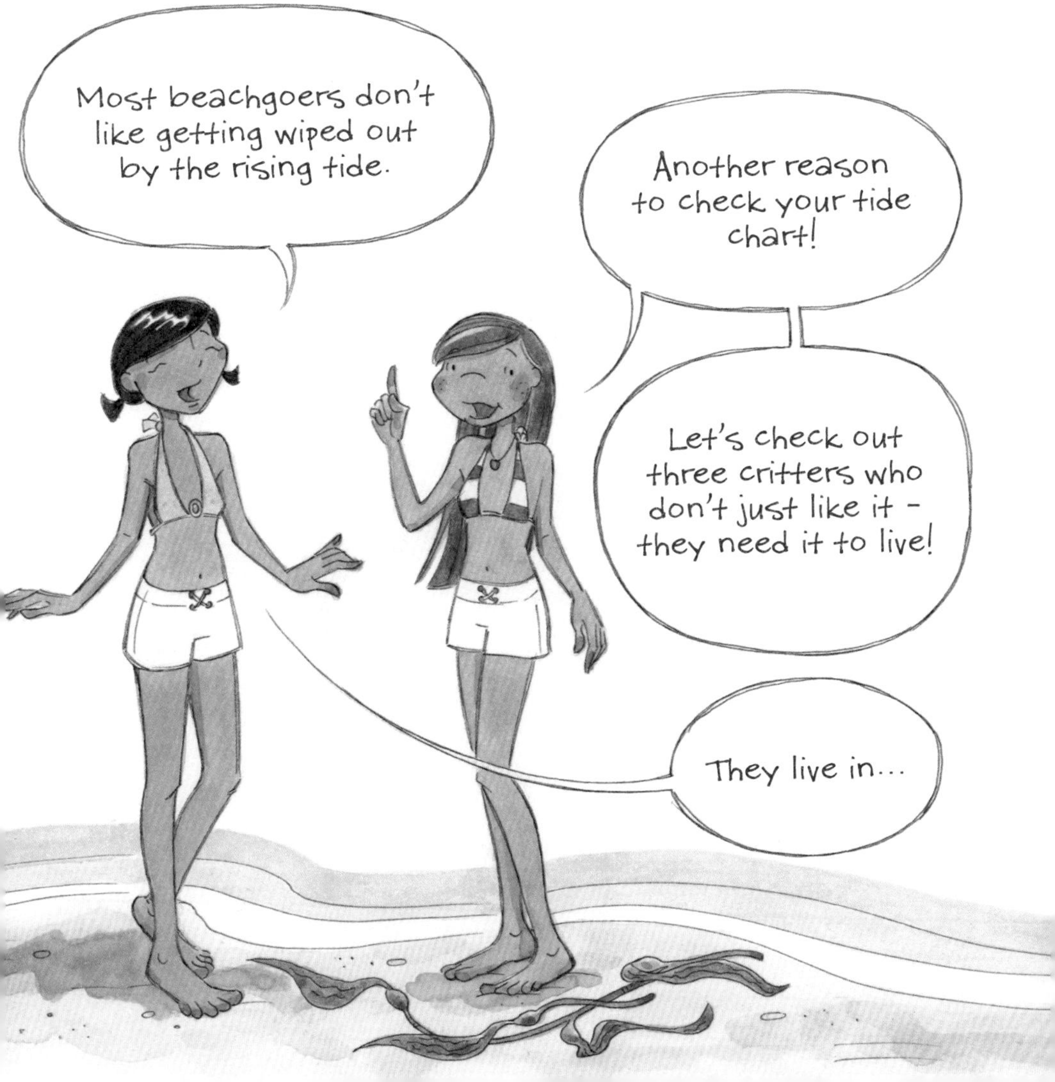
Most beachgoers don't like getting wiped out by the rising tide.
Another reason to check your tide chart!
Let's check out three critters who don't just like it - they need it to live!
They live in...

THE INTERTIDAL ZONE

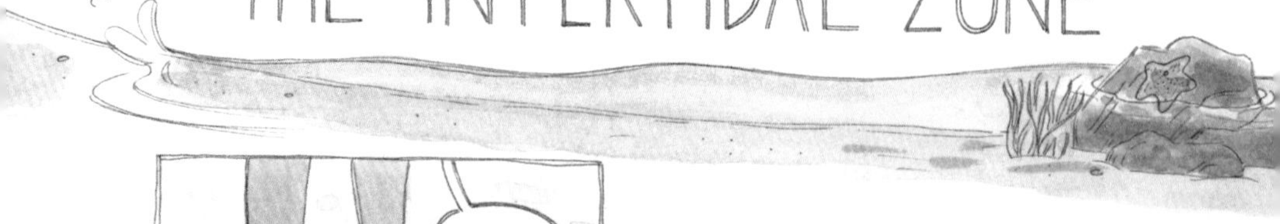

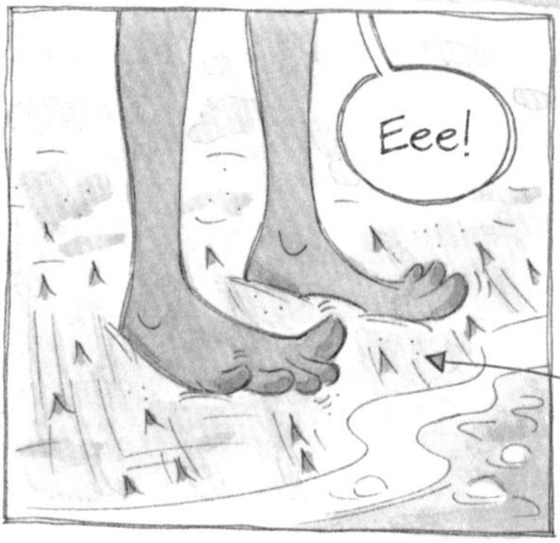
Eee!

Have you ever felt something tickle your feet as the wave pulls back out to sea?

look for the little V's

It's probably a...

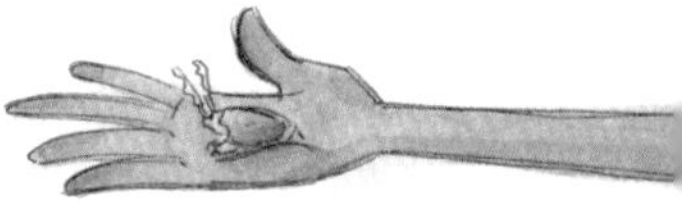

Fits in your hand.

PACIFIC SAND CRAB
Emerita analoga

1

Waves wash up and down the sand, where this guy is dug in. All of those feathery antenna and "hands" help him catch plankton and dead organic stuff to eat.

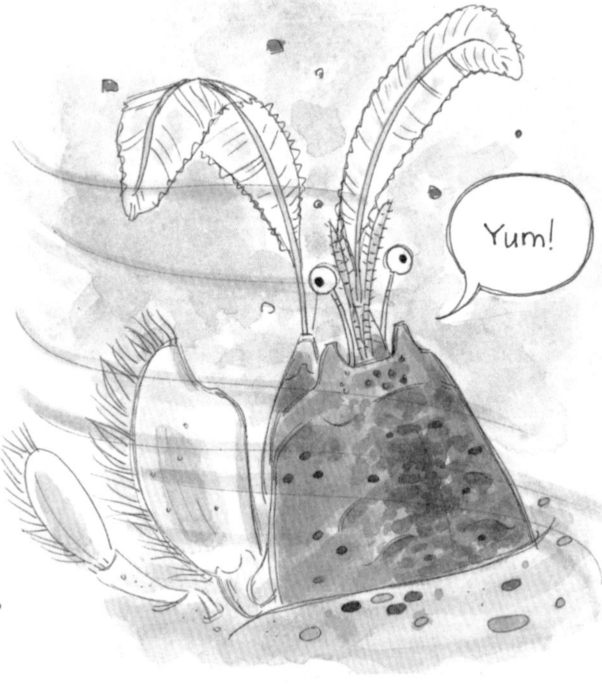
Yum!

- Neat fact: He ONLY moves backwards.

- Eaten by shorebirds like the sandpiper!

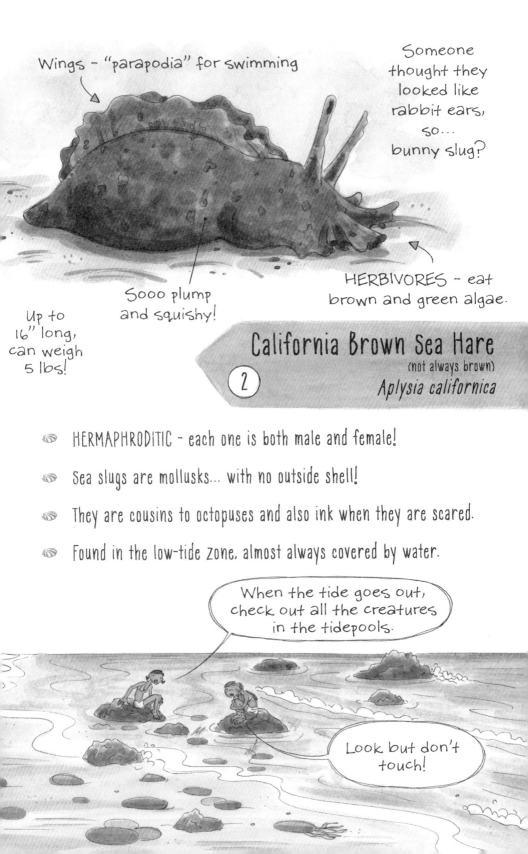

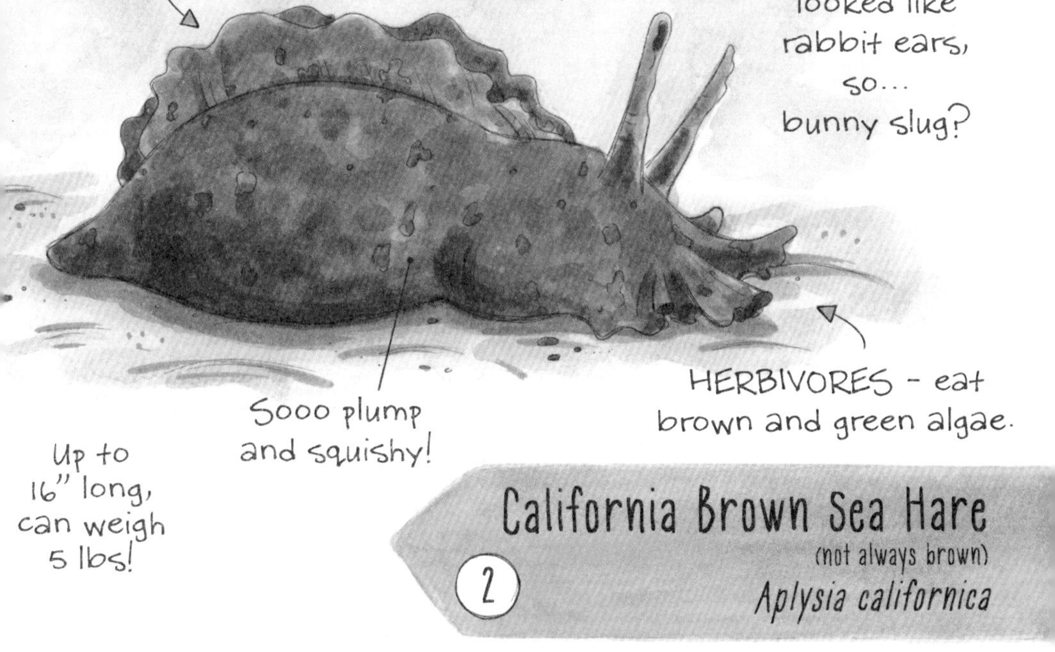
Wings - "parapodia" for swimming
Someone thought they looked like rabbit ears, so... bunny slug?
HERBIVORES - eat brown and green algae.
Sooo plump and squishy!
Up to 16" long, can weigh 5 lbs!

California Brown Sea Hare

(not always brown)

2

Aplysia californica

- HERMAPHRODITIC - each one is both male and female!
- Sea slugs are mollusks... with no outside shell!
- They are cousins to octopuses and also ink when they are scared.
- Found in the low-tide zone, almost always covered by water.

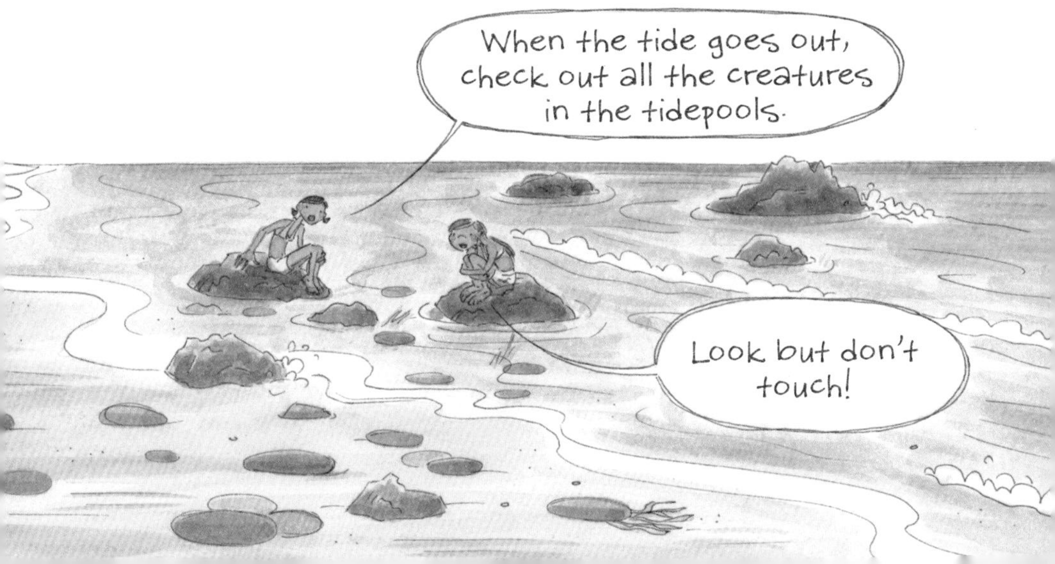
When the tide goes out, check out all the creatures in the tidepools.
Look but don't touch!

Ochre Sea Star

Pisaster ochraceus

3

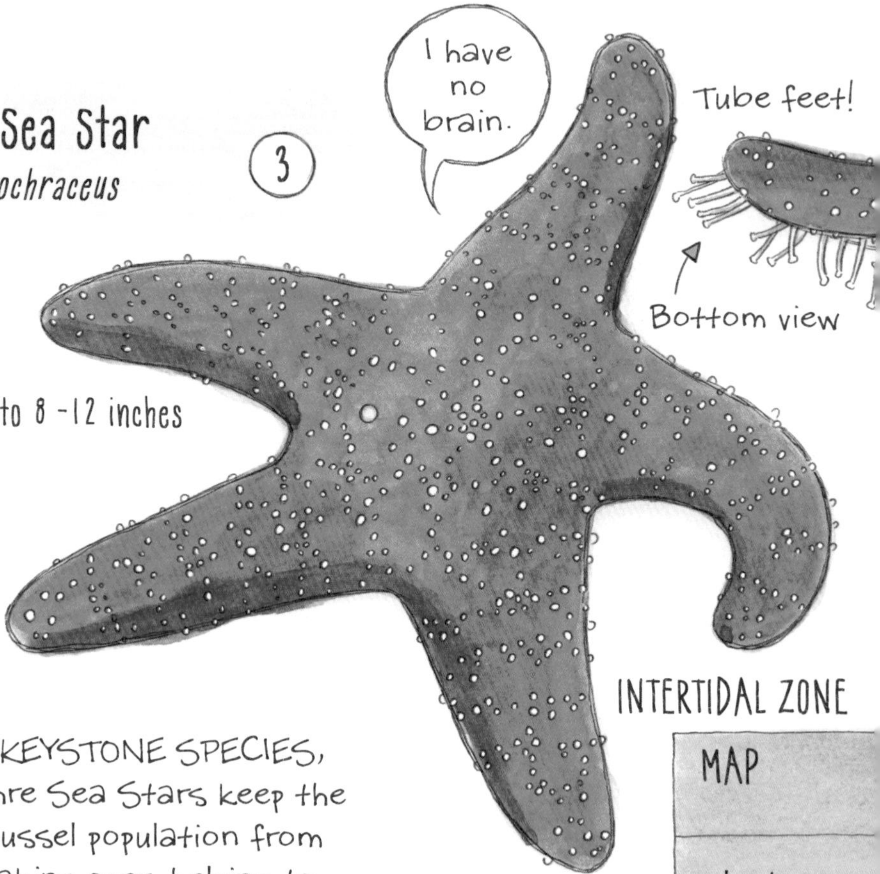
I have no brain.
Tube feet!
Bottom view

Grows to 8 -12 inches

A KEYSTONE SPECIES, Ochre Sea Stars keep the mussel population from taking over, helping to maintain BIODIVERSITY - many types of species.

INTERTIDAL ZONE

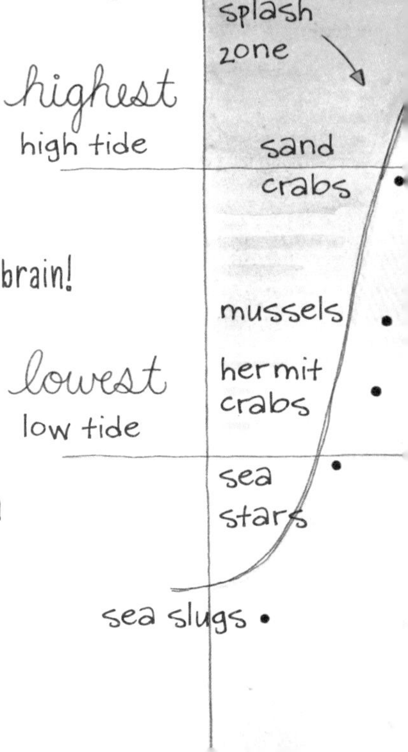
MAP
splash zone
highest
high tide
sand crabs
mussels
lowest
low tide
hermit crabs
sea stars
sea slugs

- Sea stars eat 80 mussels per year.
- Simple nervous system - they don't have a brain!
- Can live 20 years.
- Sea stars can regrow an arm if it gets cut off!
- A wasting disease, linked to warming ocean water, is threatening Ochre Sea Stars.

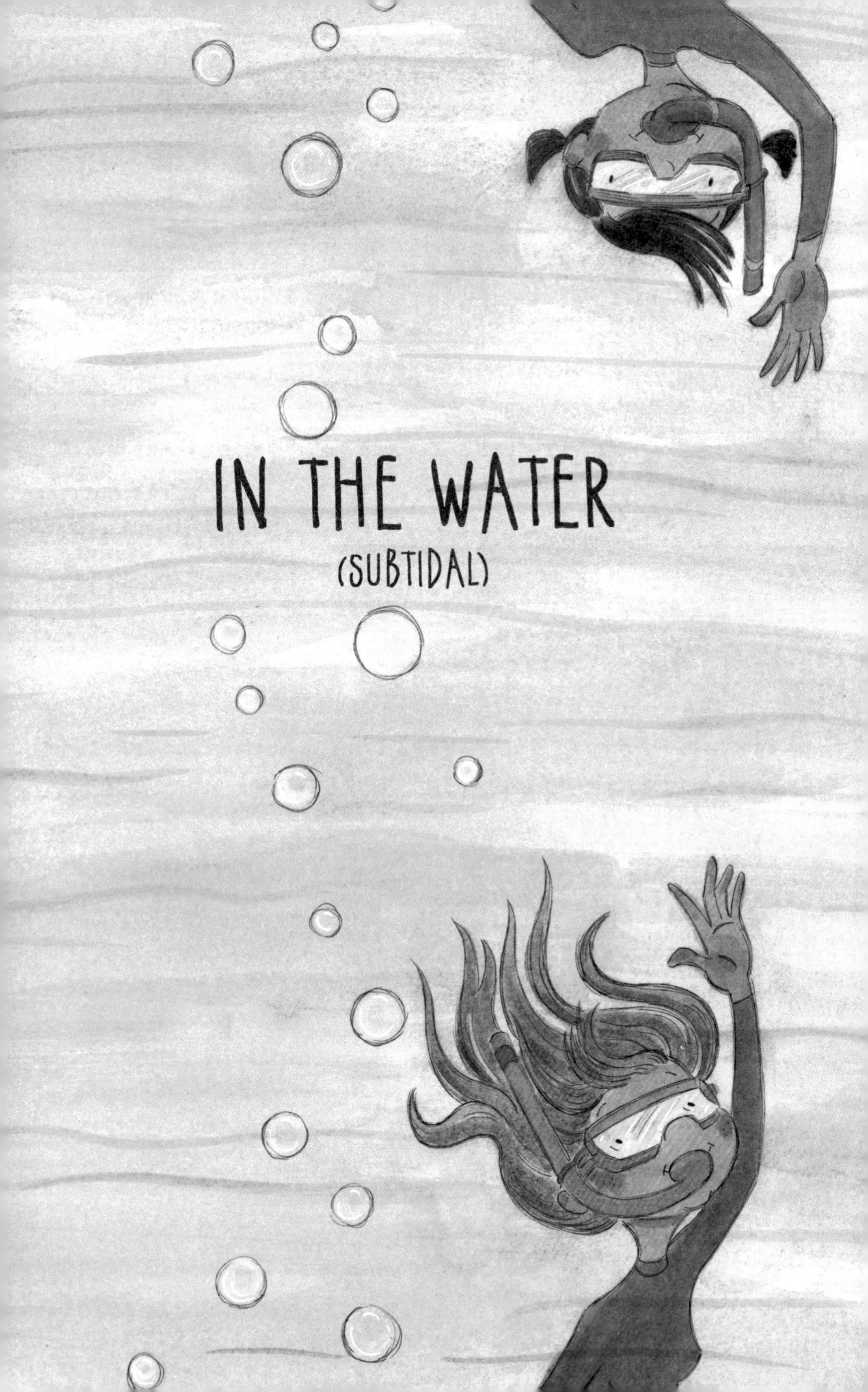
IN THE WATER
(SUBTIDAL)

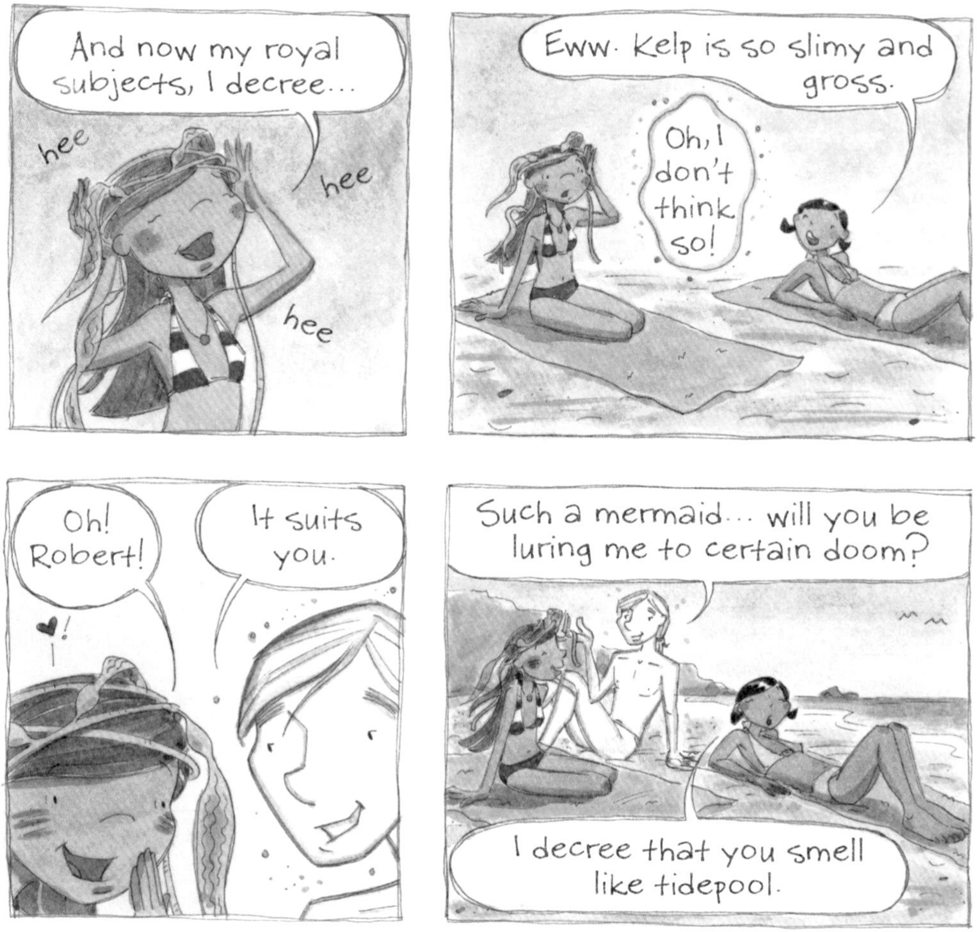
And now my royal subjects, I decree...
hee
hee
hee
Eww. Kelp is so slimy and gross.
Oh, I don't think so!
Oh! Robert!
It suits you.
Such a mermaid... will you be luring me to certain doom?
I decree that you smell like tidepool.

No way! Kelp is awesome!
In fact, it's what we're talking about next. If you've read our first book, you know we spend a lot of time at Danger Point, and underneath those perfect waves is a...

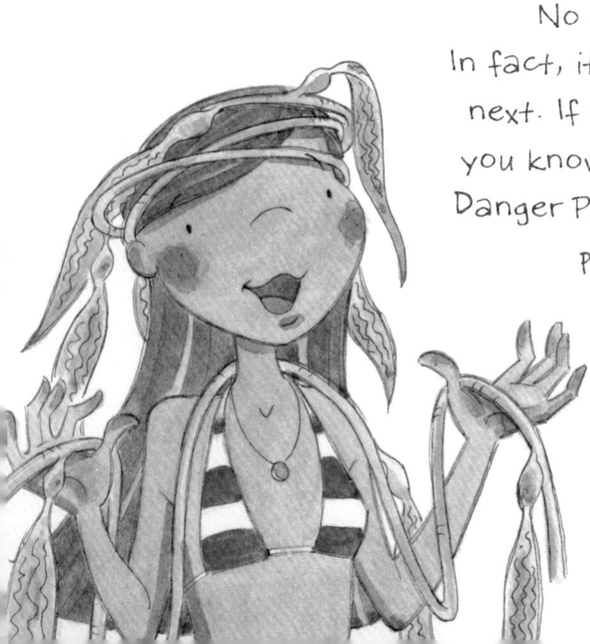

Kelp Forest!

Kelp forests are kind of like rain forests. A kelp forest is a WHOLE ECOSYSTEM, with all kinds of creatures calling it home.

And while it looks like a plant, it's actually a GIANT ALGAE.

These "roots" are called a holdfast, and it's what anchors it to the bottom.

on a rock

blade or frond

Pneumatocyst (gas bladder)

Macrocystis pyrifera

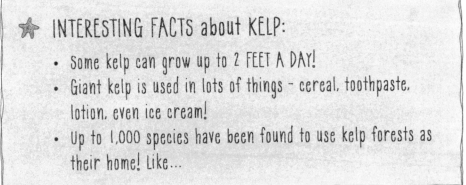

⭐ INTERESTING FACTS about KELP:

- Some kelp can grow up to 2 FEET A DAY!
- Giant kelp is used in lots of things – cereal, toothpaste, lotion, even ice cream!
- Up to 1,000 species have been found to use kelp forests as their home! Like...

INVERTEBRATES:

- abalone
- spiny lobster
- brittle stars
- urchins
- snails
- crabs
- sea stars
- jellyfish

FISH:

- rockfish
- kelp fish
- sheephead
- giant sea bass
- leopard sharks
- horn shark

MAMMALS:

- sea lions
- seals
- gray whales!
- sea otters
- Sam and Jade (occasionally)

BIRDS:

- gulls
- terns
- cormorants

...and when the kelp washes up on the beach:

- crows
- starlings
- warblers (Eat the flies, crabs and other little critters.)

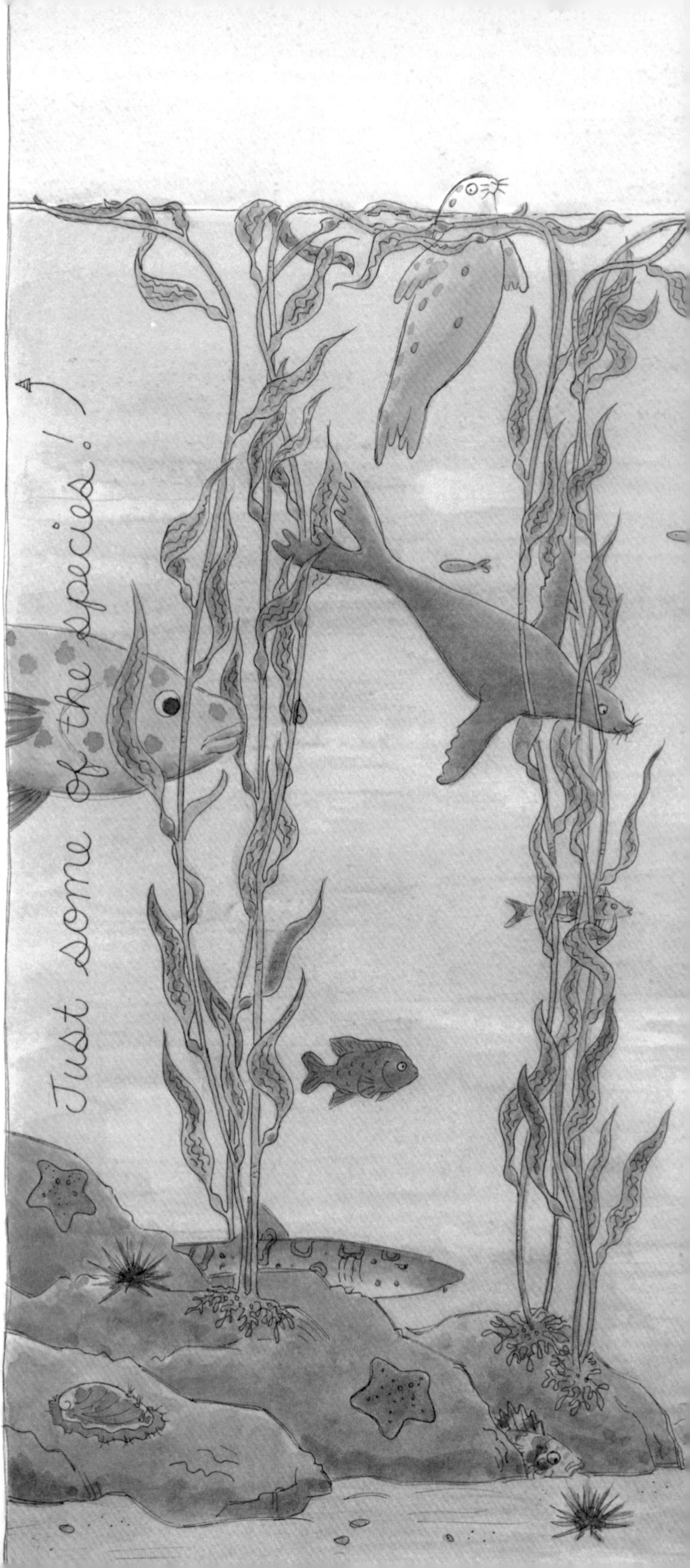
Just some of the species!

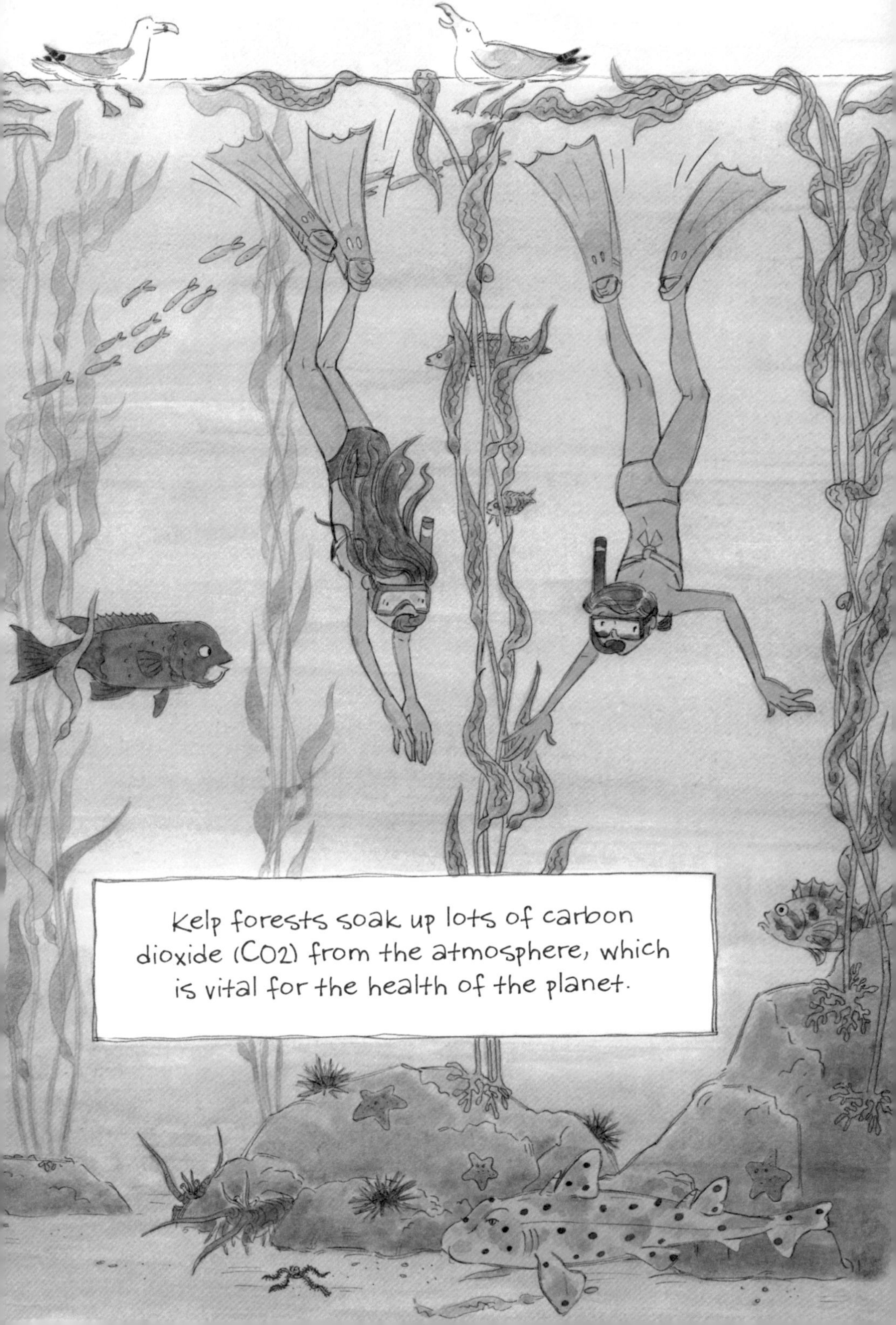
Kelp forests soak up lots of carbon dioxide (CO2) from the atmosphere, which is vital for the health of the planet.

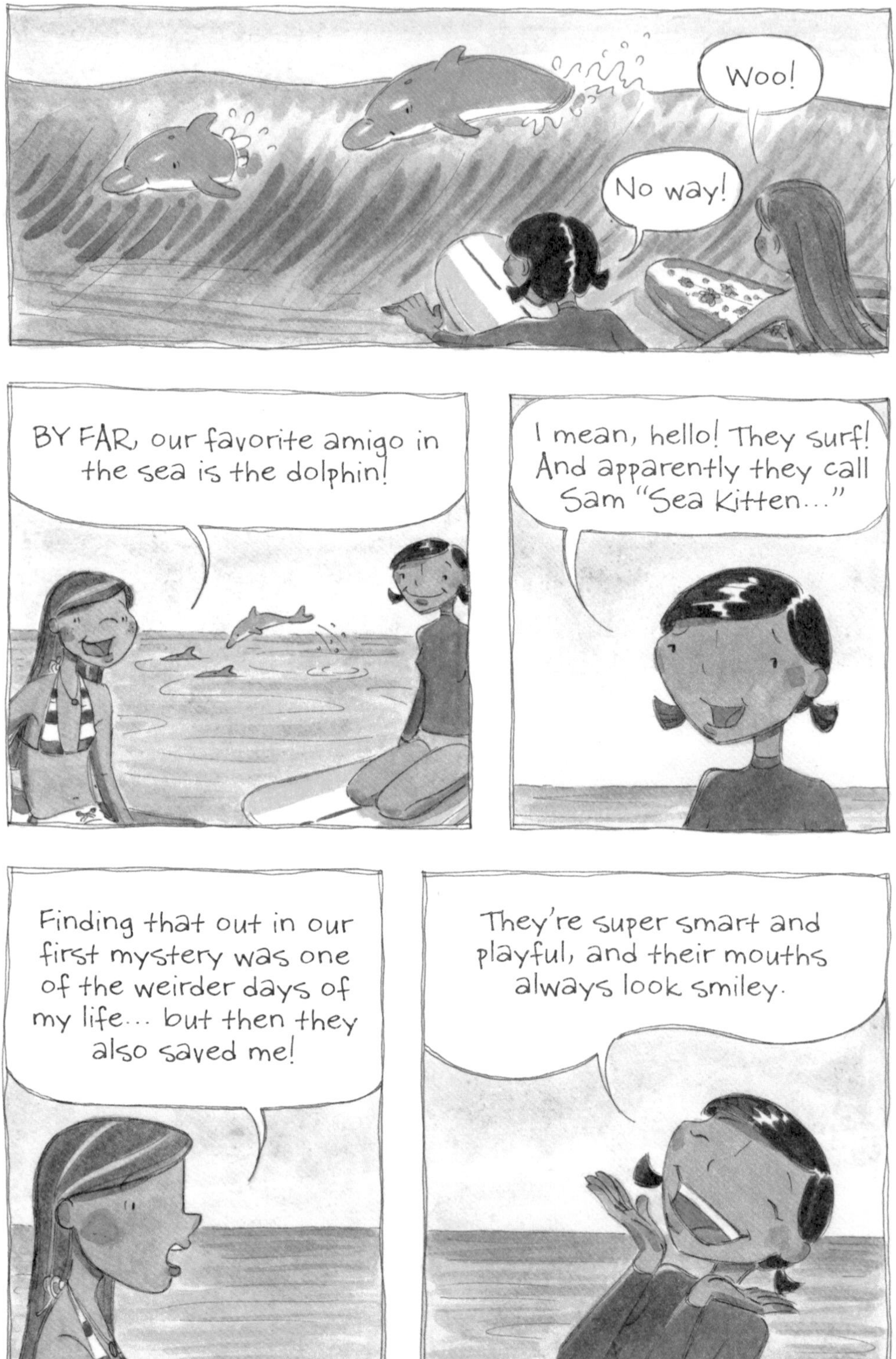
Woo!
No way!
BY FAR, our favorite amigo in the sea is the dolphin!
I mean, hello! They surf! And apparently they call Sam "Sea Kitten..."
Finding that out in our first mystery was one of the weirder days of my life... but then they also saved me!
They're super smart and playful, and their mouths always look smiley.

Who doesn't love dolphins?

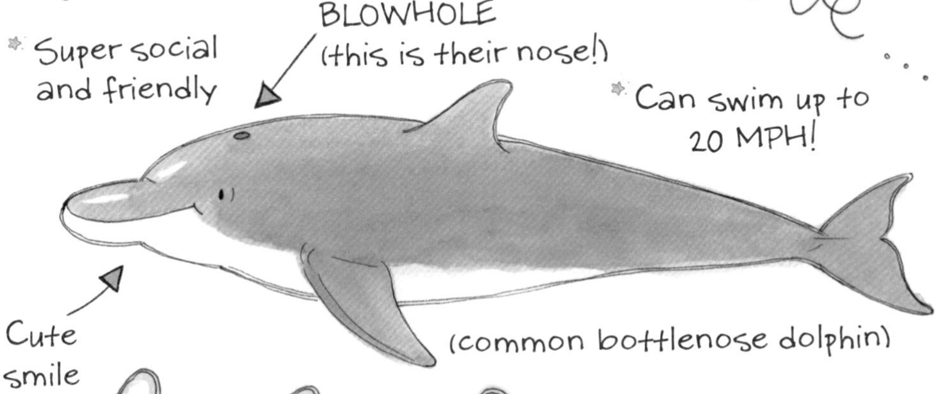
Super social and friendly
BLOWHOLE (this is their nose!)
Can swim up to 20 MPH!
Cute smile
(common bottlenose dolphin)

Tursiops truncatus

FACT:

Dolphins use ECHOLOCATION. How it works: Dolphins make sounds in air sacs near their blowhole, which pass through a fatty lump in their head called a MELON. The sounds (clicks and whistles) bounce off their surroundings - and prey - and return, giving the dolphin a kind of picture. Weird, right?!

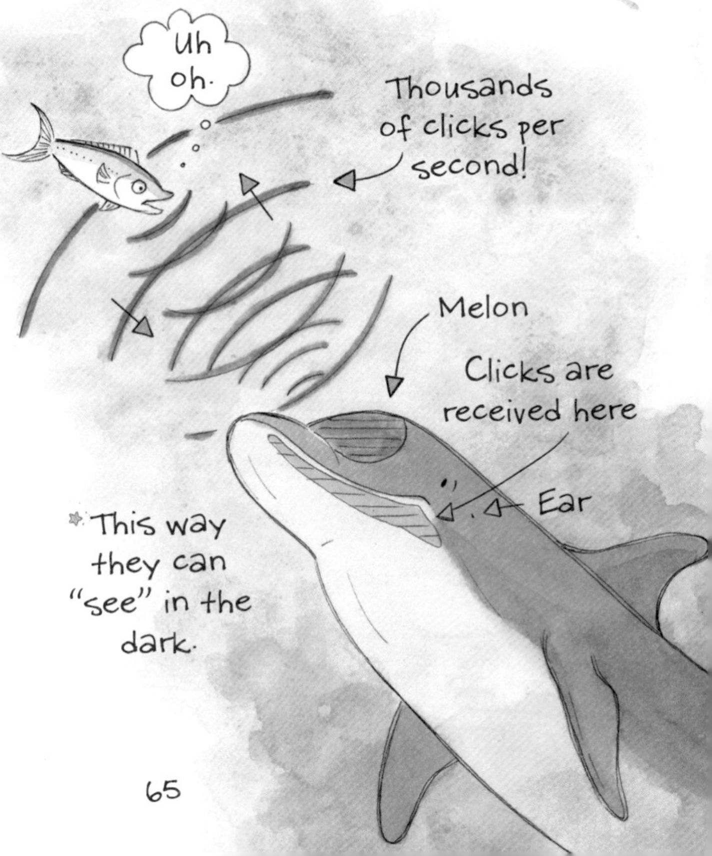
Uh oh.
Thousands of clicks per second!
Melon
Clicks are received here
Ear
This way they can "see" in the dark.

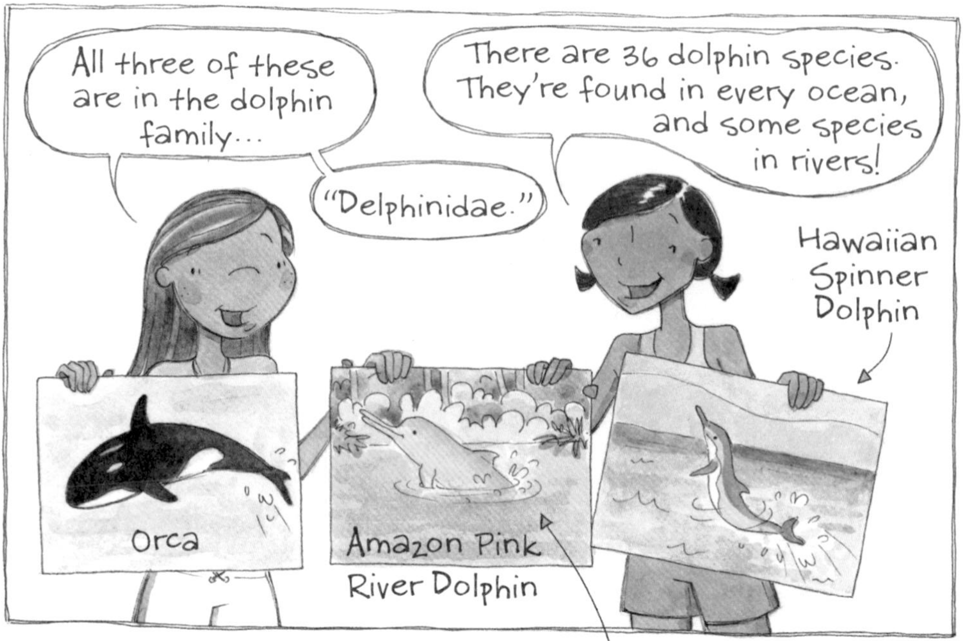
All three of these are in the dolphin family...
"Delphinidae."
There are 36 dolphin species. They're found in every ocean, and some species in rivers!
Hawaiian Spinner Dolphin
Orca
Amazon Pink River Dolphin

yes, pink!

Dolphins are MAMMALS, like we are, which means they are warm blooded, give live birth, and nurse their babies.

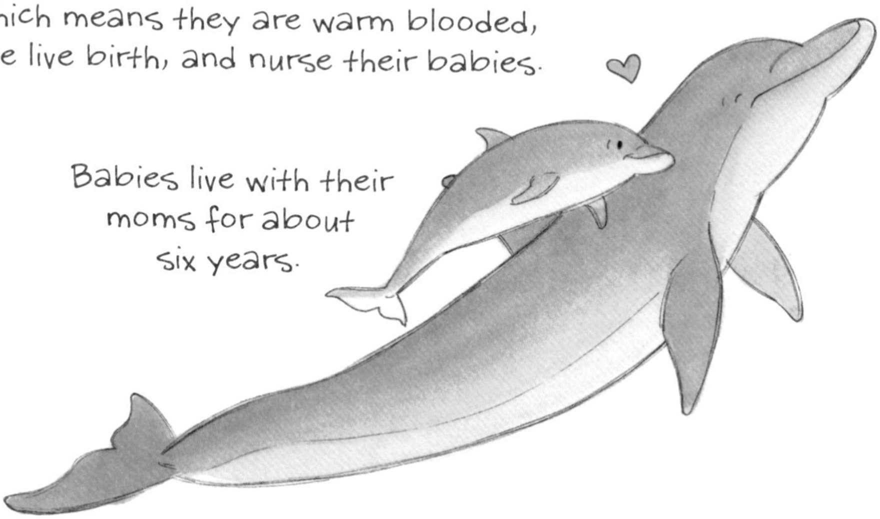

Babies live with their moms for about six years.

They are SUPER SOCIAL and can swim in PODS of up to 1,000 dolphins!

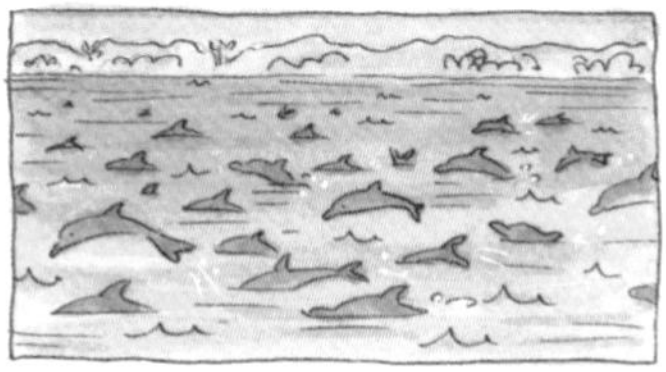

COOL FACTS:

- ♥ If you killed a dolphin in Ancient Greece, you would be executed. Dolphins were sacred.
- ♥ Dolphins sleep with half of their brain off, half on, to stay alert and breathe!
- ♥ Dolphins are mighty hunters and eat up to 33 pounds of fish a day.

c o m p a r a t i v e   a n a t o m y

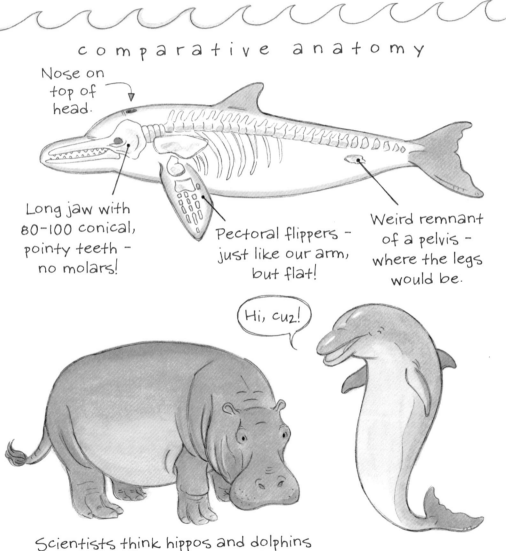

Nose on top of head.

Long jaw with 80-100 conical, pointy teeth – no molars!

Pectoral flippers – just like our arm, but flat!

Weird remnant of a pelvis – where the legs would be.

Hi, cuz!

Scientists think hippos and dolphins are distant cousins.

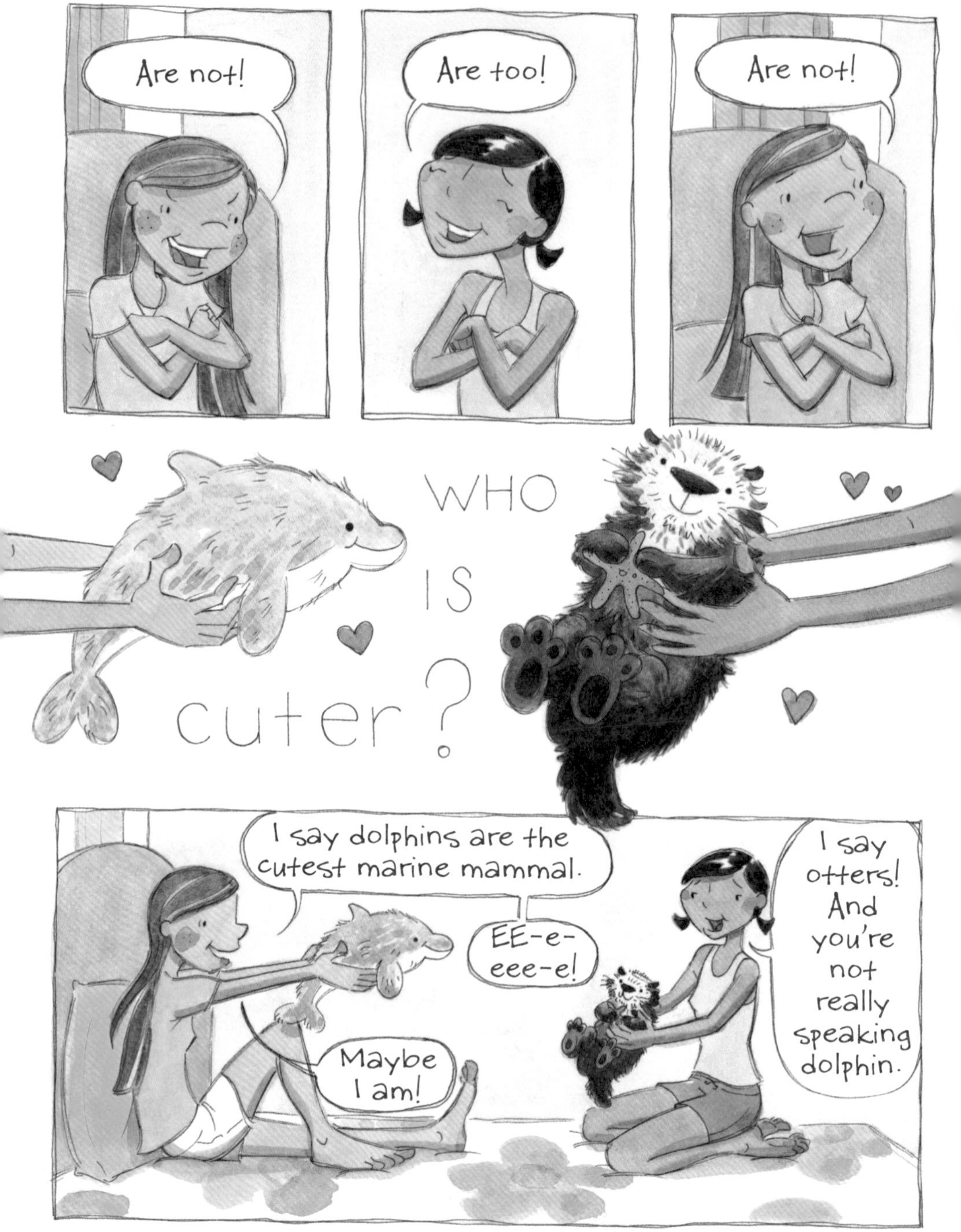
Are not!
Are too!
Are not!
WHO IS cuter?
I say dolphins are the cutest marine mammal.
EE-e-eee-e!
I say otters! And you're not really speaking dolphin.
Maybe I am!

We bought these plushies at the Aquarium. BOTH are mammals. Who's your favorite?

Sea Otters: The *Cutest* Marine Mammal

* Says Jade

Enhydra lutris

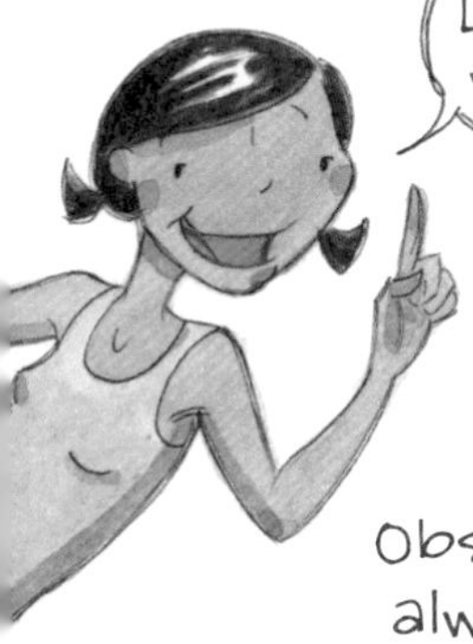

Let me explain why I'm right.

1. SOOO FLUFFY!

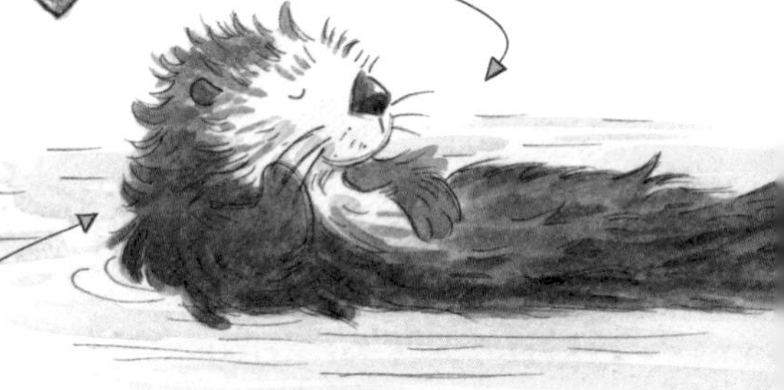

Obsessively clean, always grooming!

2. THEY WRAP THEIR BABIES IN KELP WHEN THEY HAVE TO GO HUNTING.

(so they stay hidden and don't drift away)

Sea otters have the thickest fur of any mammal - millions of hairs per square inch!

Eeee!

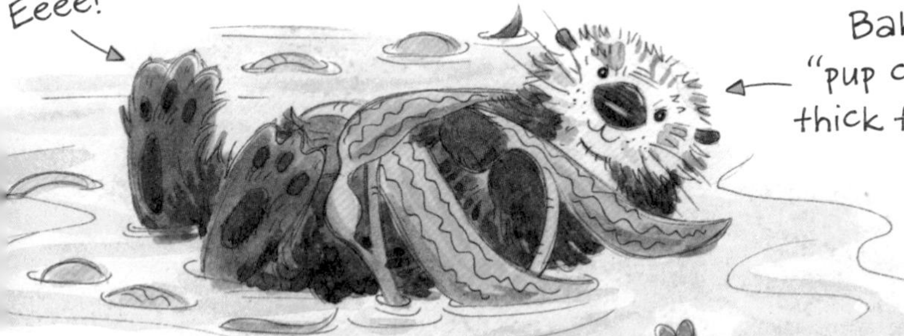

Baby otters' "pup coats" are so thick they bob like corks.

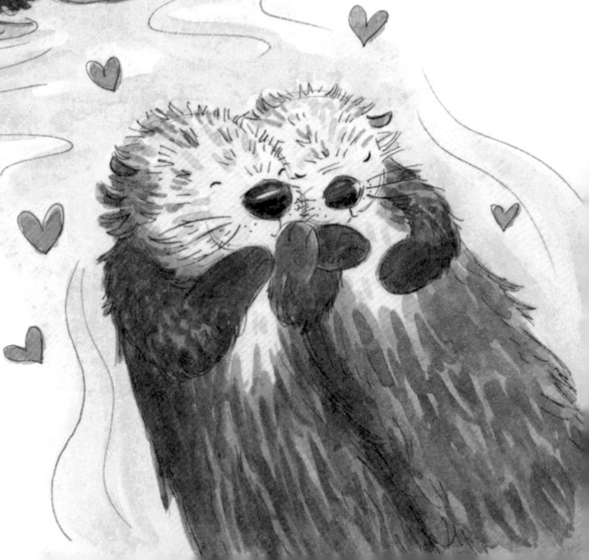

3. THEY HOLD HANDS WHEN THEY SLEEP!

(so they don't get separated)

Stop it! The cuteness!

PROTECTOR of the REALM

Sea otters are in the weasel family. Water weasels!

Otters are considered a

KEYSTONE SPECIES,

"Keepers of the Kelp Forest."

Sea otters need to eat A LOT to keep warm. One of their favorite foods to eat is sea urchin. If no one was eating the urchins, they would eat the roots off of an entire kelp forest! We know how important kelp forests are... so many species live there! Sea otters maintain the balance and health of a whole ecosystem!

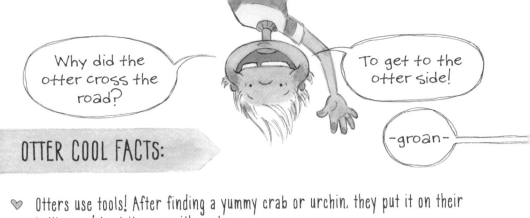

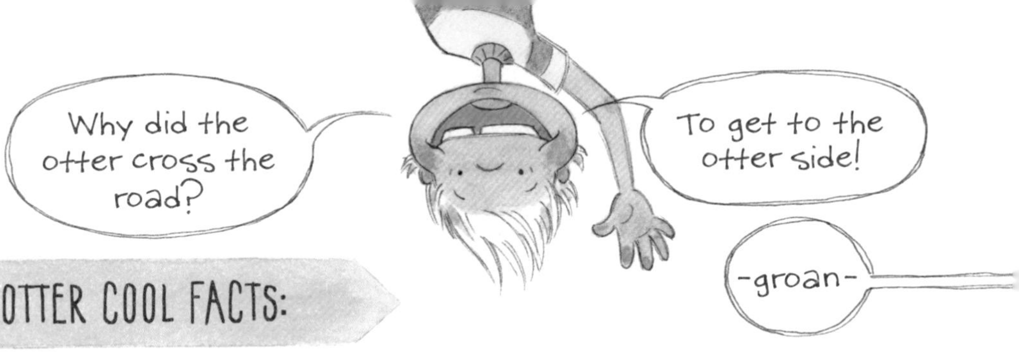
Why did the otter cross the road?
To get to the otter side!
-groan-

OTTER COOL FACTS:

- Otters use tools! After finding a yummy crab or urchin, they put it on their bellies and bust it open with a stone.
- Sea otters grow to 4 feet and can weigh 65 lbs.
- Otters can live their whole life without leaving the ocean!

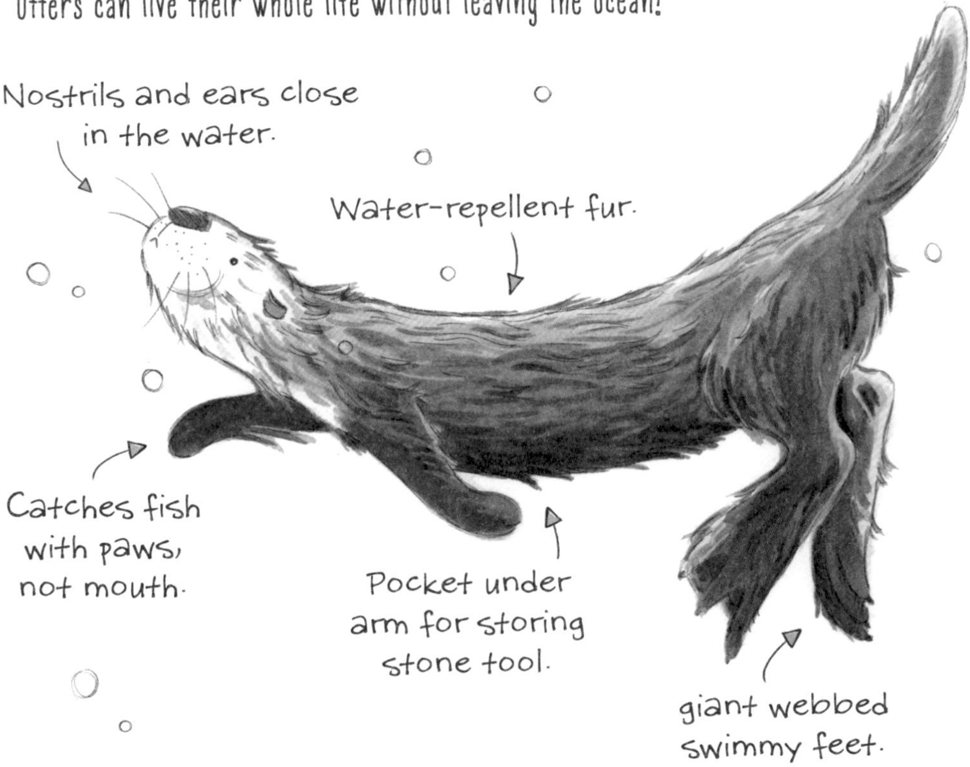
Nostrils and ears close in the water.
Water-repellent fur.
Catches fish with paws, not mouth.
Pocket under arm for storing stone tool.
giant webbed swimmy feet.

Sadly, sea otters were nearly hunted to extinction for their fur. Now they are PROTECTED under the Endangered Species Act.

Yay! The cuteness lives on!

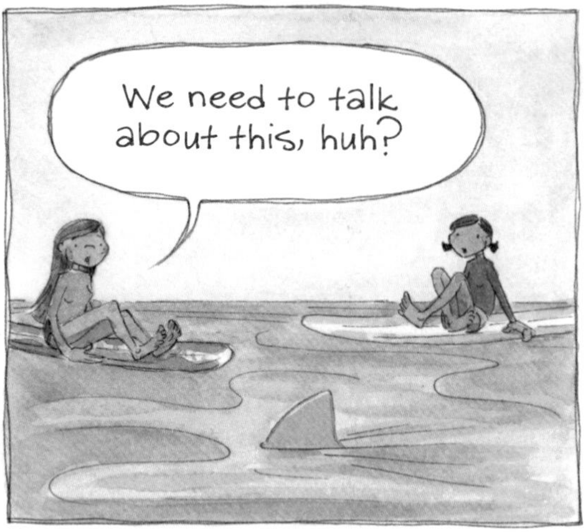
We need to talk about this, huh?

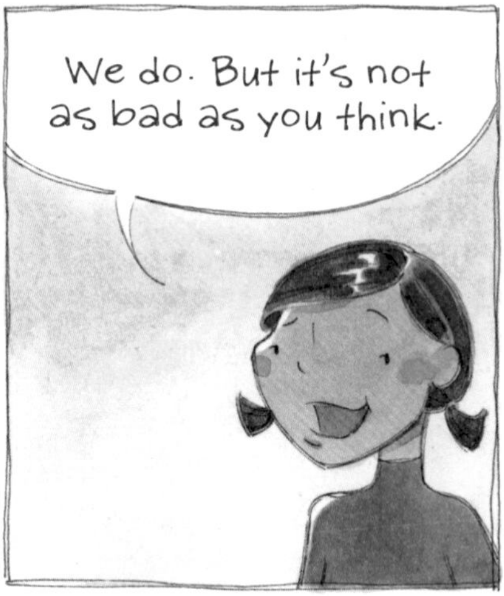
We do. But it's not as bad as you think.

sharks

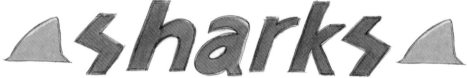

We'll admit... seeing a fin when you're out in the lineup can definitely make your heart race! But we share the ocean with these creatures, and they deserve our respect. They're actually pretty amazing! Let's look at three...

LEOPARD SHARK

Triakis semifasciata

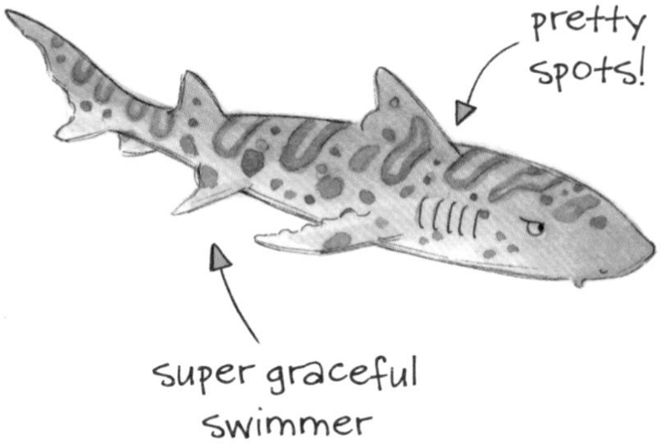
pretty spots!
super graceful swimmer

COOL FACTS:

- Lives in kelp forests.
- Grows to 6.5 feet.
- Eats fish eggs, crabs, clams, and innkeeper worms.

HORN SHARK

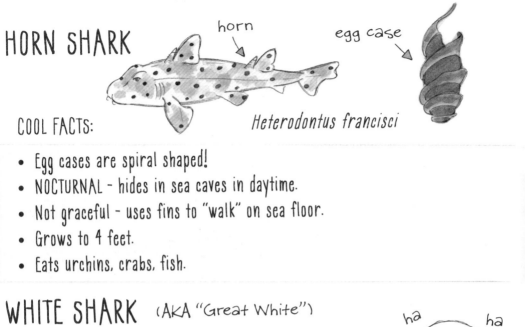

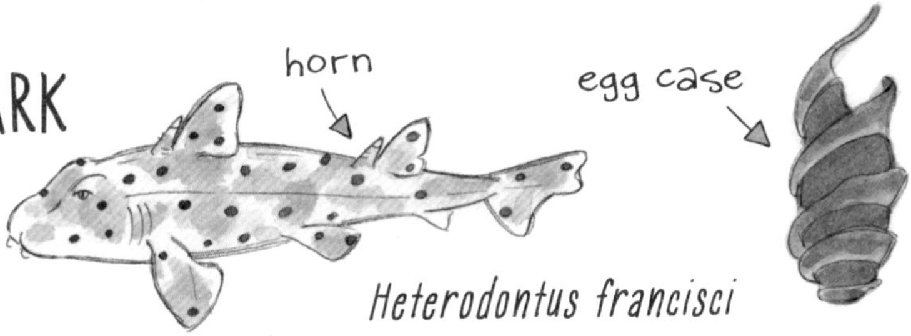
horn
egg case

Heterodontus francisci

COOL FACTS:

- Egg cases are spiral shaped!
- NOCTURNAL - hides in sea caves in daytime.
- Not graceful - uses fins to "walk" on sea floor.
- Grows to 4 feet.
- Eats urchins, crabs, fish.

WHITE SHARK (AKA "Great White")

Carcharodon carcharias

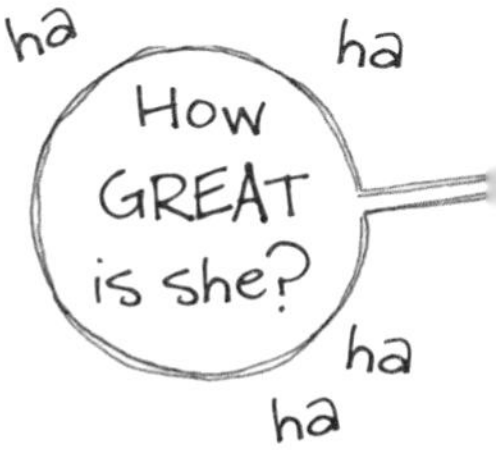
ha
ha
How GREAT is she?
ha
ha

Statistically, you're more likely to die from a cow attack, a dog bite, or a car accident than in an encounter with a White Shark. So check out these facts about why this apex predator is so mighty awesome:

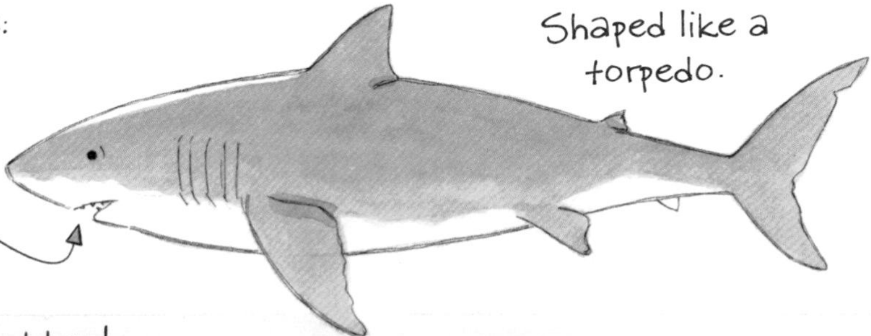
Shaped like a torpedo.
Sharp teeth can be 3 inches long!

COOL FACTS:

- Can grow to 20 feet long!
- Babies are born alive, at 4 feet, with a full set of teeth!
- The world's largest predatory fish, the White Shark keeps the seal and sea lion populations under control.
- They're only scared of Orcas!

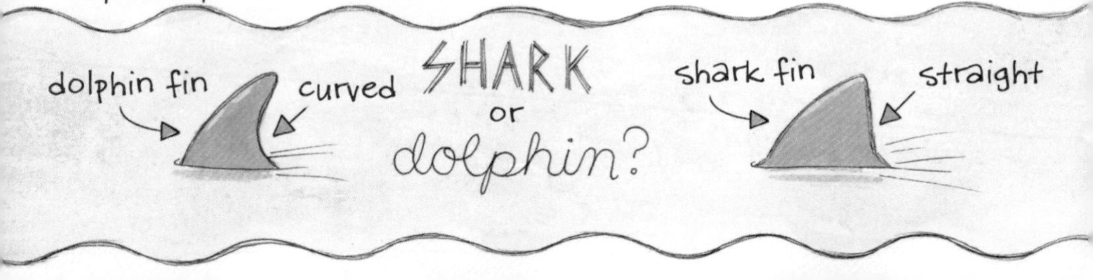
SHARK or dolphin?
dolphin fin
curved
shark fin
straight

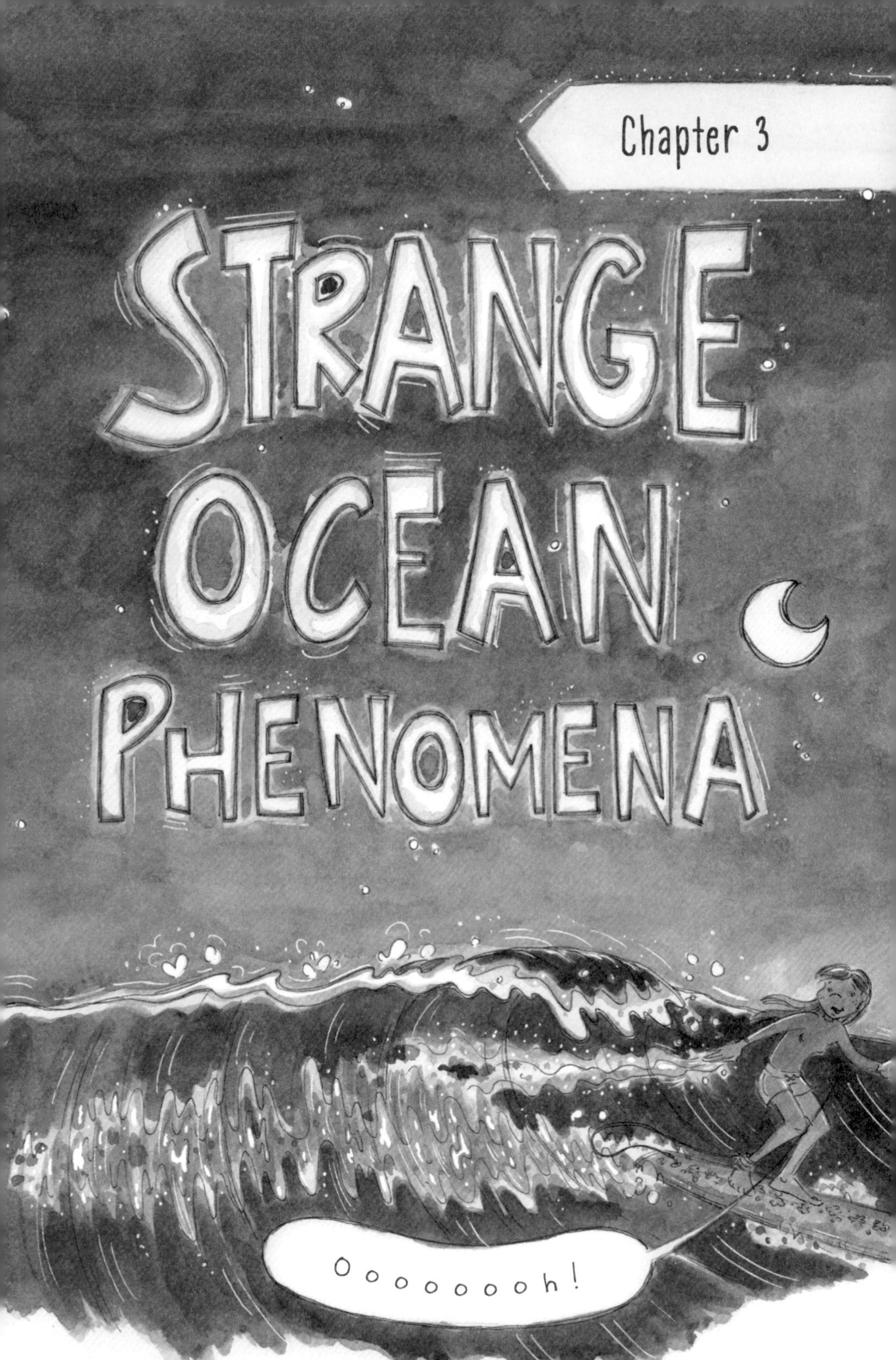
Chapter 3
STRANGE OCEAN PHENOMENA
Oooooooh!

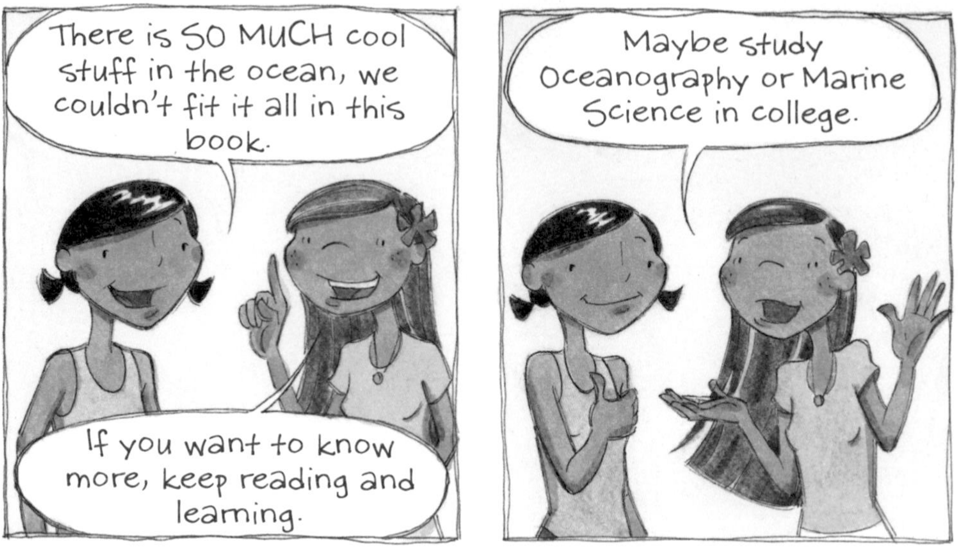
There is SO MUCH cool stuff in the ocean, we couldn't fit it all in this book.
If you want to know more, keep reading and learning.
Maybe study Oceanography or Marine Science in college.

Here are some super bizarre phenomena to ponder...

1. The World's Largest Surfed Wave.

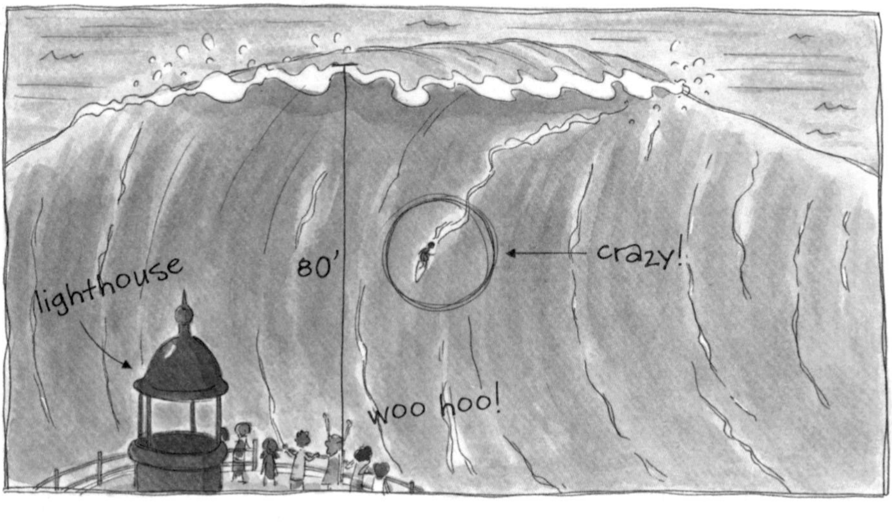
lighthouse
80'
crazy!
woo hoo!

The World Record for the largest wave ever surfed was set in 2017 by Brazilian surfer Rodrigo Koxa at Nazare, Portugal. It was 80 FEET! A swell hitting the underwater "Nazare Canyon" is what makes these giants form.

2. Bait Balls.

Bait balls happen when small, schooling fish are threatened by predators. They wind themselves into a tight ball, with every fish trying to get into the middle.

This movement attracts MORE predators – seals, dolphins, tuna, sharks, whales and diving seabirds – who join the feast. Oddly, the predators don't attack each other but work together!

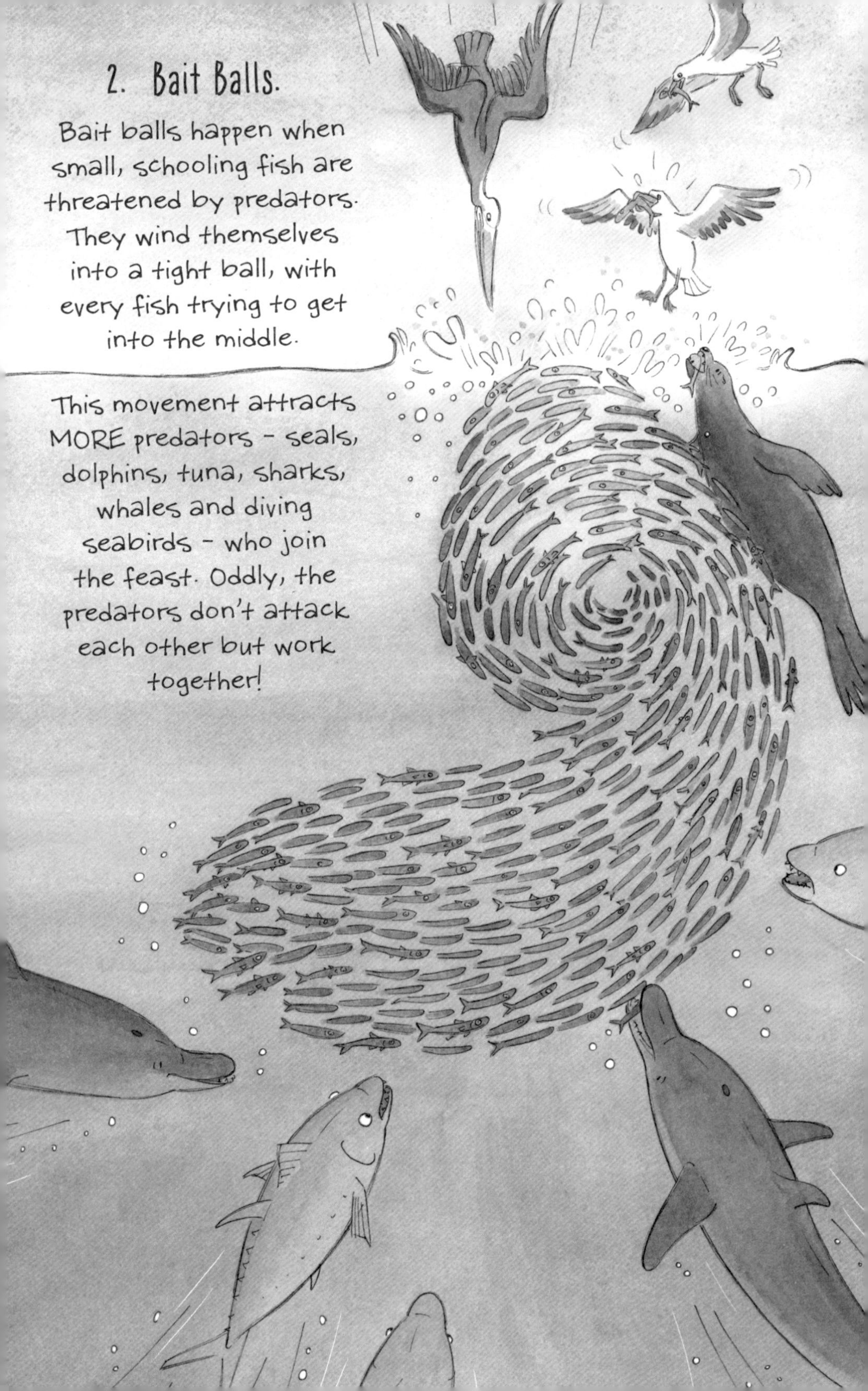

And last but not least...

3. Bioluminescence.

Magical glowing ocean!

Every so often, if you go down to the beach at night, you'll think you're in fairyland. When waves break... they glow! And if you run down the beach in the wet sand, your footsteps glow. WHAT is this?!

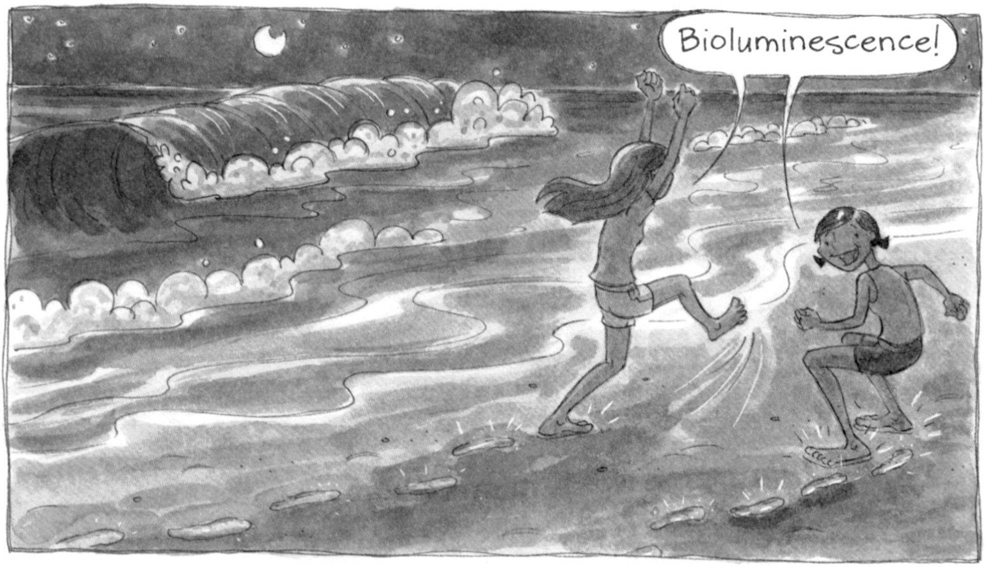
Bioluminescence!

Bioluminescence actually comes with another phenomenon called

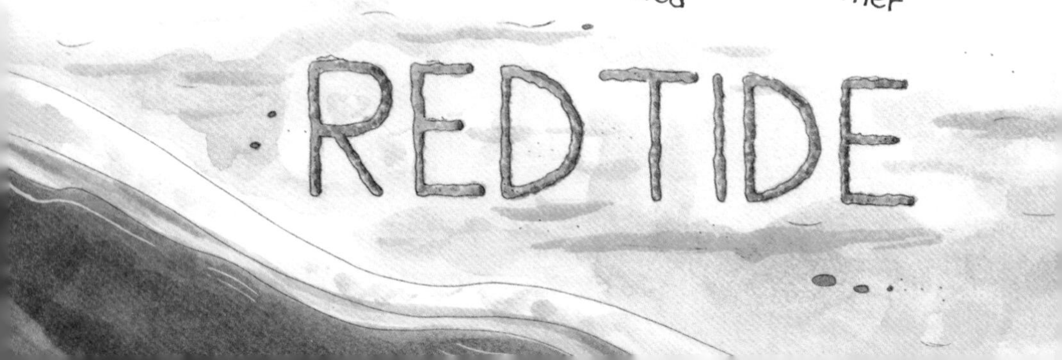
RED TIDE

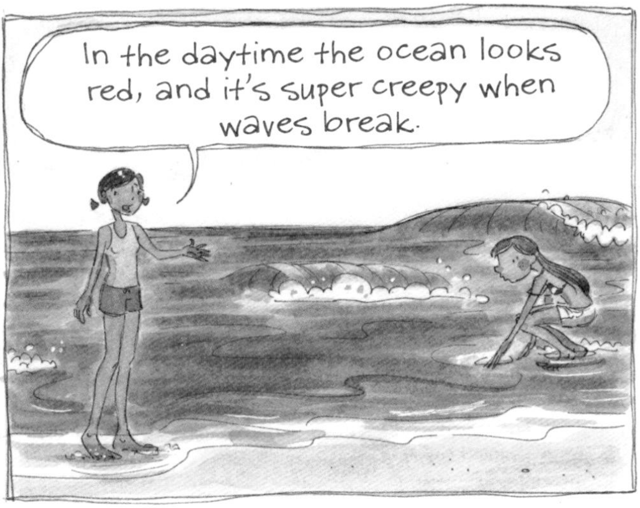
In the daytime the ocean looks red, and it's super creepy when waves break.

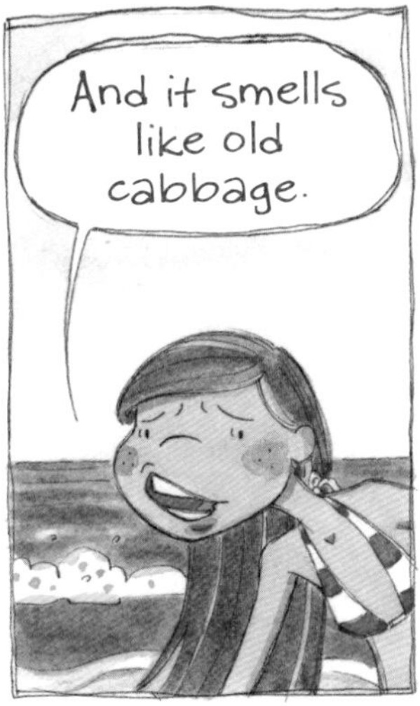
And it smells like old cabbage.

This is actually due to MILLIONS of teeny tiny creatures called DINOFLAGELLATES in the ocean.

Lingulodinium polyedra
(microscopic)

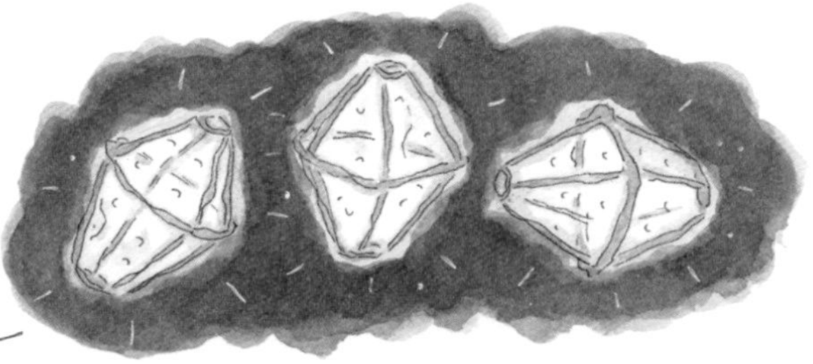

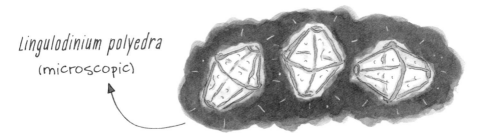

There are lots of species that cause red tide, but *Lingulodinium polyedra* is SUPER SPECIAL. At night, when they are disturbed by waves or footsteps or swimming or surfing, they glow! Like teeny ocean lightning bugs!

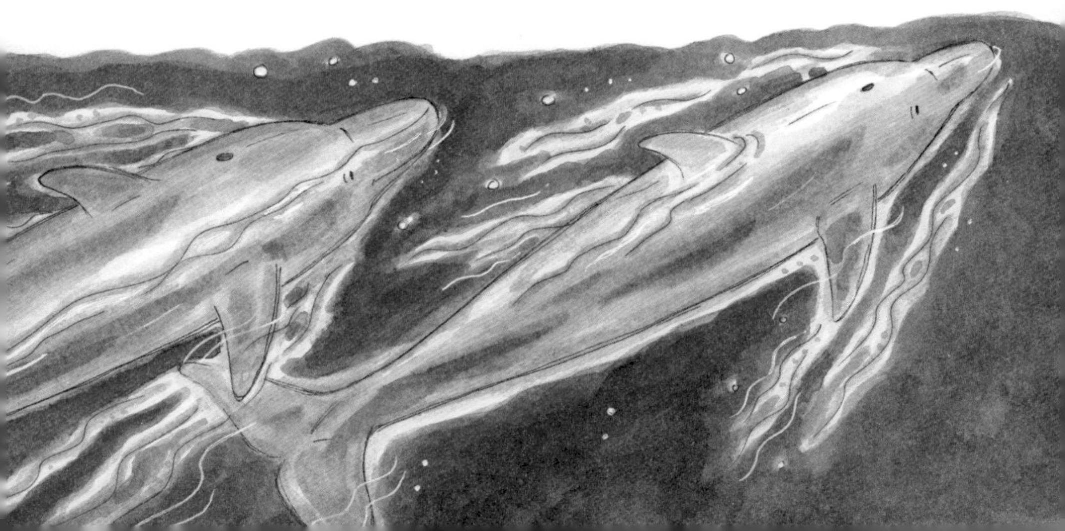

NOTE: While surfing is super fun, make sure you stay safe.
Always have an adult with you, and surf at a beach with a lifeguard.

Chapter 4

…and now…

HOW TO SURF

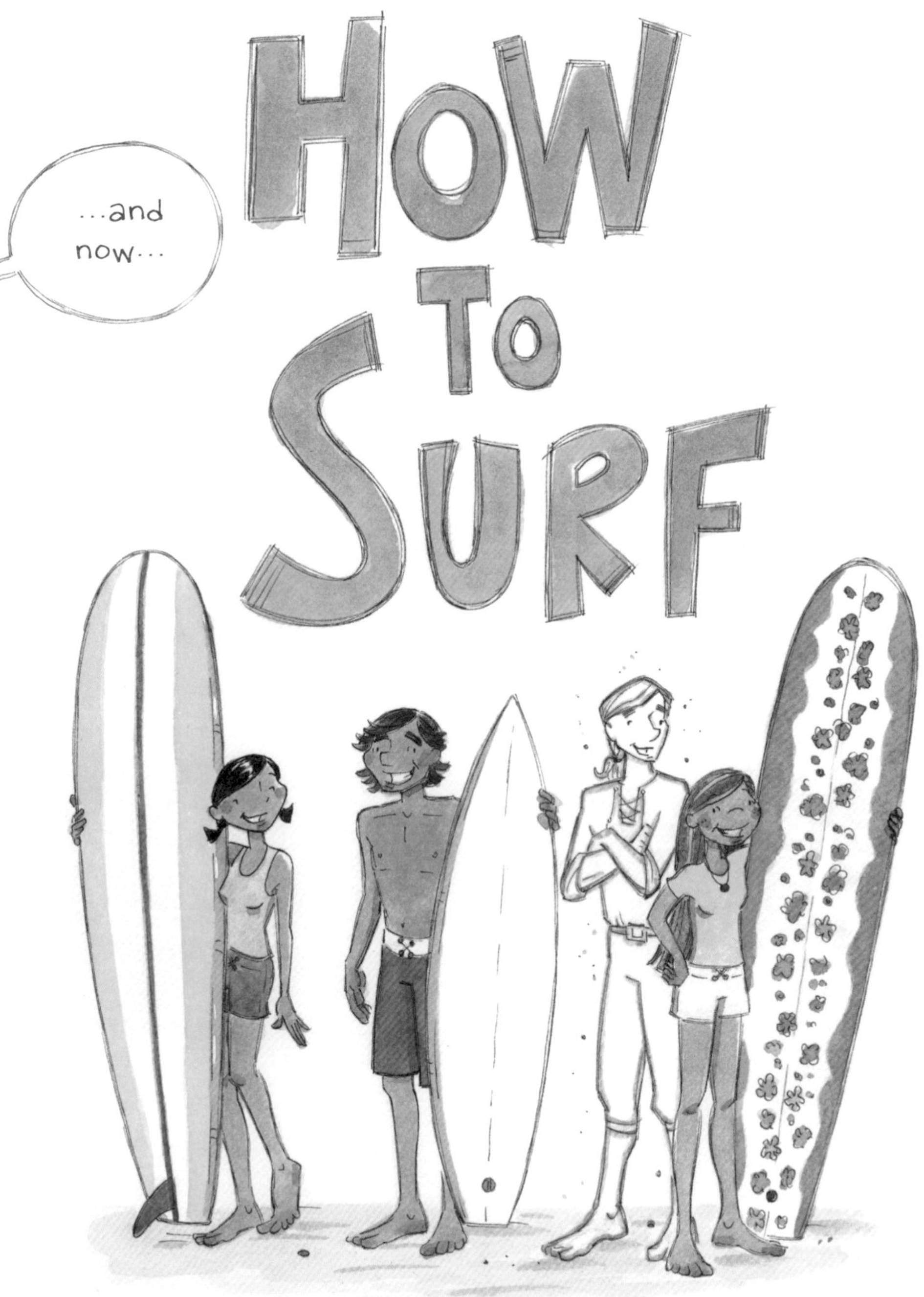

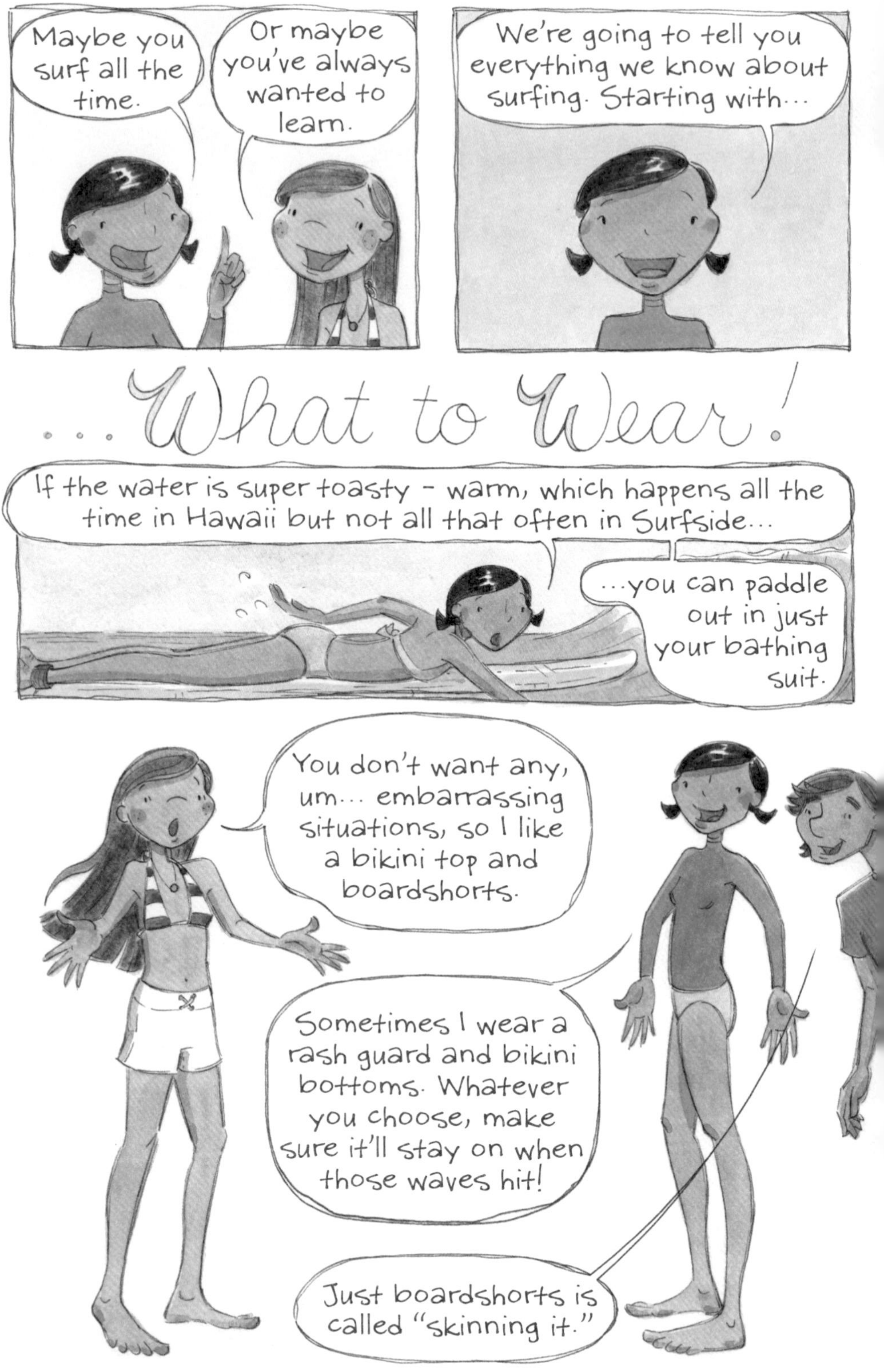
Maybe you surf all the time.
Or maybe you've always wanted to learn.
We're going to tell you everything we know about surfing. Starting with...
...What to Wear!
If the water is super toasty - warm, which happens all the time in Hawaii but not all that often in Surfside...
...you can paddle out in just your bathing suit.
You don't want any, um... embarrassing situations, so I like a bikini top and boardshorts.
Sometimes I wear a rash guard and bikini bottoms. Whatever you choose, make sure it'll stay on when those waves hit!
Just boardshorts is called "skinning it."

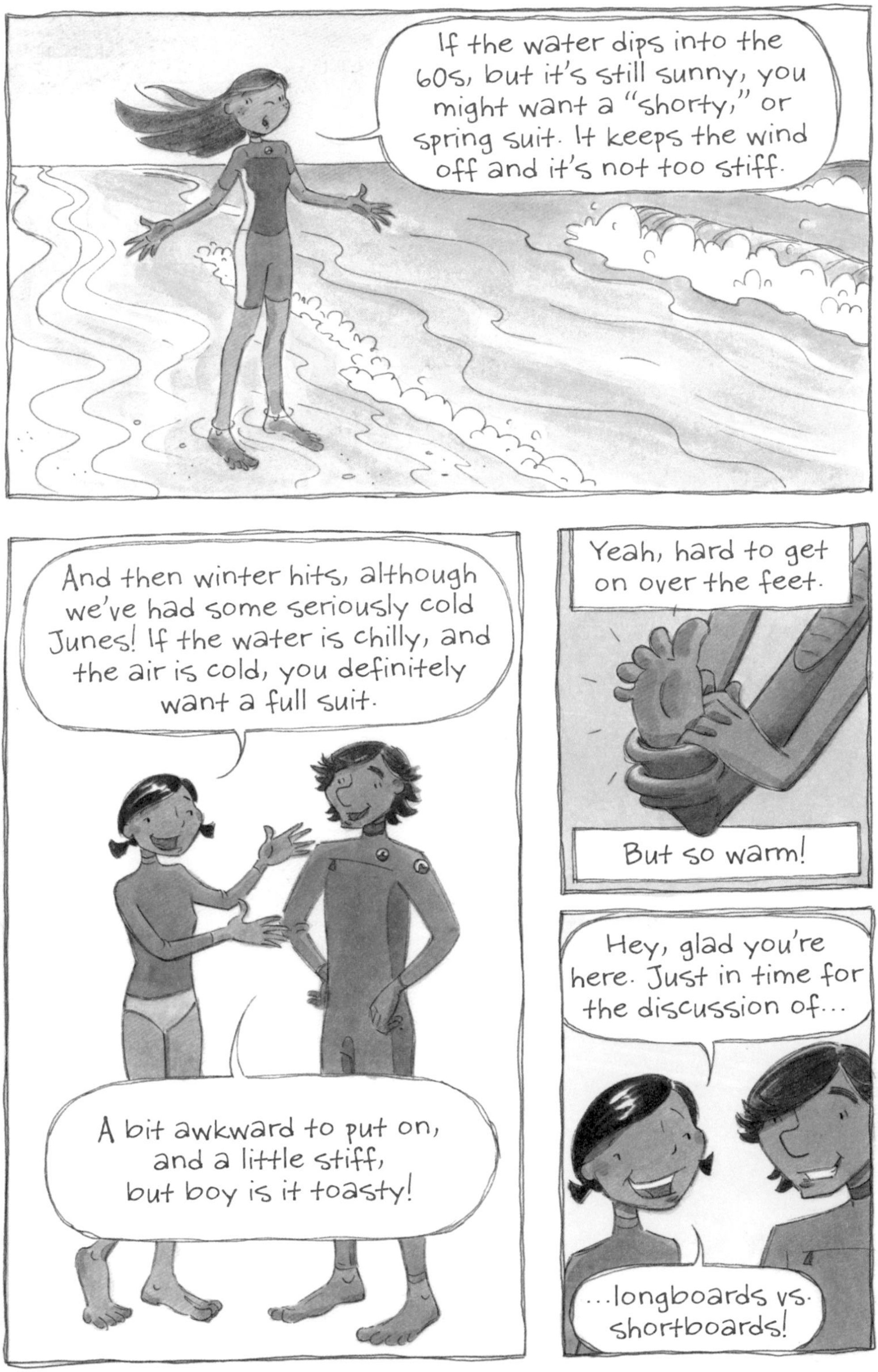
If the water dips into the 60s, but it's still sunny, you might want a "shorty," or spring suit. It keeps the wind off and it's not too stiff.
And then winter hits, although we've had some seriously cold Junes! If the water is chilly, and the air is cold, you definitely want a full suit.
A bit awkward to put on, and a little stiff, but boy is it toasty!
Yeah, hard to get on over the feet.
But so warm!
Hey, glad you're here. Just in time for the discussion of...
...longboards vs. shortboards!

LONGBOARD OR shortboard?

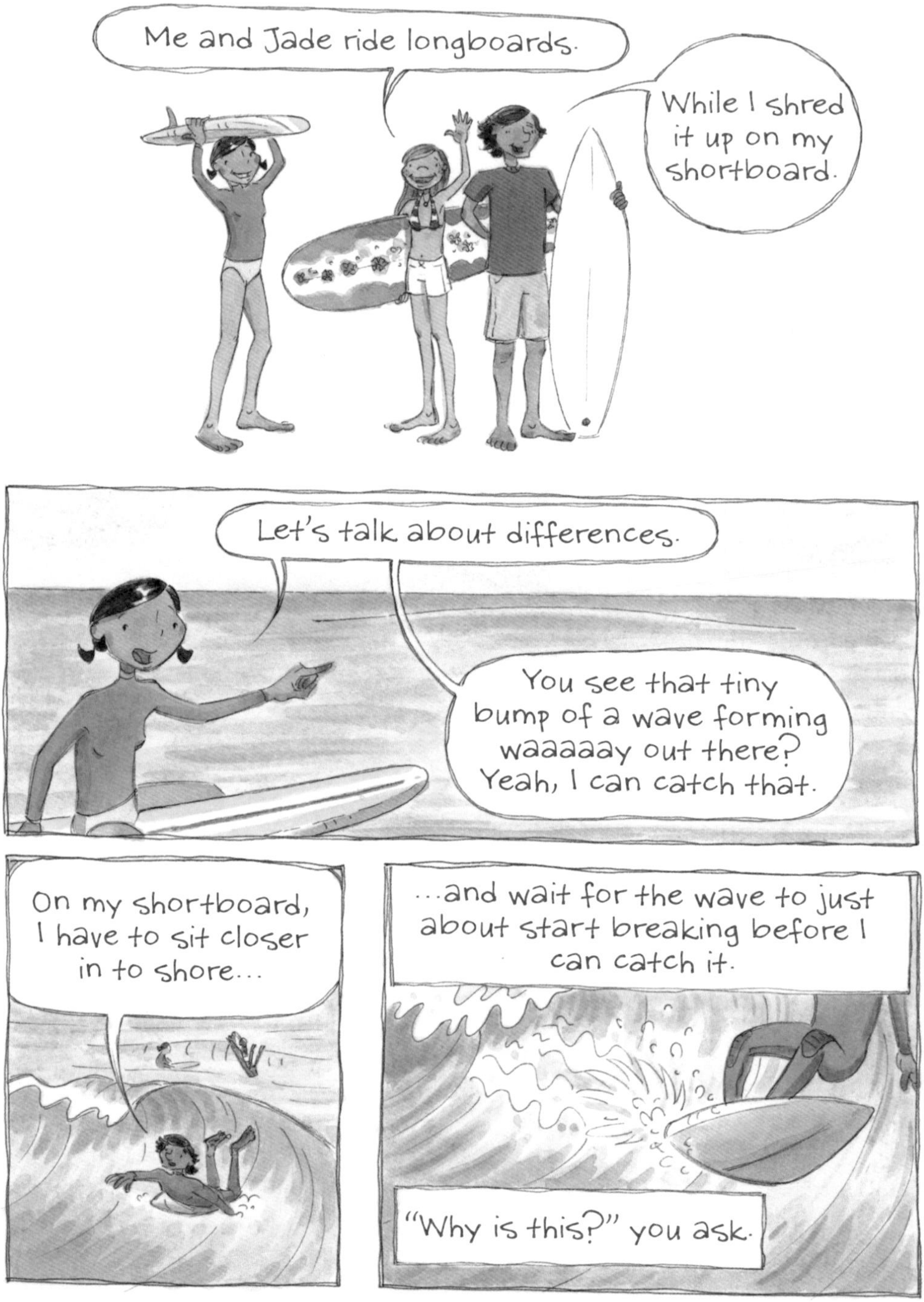
Me and Jade ride longboards.
While I shred it up on my shortboard.
Let's talk about differences.
You see that tiny bump of a wave forming waaaaay out there? Yeah, I can catch that.
On my shortboard, I have to sit closer in to shore...
...and wait for the wave to just about start breaking before I can catch it.
"Why is this?" you ask.

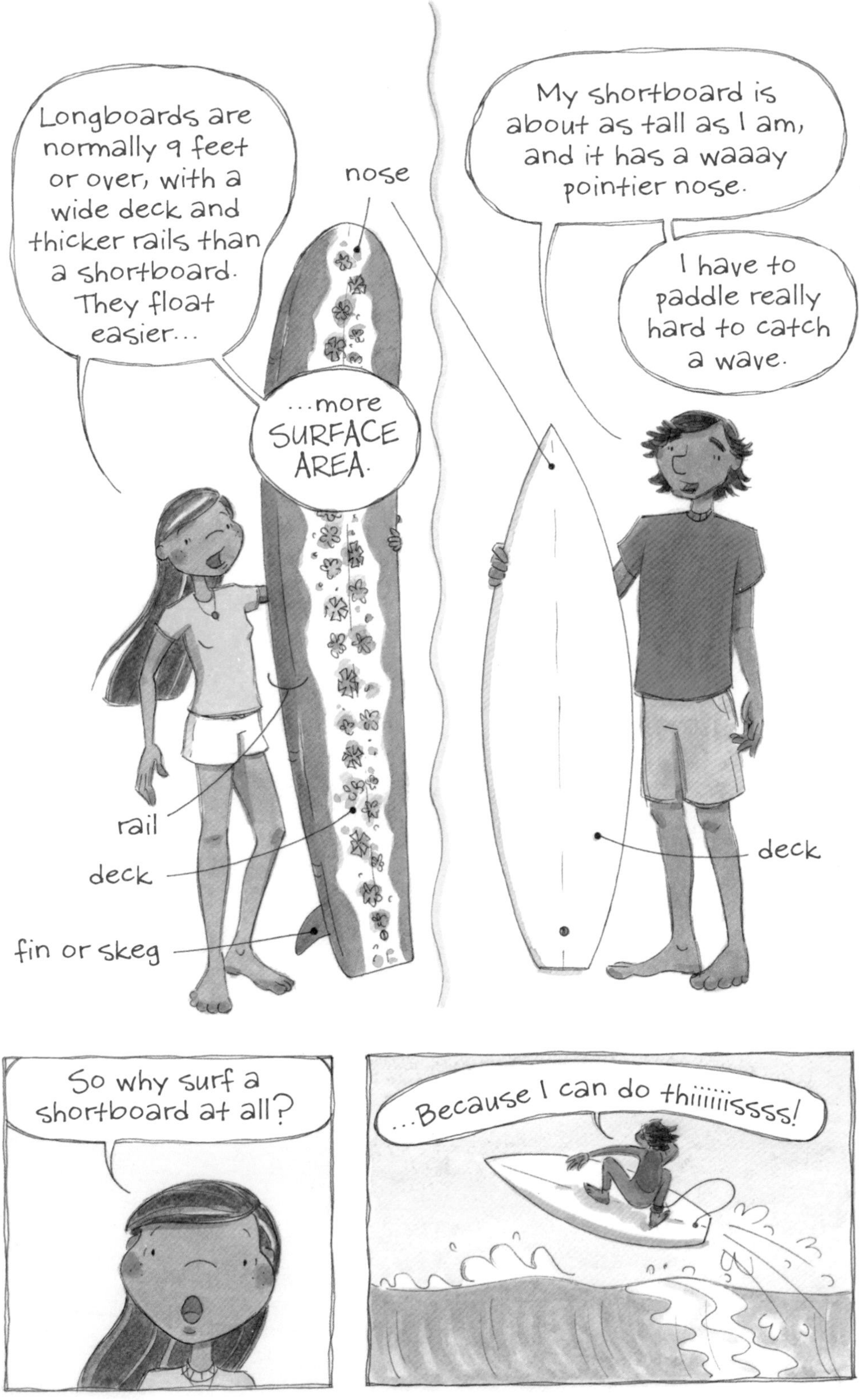
Longboards are normally 9 feet or over, with a wide deck and thicker rails than a shortboard. They float easier...
...more SURFACE AREA.
nose
rail
deck
fin or skeg
My shortboard is about as tall as I am, and it has a waaay pointier nose.
I have to paddle really hard to catch a wave.
deck
So why surf a shortboard at all?
...Because I can do thiiiiiissss!

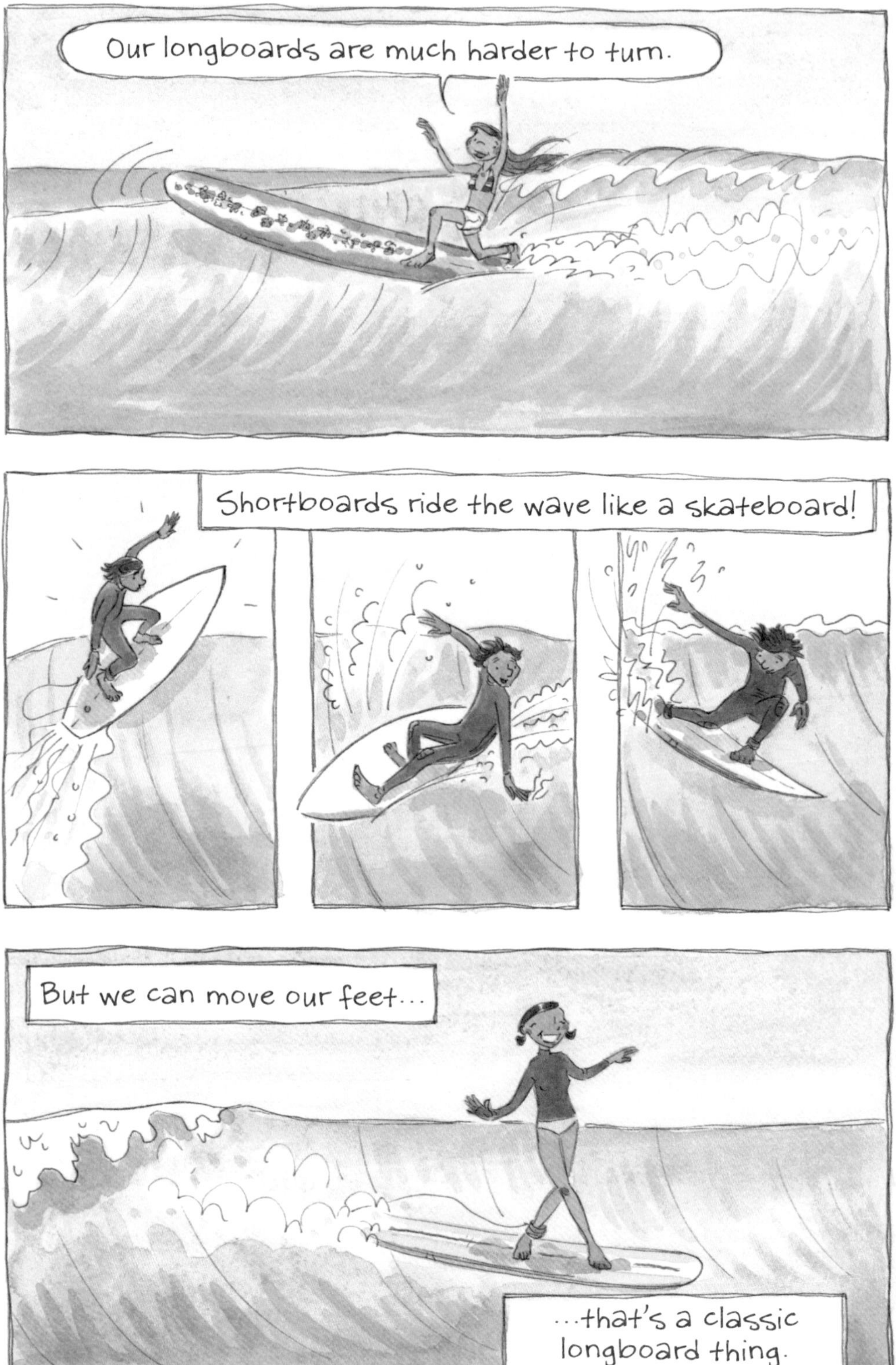
Our longboards are much harder to turn.
Shortboards ride the wave like a skateboard!
But we can move our feet...
...that's a classic longboard thing.

See how both boards are slightly banana shaped? That's called ROCKER, and it helps the board fit into the shape of the wave.

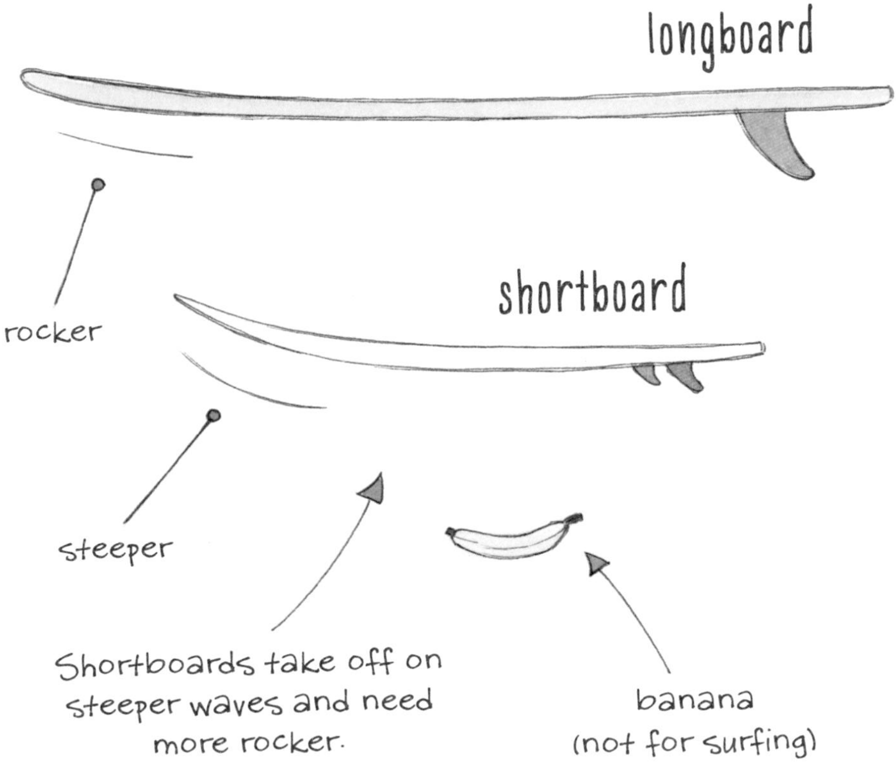
longboard
rocker
shortboard
steeper
Shortboards take off on steeper waves and need more rocker.
banana
(not for surfing)

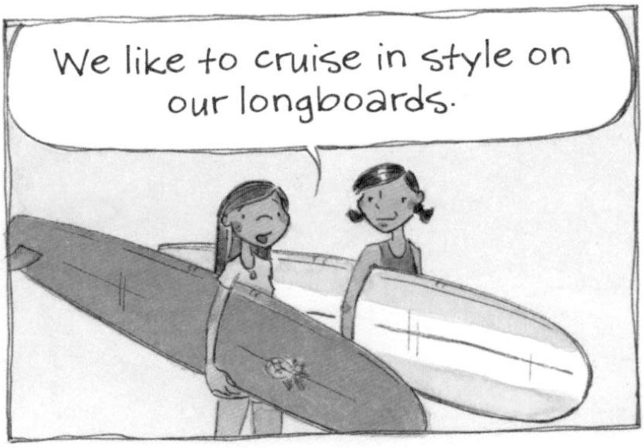
We like to cruise in style on our longboards.

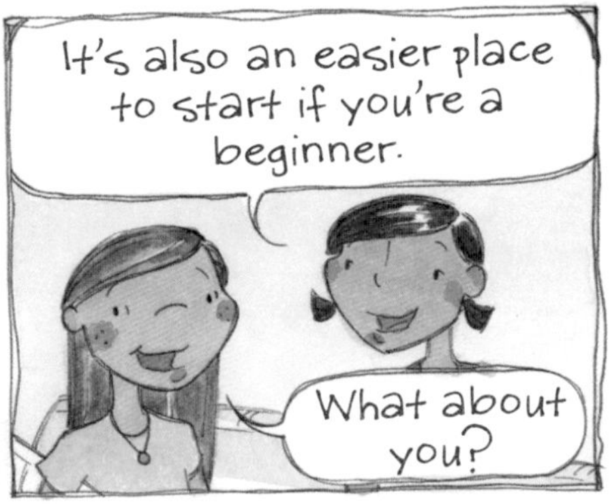
It's also an easier place to start if you're a beginner.
What about you?

Goofy or Regular? (or, Where Do I Put My Leash?)

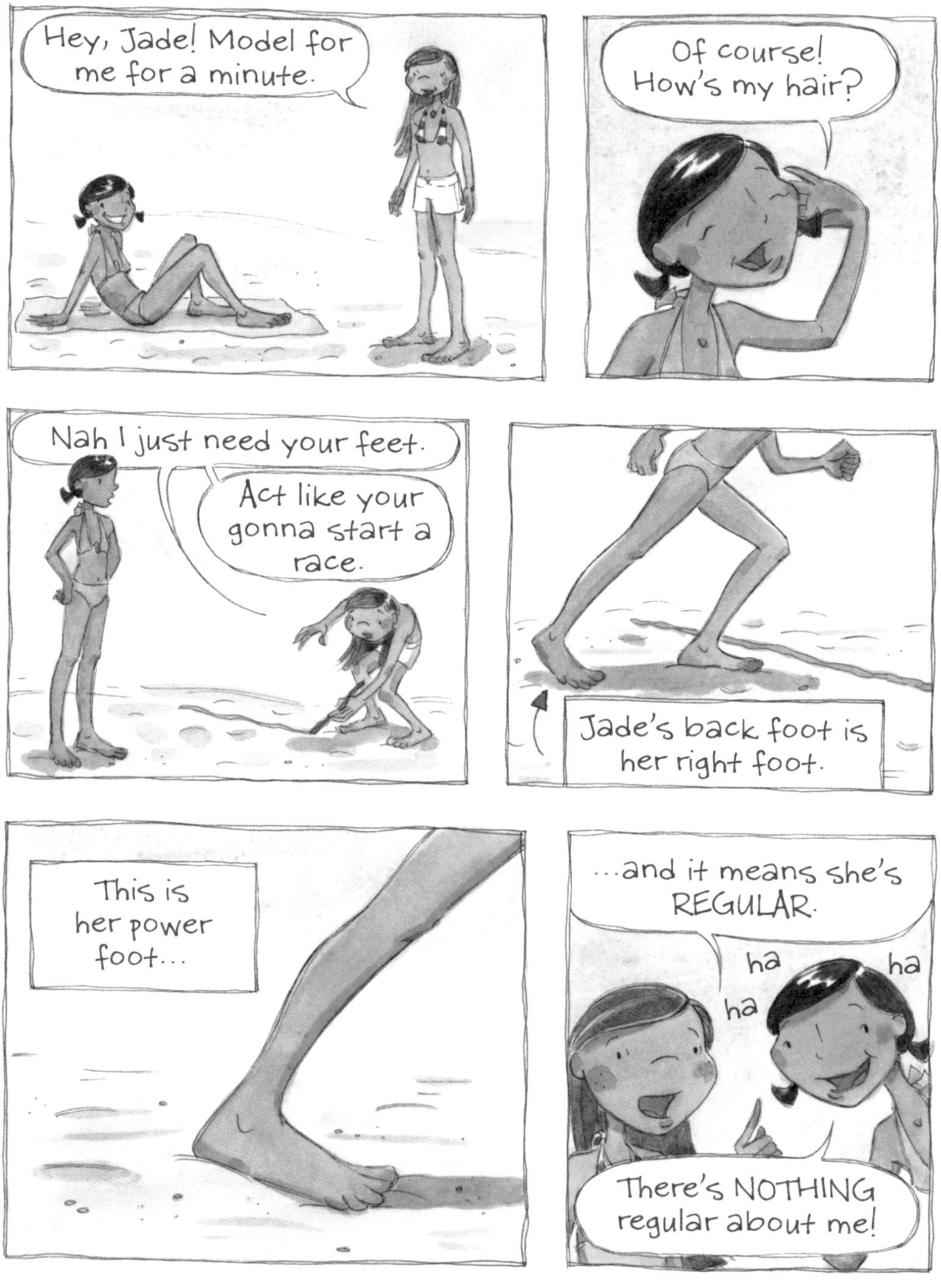
Hey, Jade! Model for me for a minute.
Of course! How's my hair?
Nah I just need your feet.
Act like your gonna start a race.
Jade's back foot is her right foot.
This is her power foot...
...and it means she's REGULAR.
ha
ha
ha
There's NOTHING regular about me!

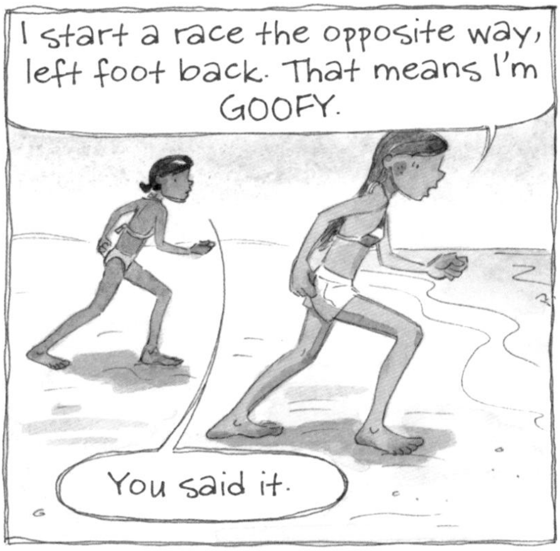
I start a race the opposite way, left foot back. That means I'm GOOFY.
You said it.
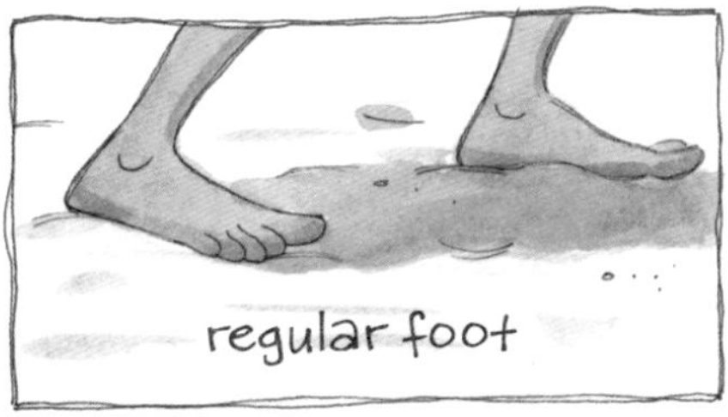
regular foot
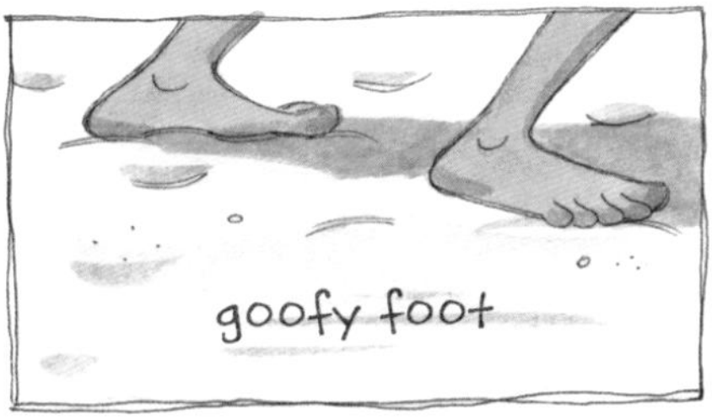
goofy foot
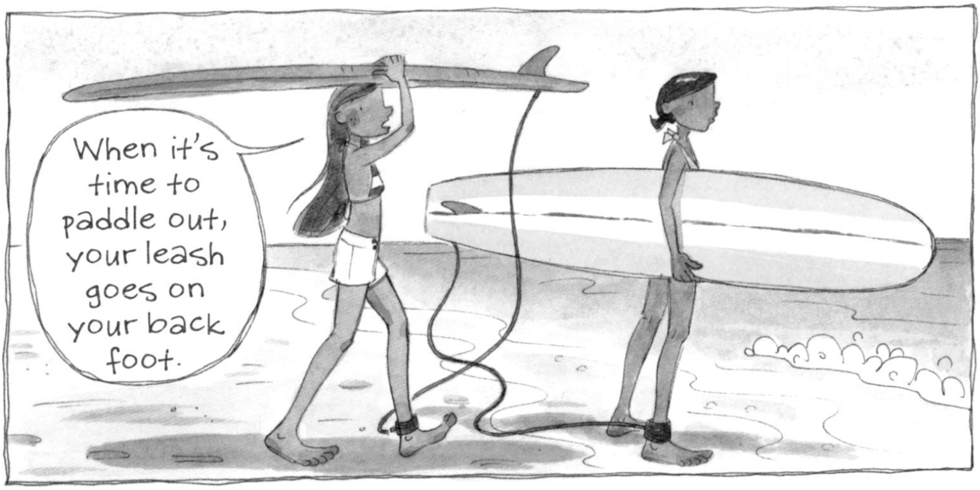
When it's time to paddle out, your leash goes on your back foot.
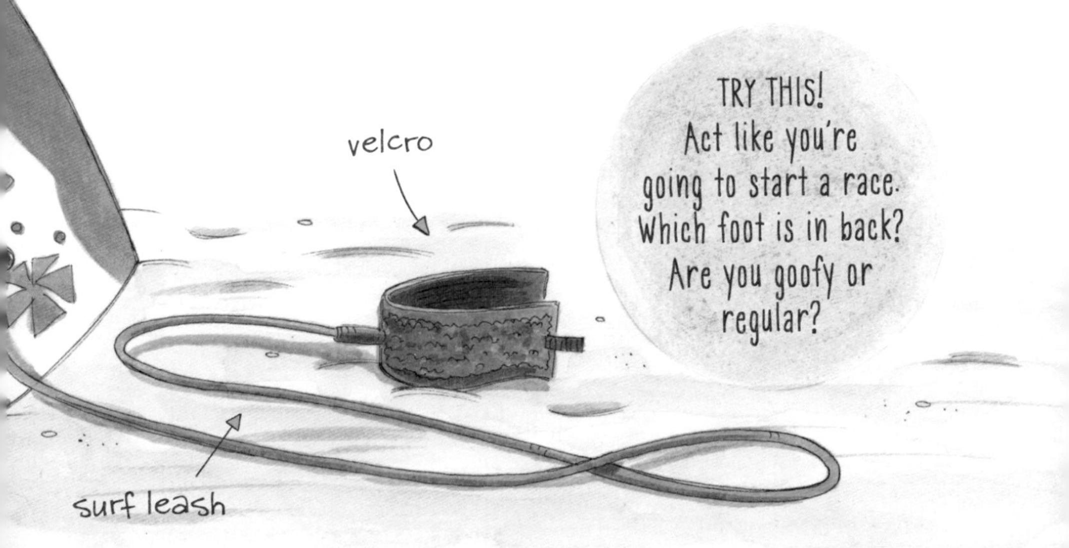
velcro
surf leash
TRY THIS!
Act like you're going to start a race. Which foot is in back? Are you goofy or regular?

DRY LAND PRACTICE

Feet! No Knees!

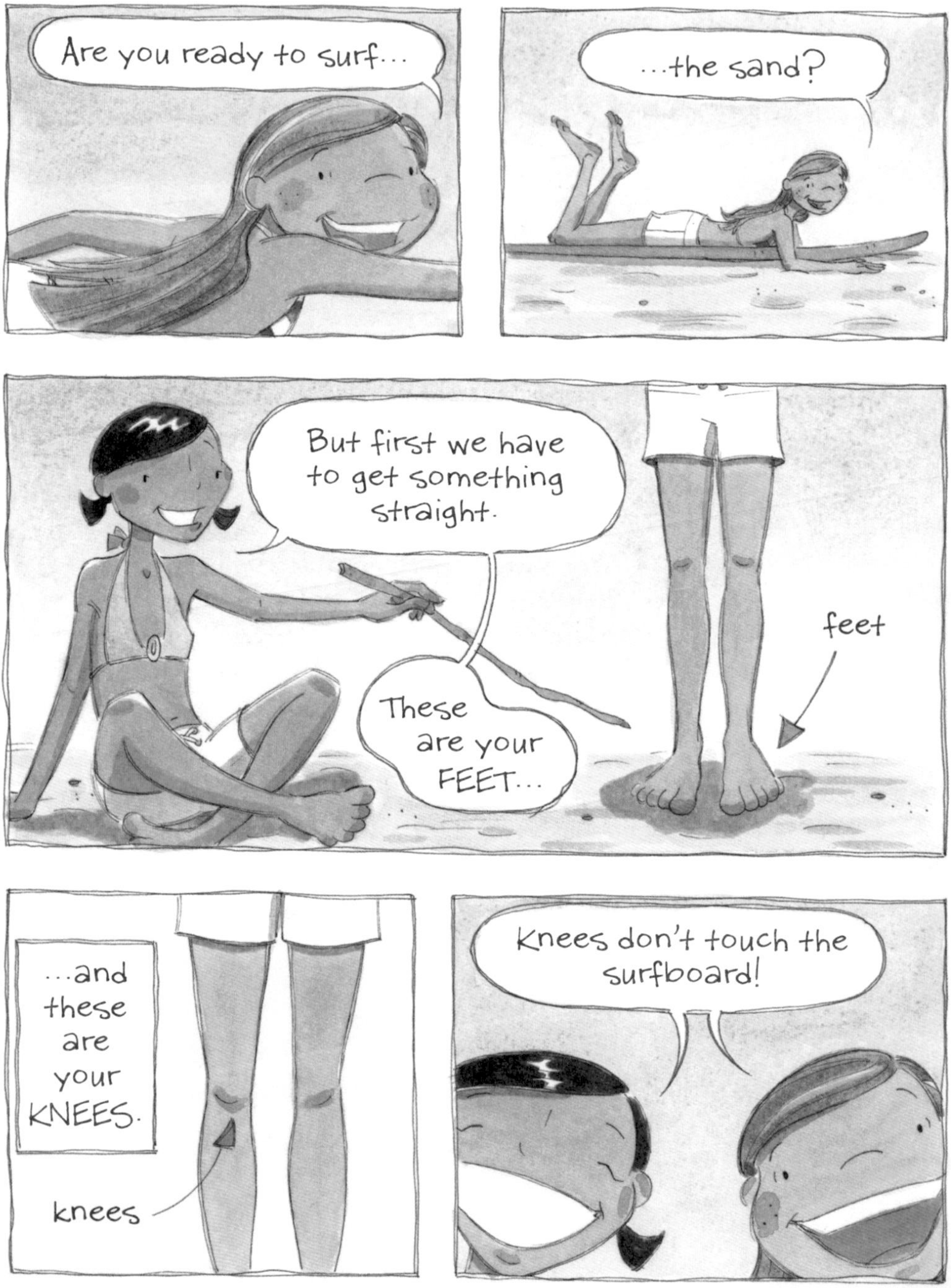
Are you ready to surf...
...the sand?
But first we have to get something straight.
These are your FEET...
feet
...and these are your KNEES.
knees
Knees don't touch the surfboard!

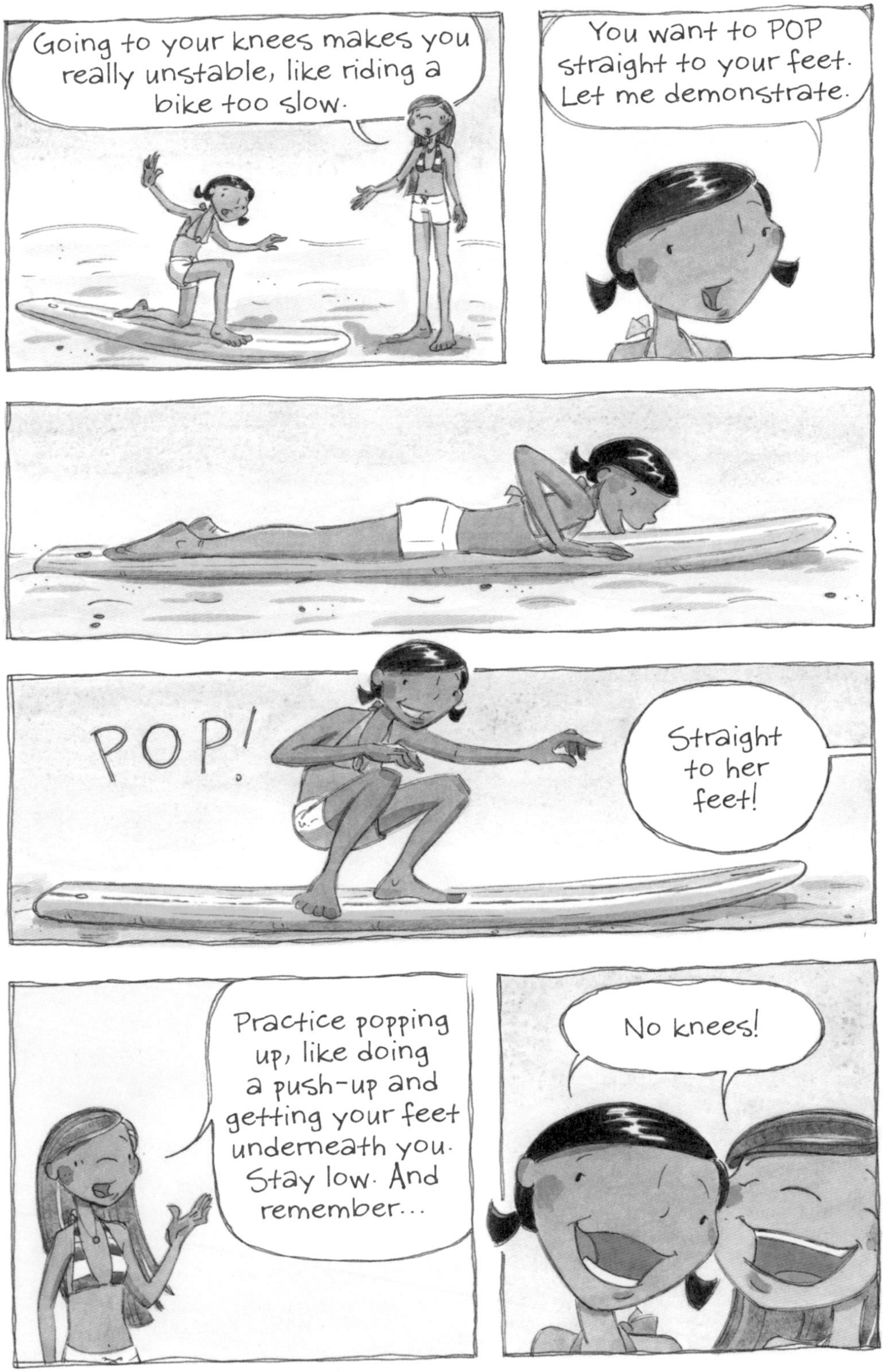
Going to your knees makes you really unstable, like riding a bike too slow.
You want to POP straight to your feet. Let me demonstrate.
POP!
Straight to her feet!
Practice popping up, like doing a push-up and getting your feet underneath you. Stay low. And remember...
No knees!

How to Paddle

AND SIT ON YOUR BOARD

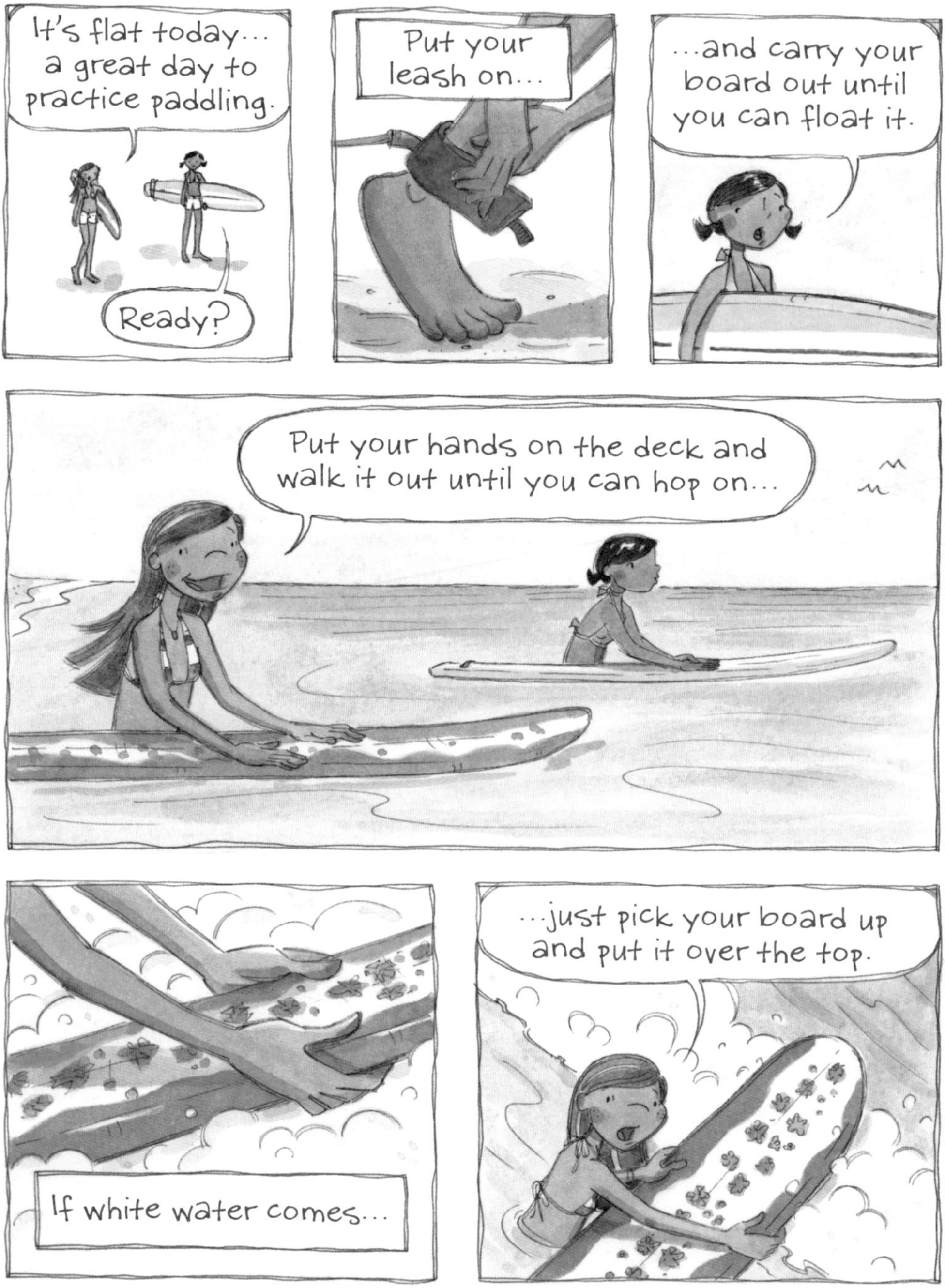

It's flat today... a great day to practice paddling.
Ready?
Put your leash on...
...and carry your board out until you can float it.
Put your hands on the deck and walk it out until you can hop on...
If white water comes...
...just pick your board up and put it over the top.

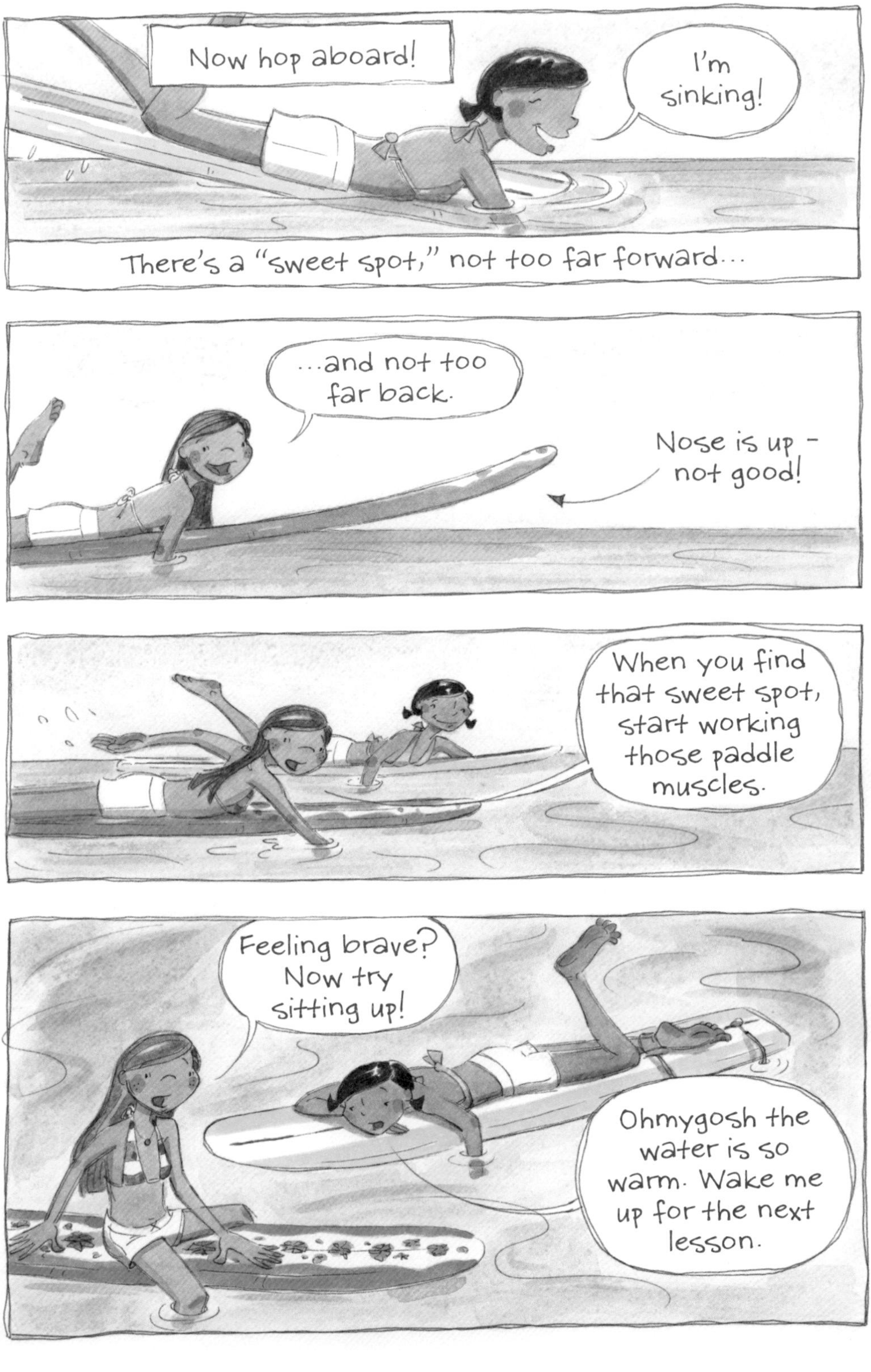
Now hop aboard!
I'm sinking!
There's a "sweet spot," not too far forward...
...and not too far back.
Nose is up - not good!
When you find that sweet spot, start working those paddle muscles.
Feeling brave? Now try sitting up!
Ohmygosh the water is so warm. Wake me up for the next lesson.

Riding the White Water

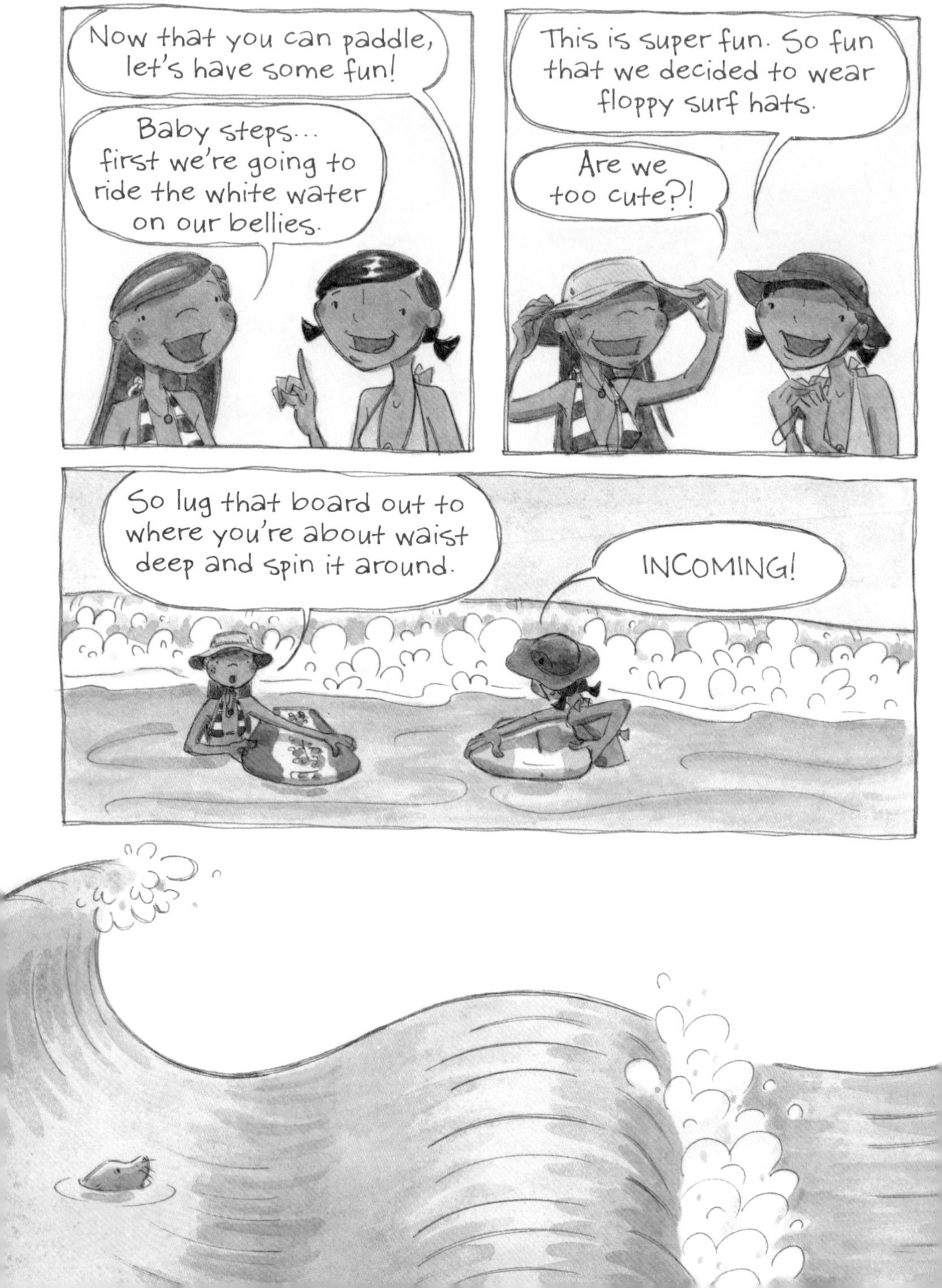
Now that you can paddle, let's have some fun!
Baby steps... first we're going to ride the white water on our bellies.
This is super fun. So fun that we decided to wear floppy surf hats.
Are we too cute?!
So lug that board out to where you're about waist deep and spin it around.
INCOMING!

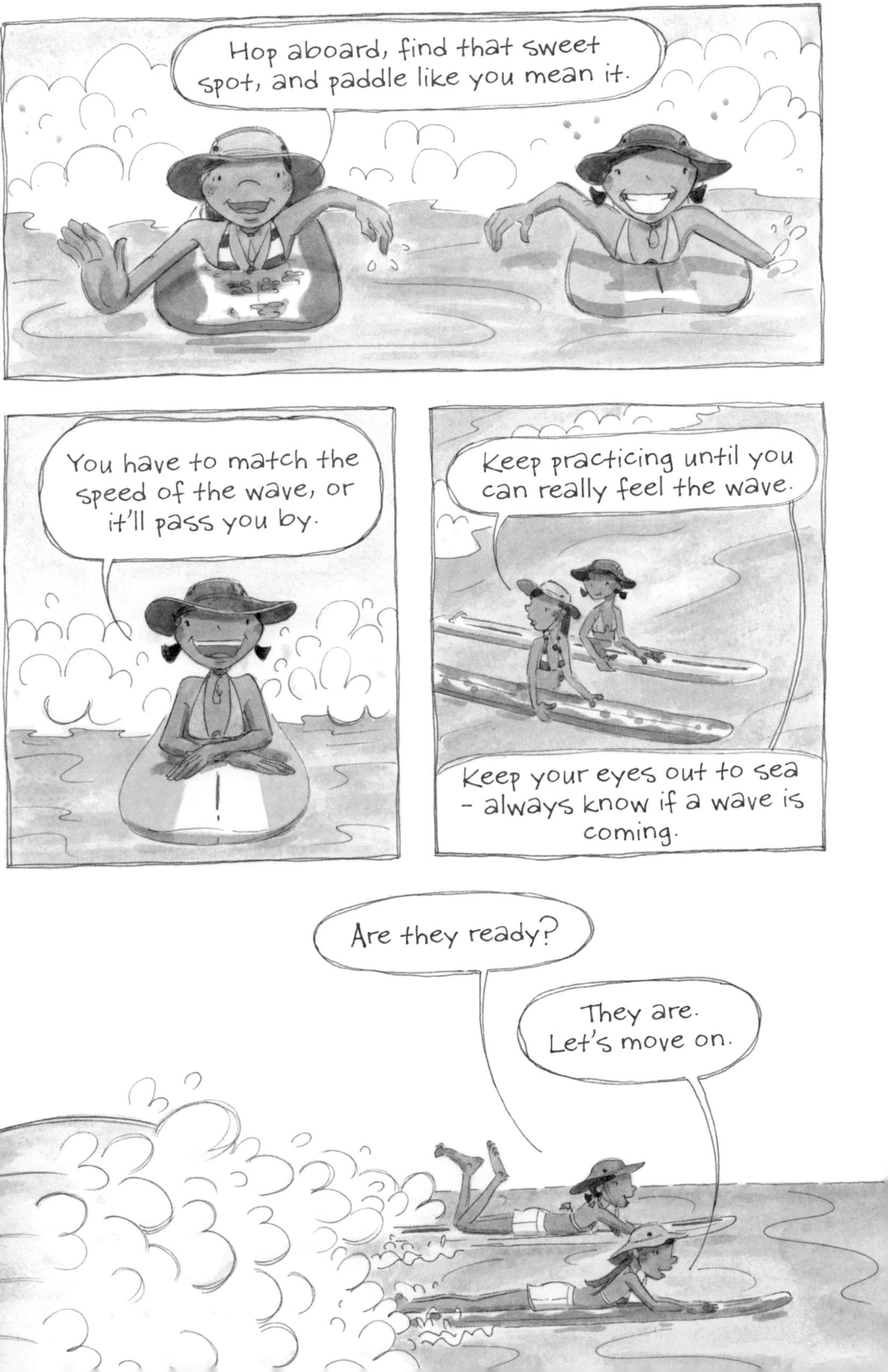
Hop aboard, find that sweet spot, and paddle like you mean it.
You have to match the speed of the wave, or it'll pass you by.
Keep practicing until you can really feel the wave.
Keep your eyes out to sea - always know if a wave is coming.
Are they ready?
They are. Let's move on.

Surfing the White Water

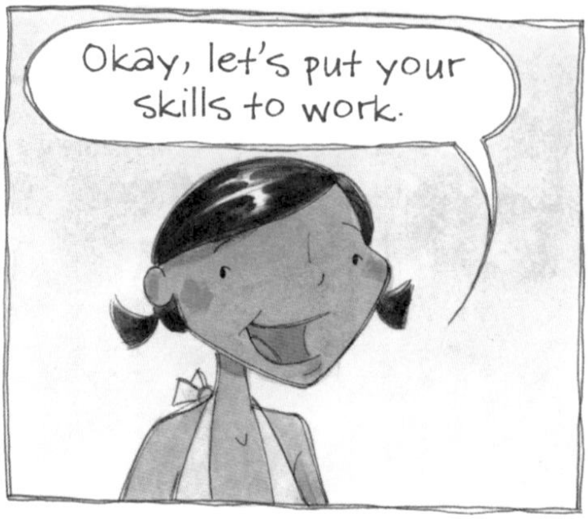
Okay, let's put your skills to work.

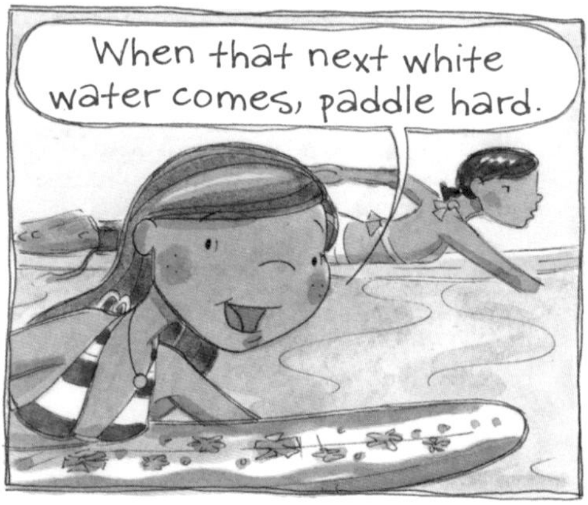
When that next white water comes, paddle hard.

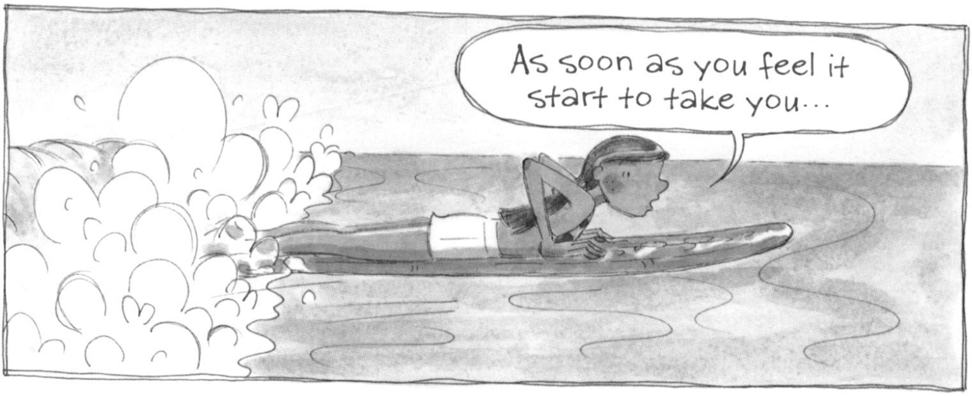
As soon as you feel it start to take you...

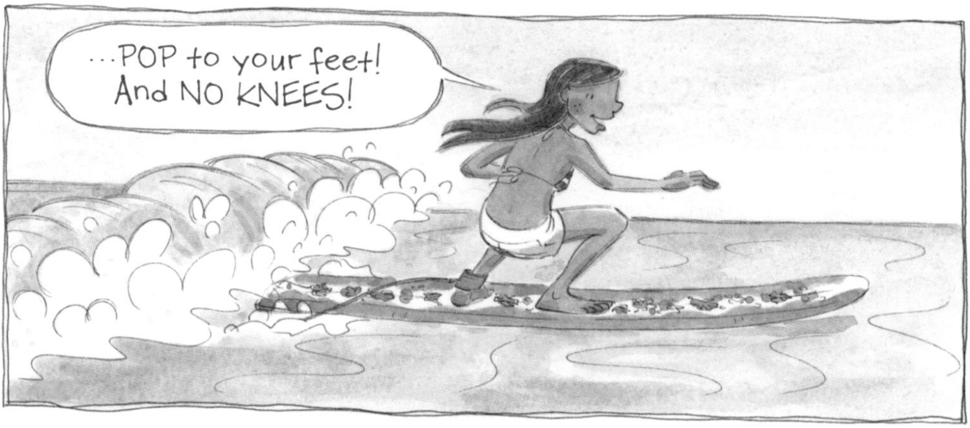
...POP to your feet! And NO KNEES!

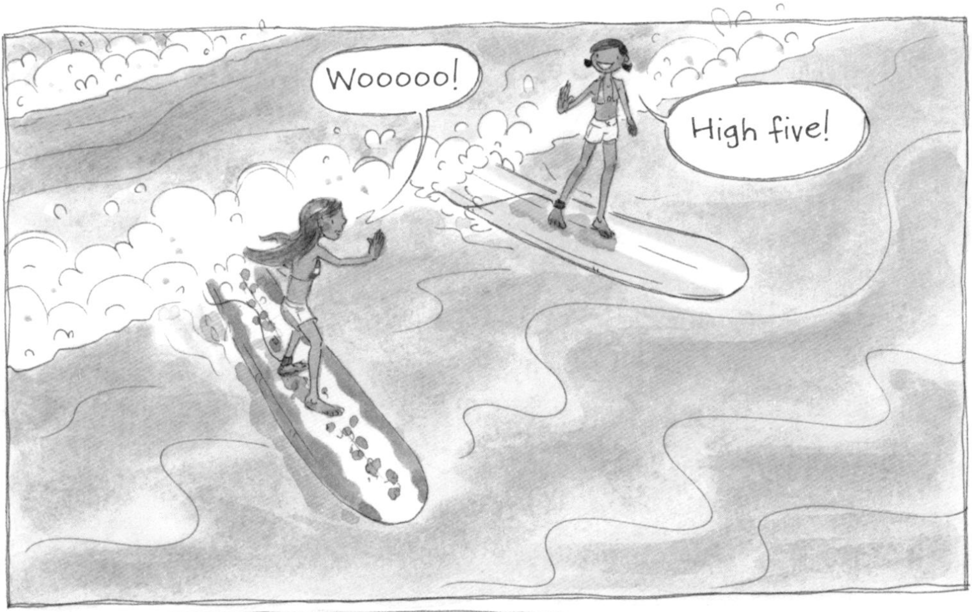
Wooooo!
High five!

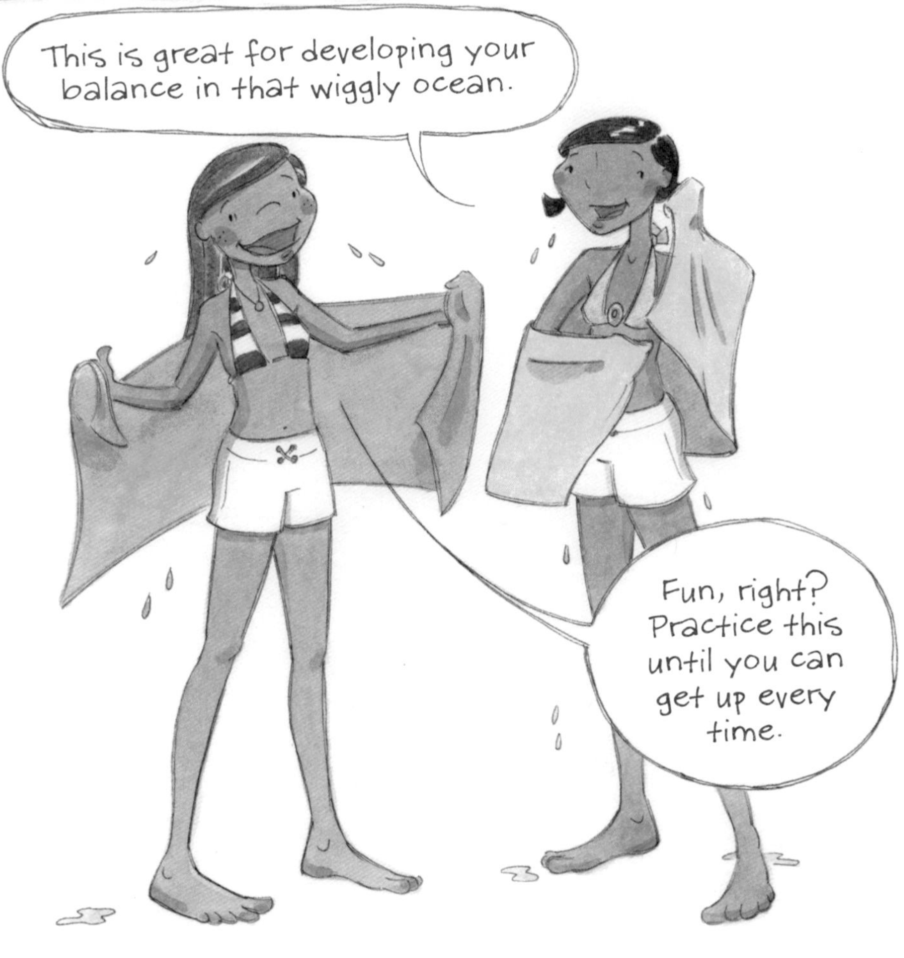
This is great for developing your balance in that wiggly ocean.
Fun, right? Practice this until you can get up every time.

HOW to get OUTSIDE

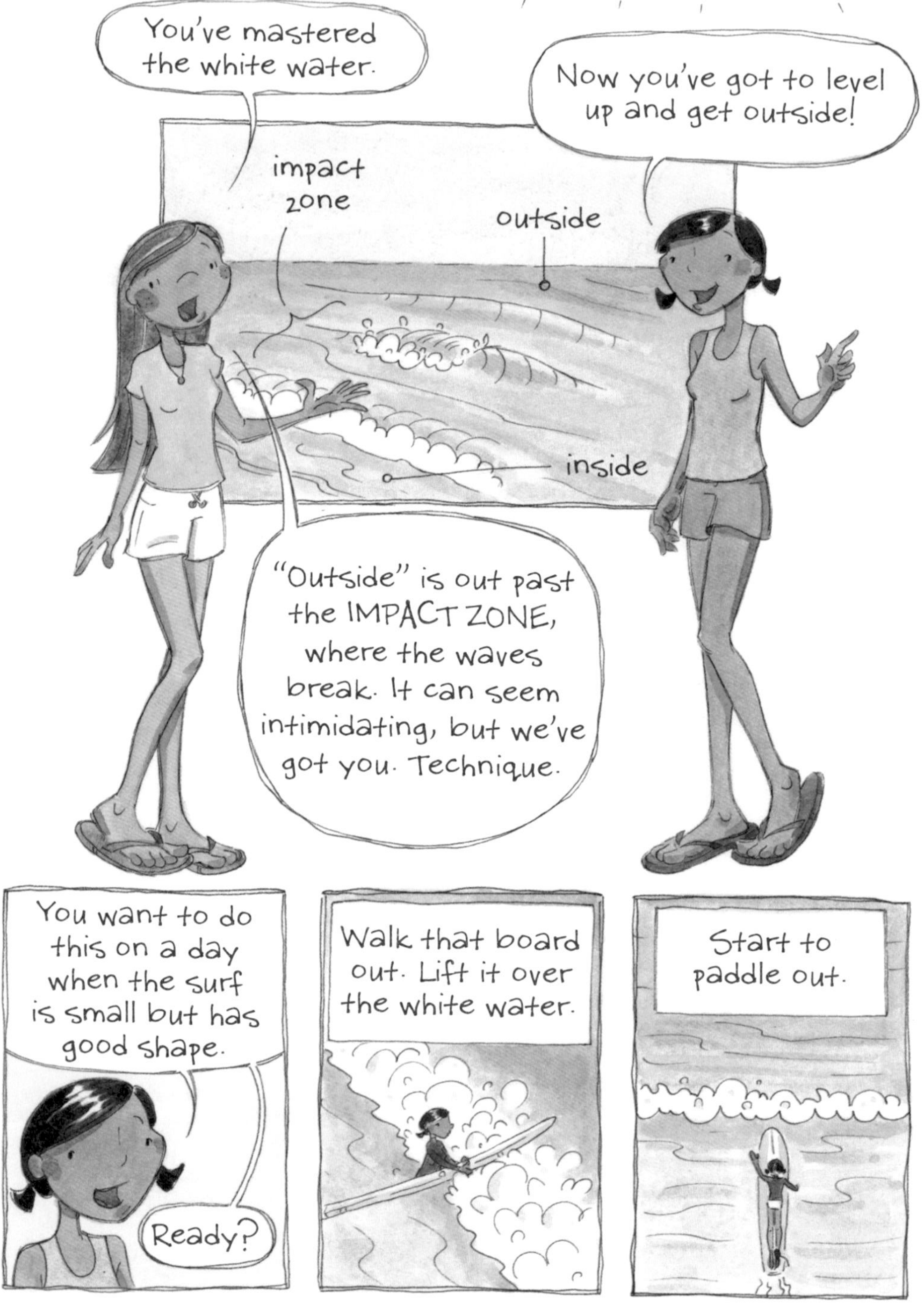
You've mastered the white water.
Now you've got to level up and get outside!
impact zone
outside
inside
"Outside" is out past the IMPACT ZONE, where the waves break. It can seem intimidating, but we've got you. Technique.
You want to do this on a day when the surf is small but has good shape.
Ready?
Walk that board out. Lift it over the white water.
Start to paddle out.

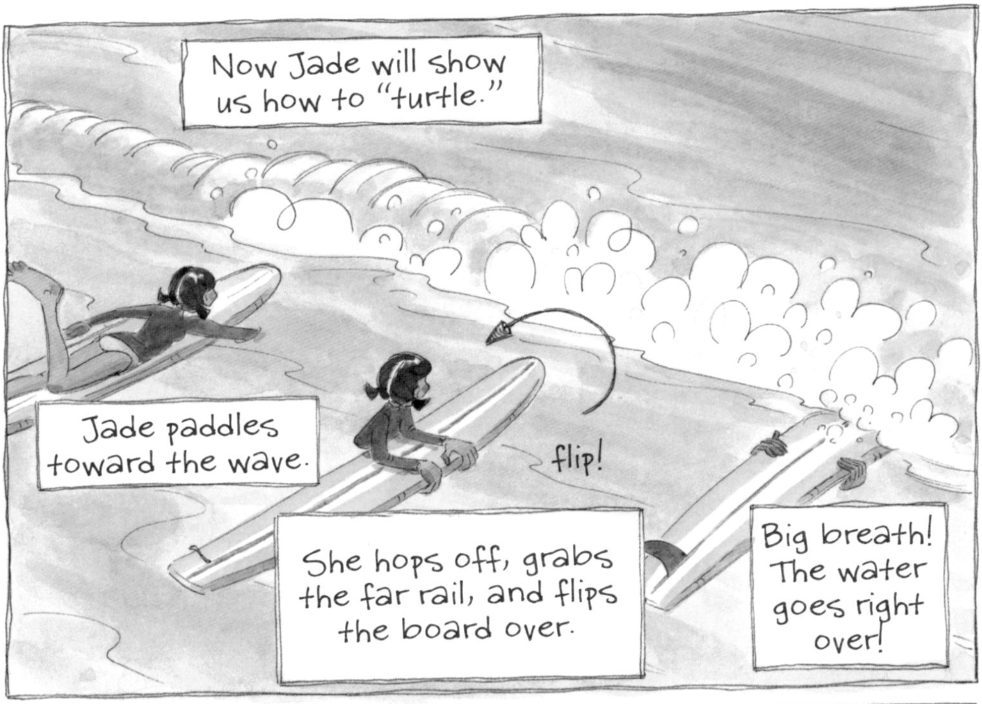
Now Jade will show us how to "turtle."
Jade paddles toward the wave.
flip!
She hops off, grabs the far rail, and flips the board over.
Big breath! The water goes right over!

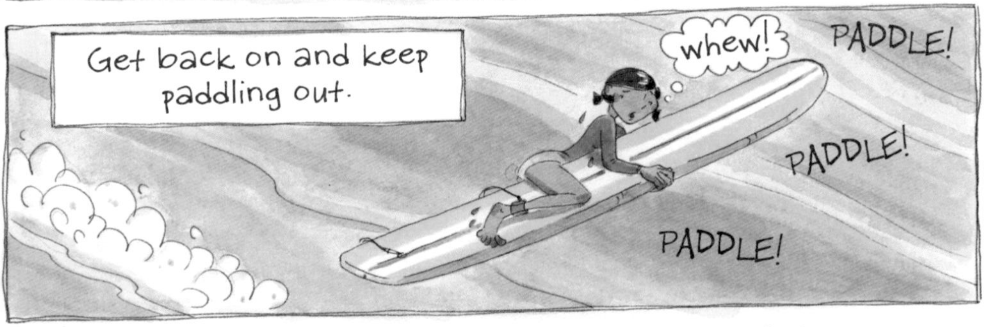
Get back on and keep paddling out.
whew!
PADDLE!
PADDLE!
PADDLE!

You're going to have to do this a bunch of times before you get out. Don't give up!

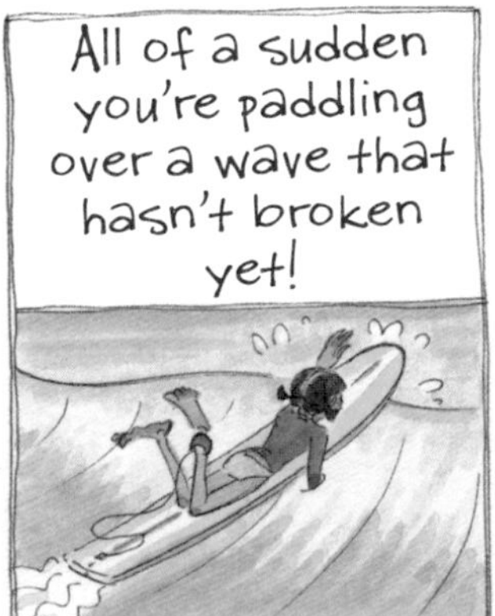
All of a sudden you're paddling over a wave that hasn't broken yet!

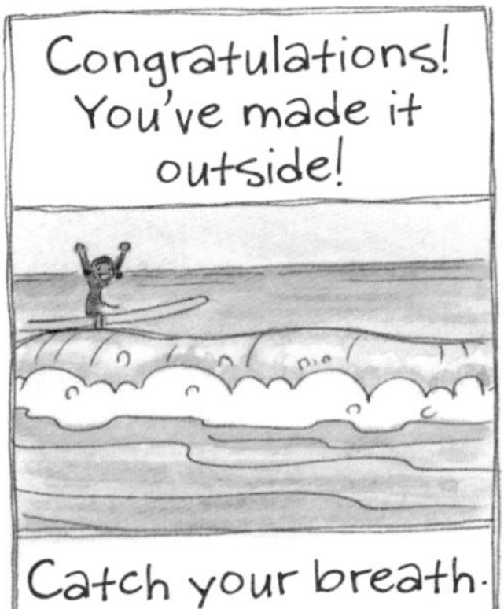
Congratulations! You've made it outside!
Catch your breath.

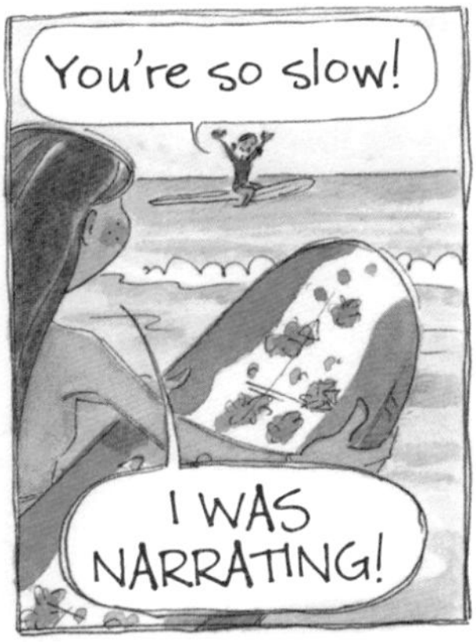
You're so slow!
I WAS NARRATING!

RULES of the ROAD

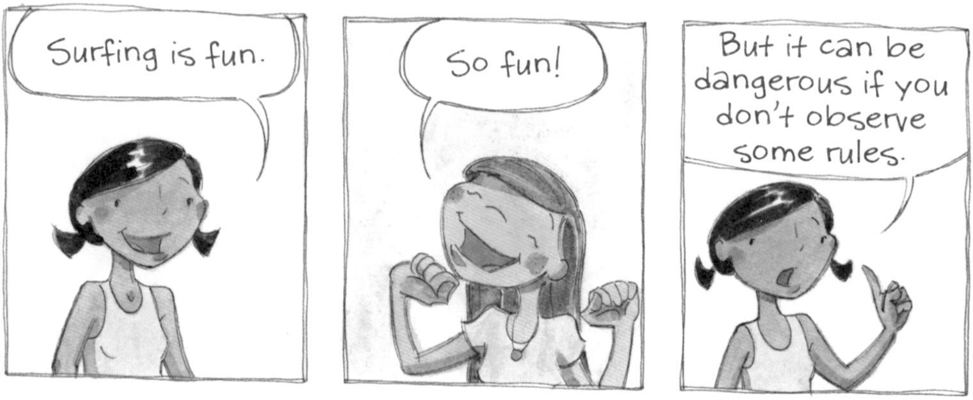
Surfing is fun.
So fun!
But it can be dangerous if you don't observe some rules.

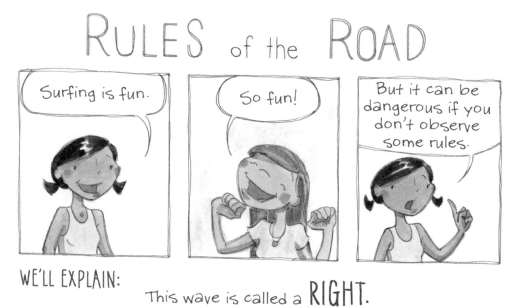

WE'LL EXPLAIN:

This wave is called a **RIGHT**.

If you're OUTSIDE looking at shore, the direction you would ride it is RIGHT. From the sand it is breaking from right to left.

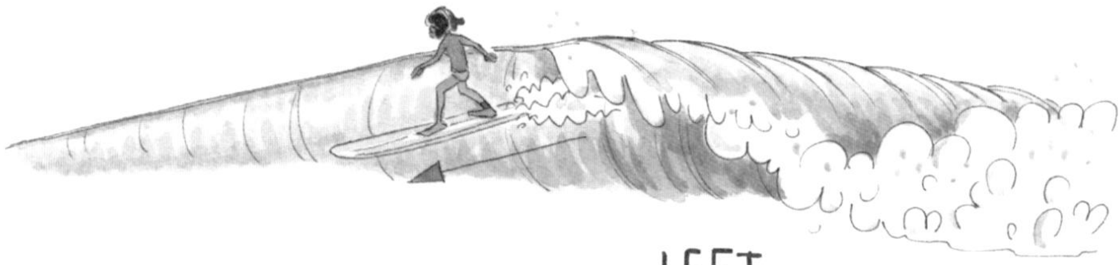

This wave is called a **LEFT**.

As a surfer, you would ride this to the left.

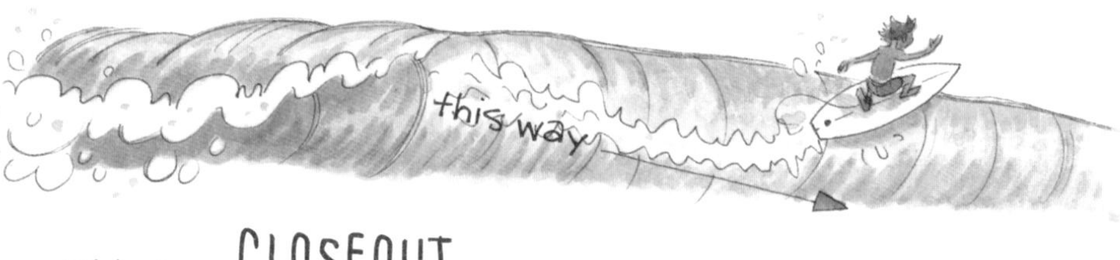
this way

This is a **CLOSEOUT**, nowhere to go. Don't take off!

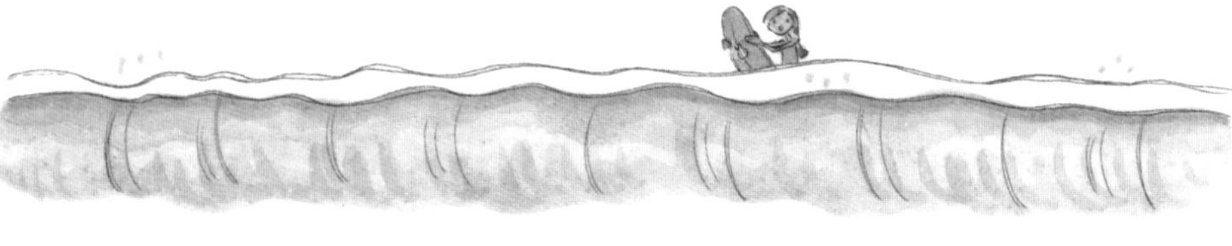

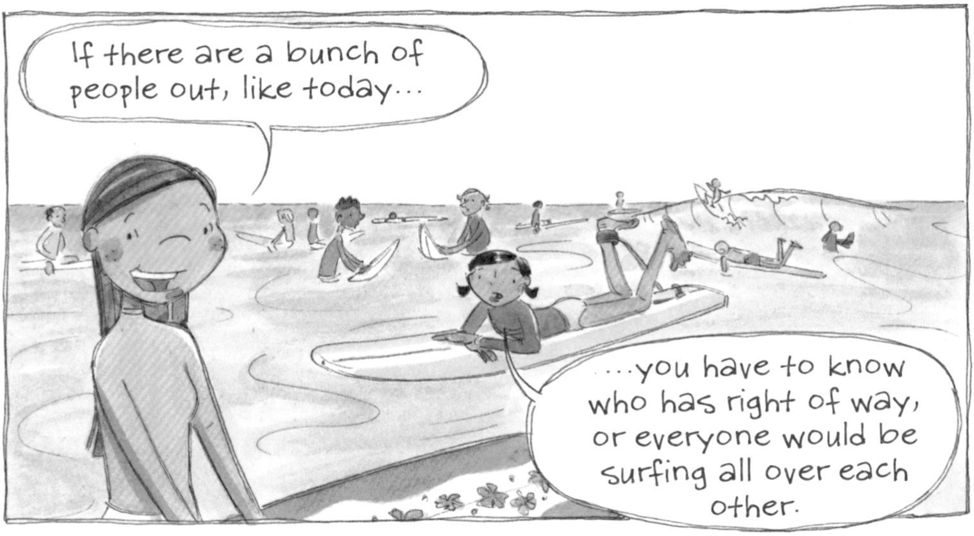
If there are a bunch of people out, like today...
...you have to know who has right of way, or everyone would be surfing all over each other.

You don't want to get run over by a fin - ouch! It's easy - the person who is closest to the curl has the right-of-way.

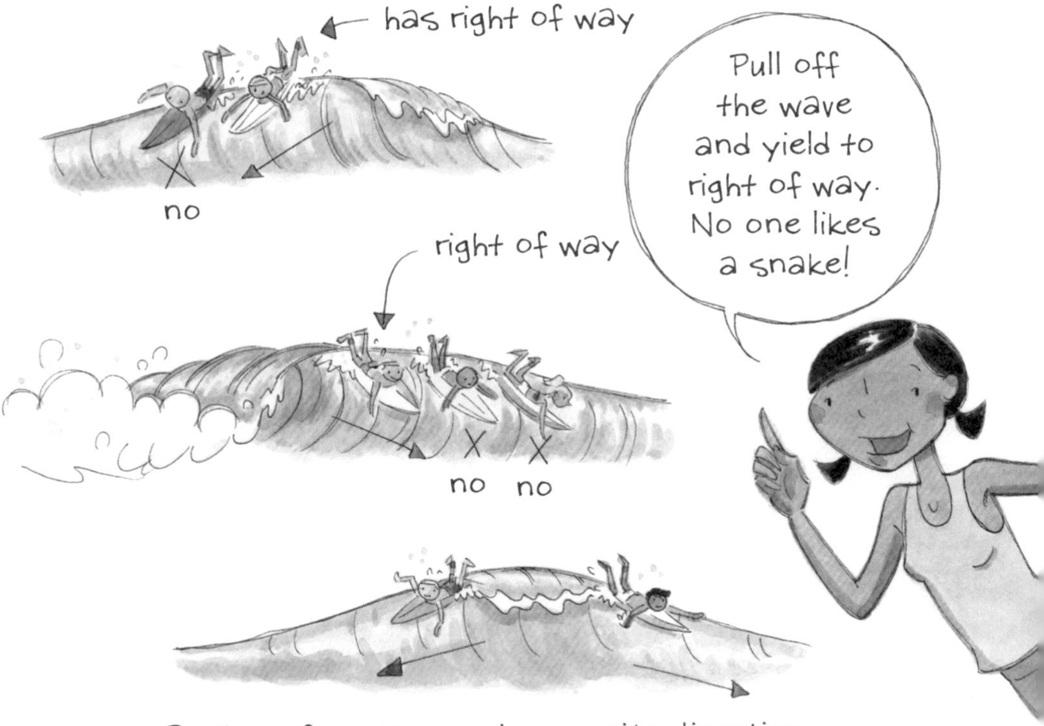
has right of way
no
Pull off the wave and yield to right of way. No one likes a snake!
right of way
no
no

Both surfers can go, in opposite directions.

Paddle, POP! AND AIM FOR THE SHOULDER

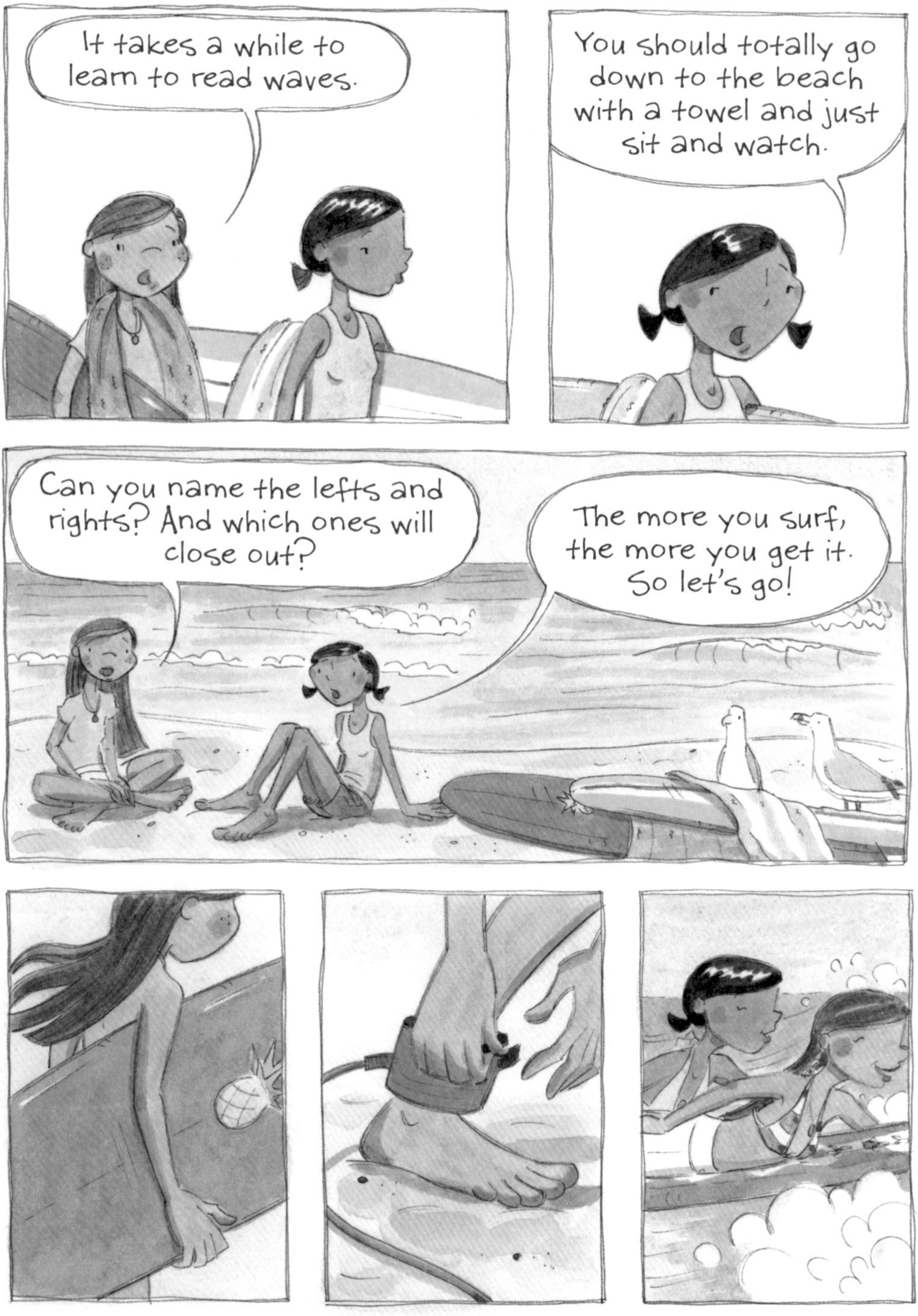
It takes a while to learn to read waves.
You should totally go down to the beach with a towel and just sit and watch.
Can you name the lefts and rights? And which ones will close out?
The more you surf, the more you get it. So let's go!

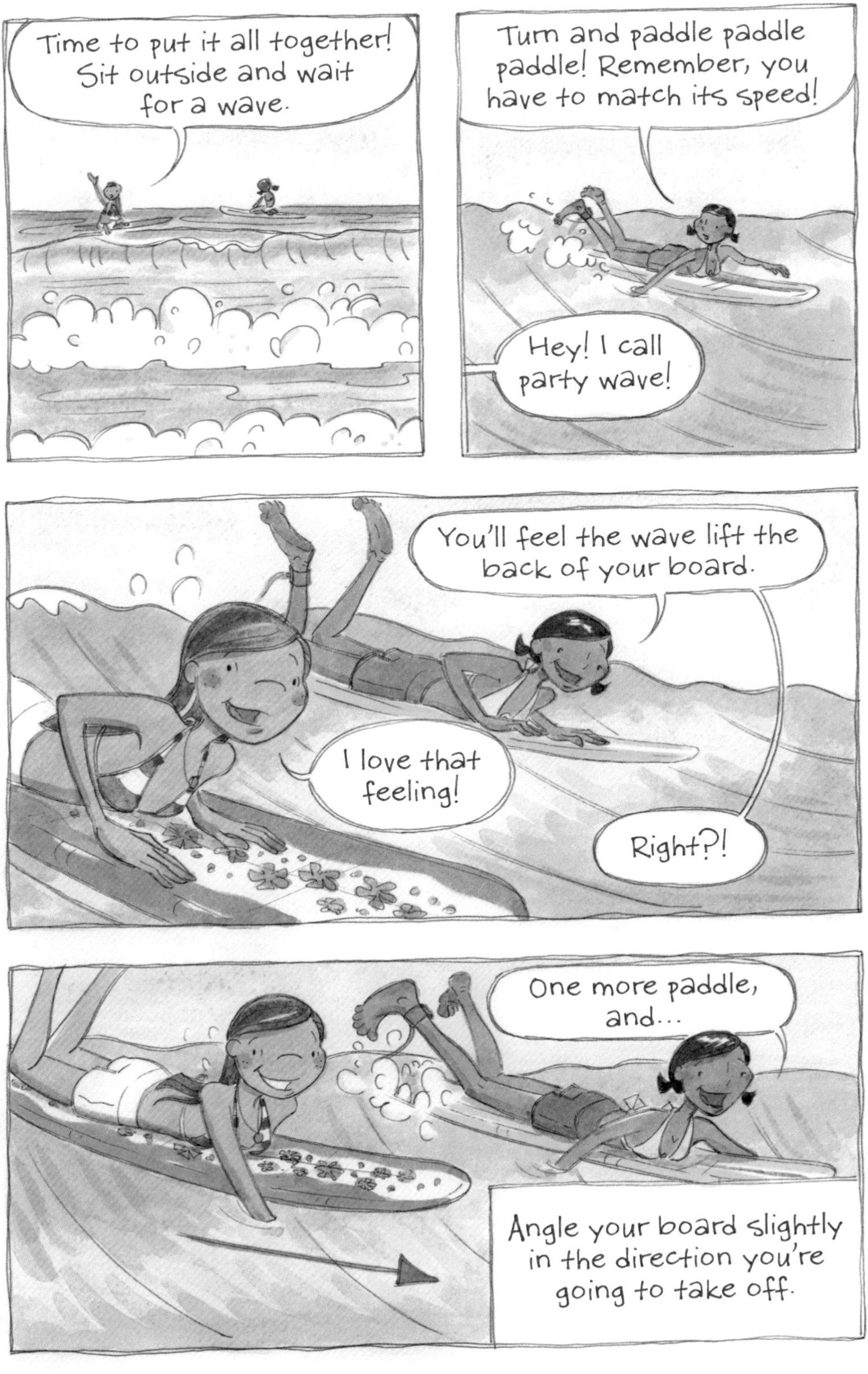
Time to put it all together! Sit outside and wait for a wave.
Turn and paddle paddle paddle! Remember, you have to match its speed!
Hey! I call party wave!
You'll feel the wave lift the back of your board.
I love that feeling!
Right?!
One more paddle, and...
Angle your board slightly in the direction you're going to take off.

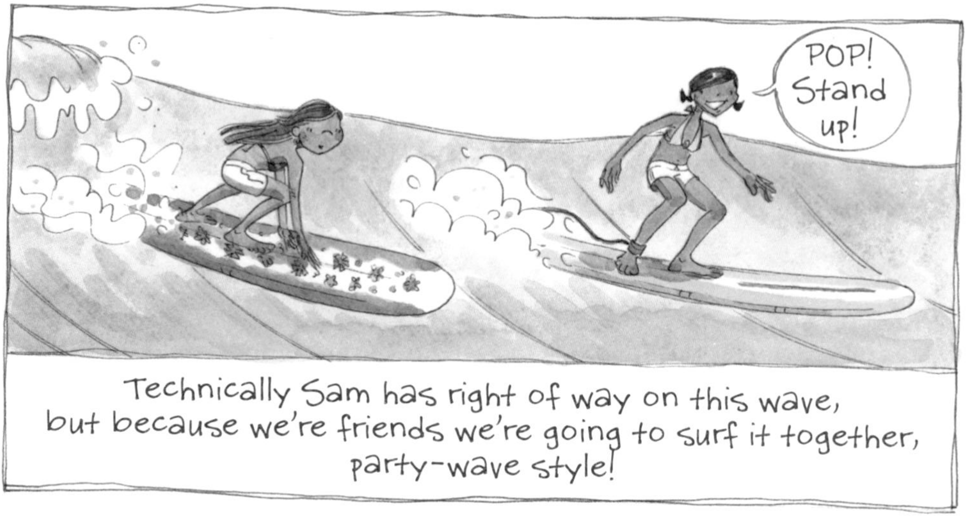
POP! Stand up!
Technically Sam has right of way on this wave, but because we're friends we're going to surf it together, party-wave style!

Just like paddling, you have to stand in the sweet spot.

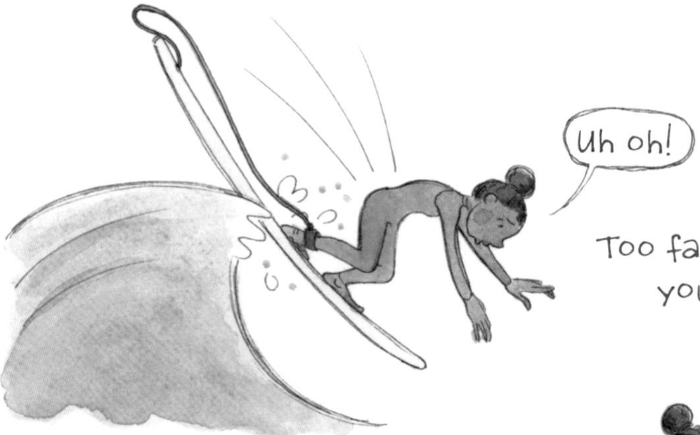
Uh oh!

Too far forward and you'll endo...

...and too far back and the wave won't take you.

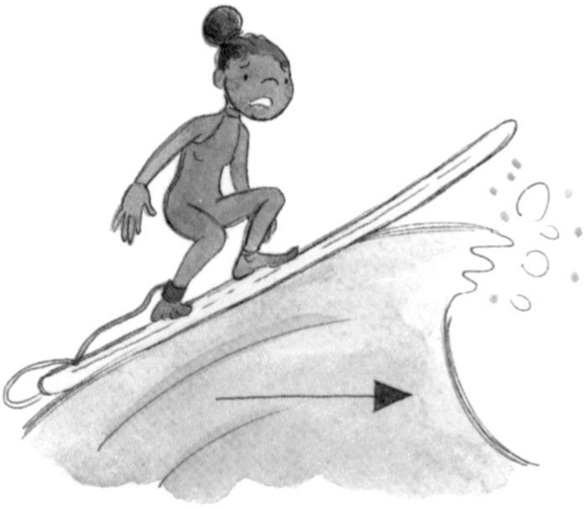

But then you're in the sweet spot and it's like...

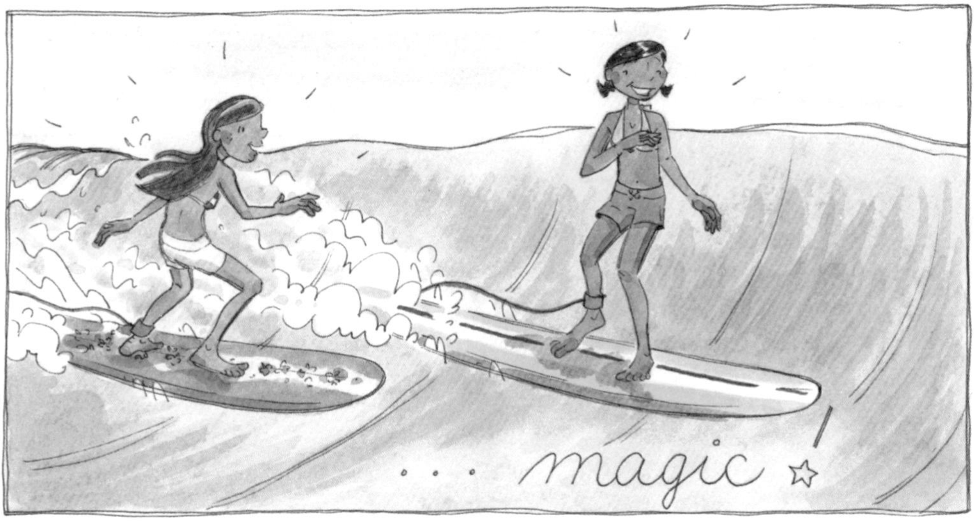
. . . magic ☆!

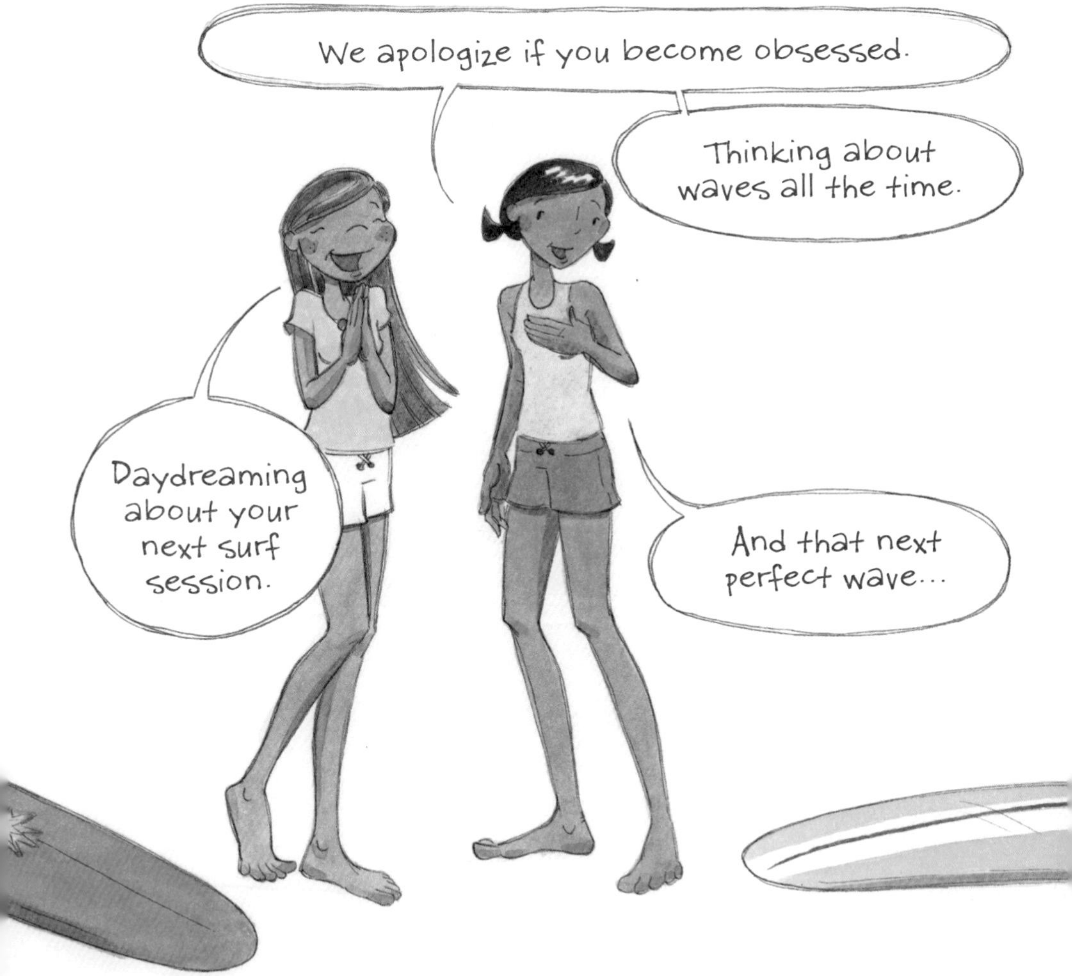
We apologize if you become obsessed.
Thinking about waves all the time.
Daydreaming about your next surf session.
And that next perfect wave...

Chapter 5

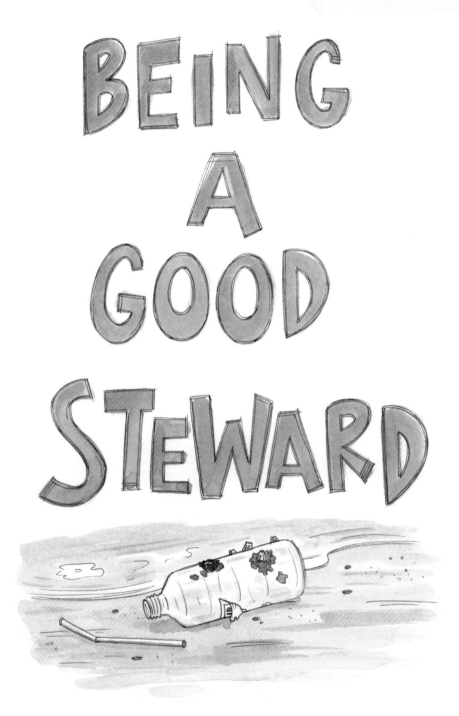

BEING A GOOD STEWARD

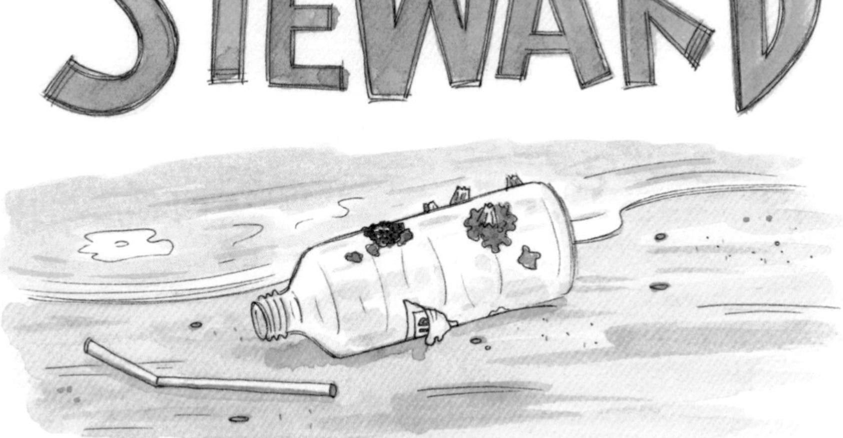

The Ocean is super important to our planet. It does so much for us - what can we do for it? LOTS! Here are some ways you can be a good ocean steward:

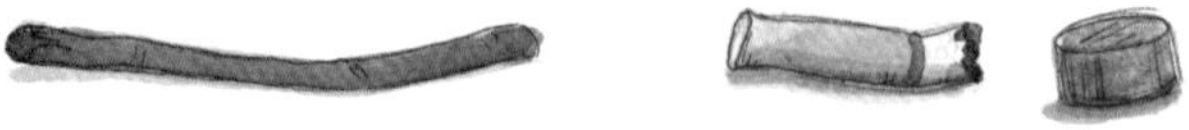

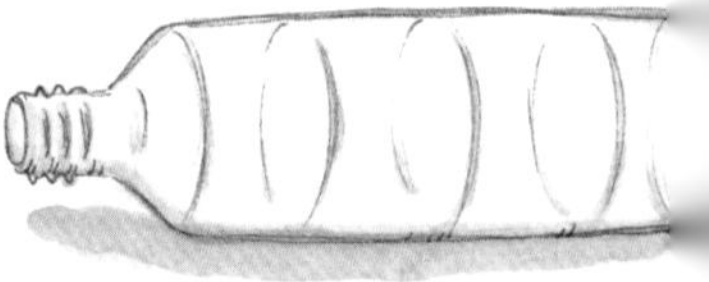

1. BEACH CLEAN-UPS

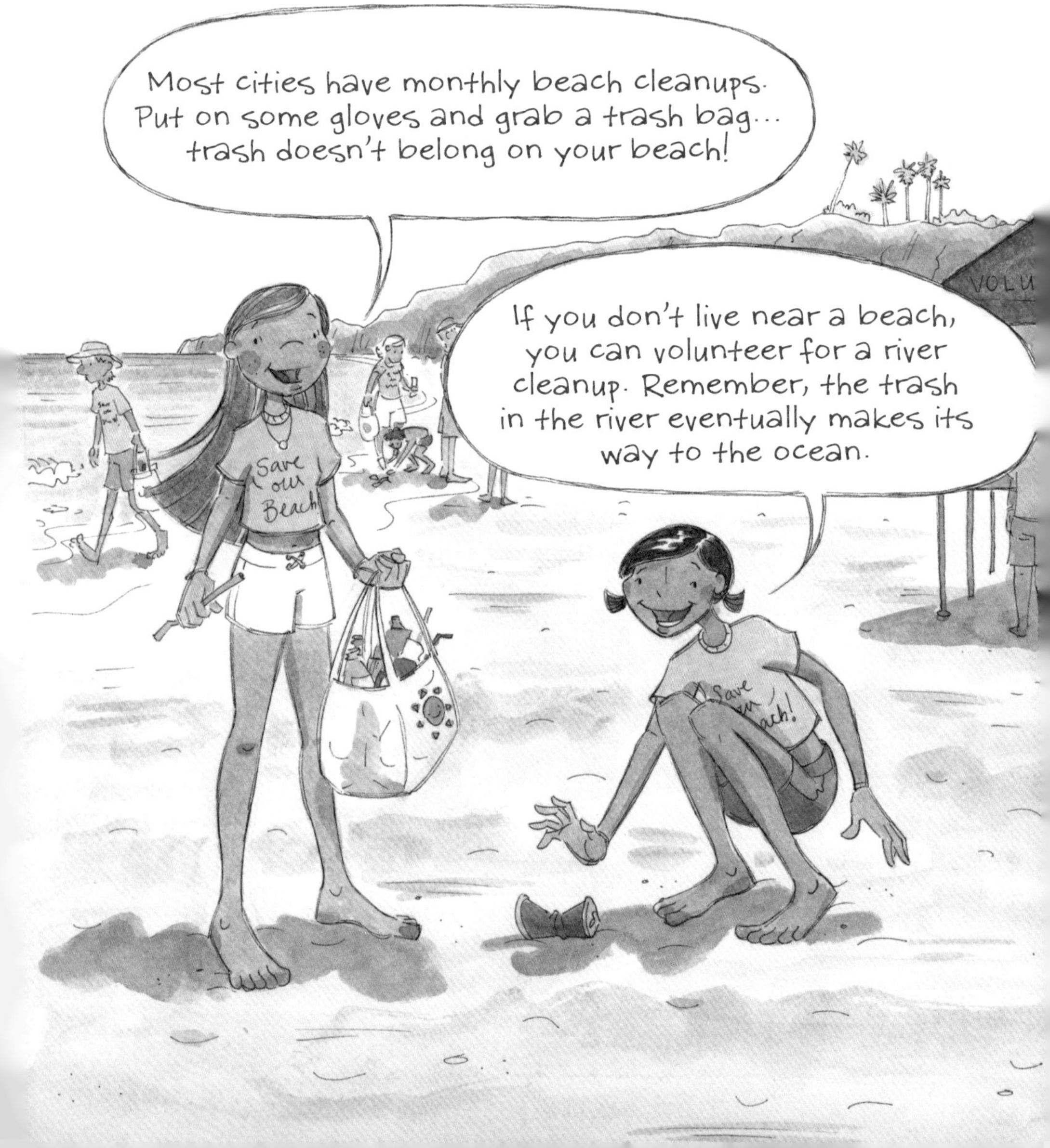
Most cities have monthly beach cleanups. Put on some gloves and grab a trash bag... trash doesn't belong on your beach!
If you don't live near a beach, you can volunteer for a river cleanup. Remember, the trash in the river eventually makes its way to the ocean.
Save our Beach!
VOLU

2. REDUCE, REUSE, AND RECYCLE.

Plastic is an ENORMOUS problem on our planet, and in the ocean in particular.

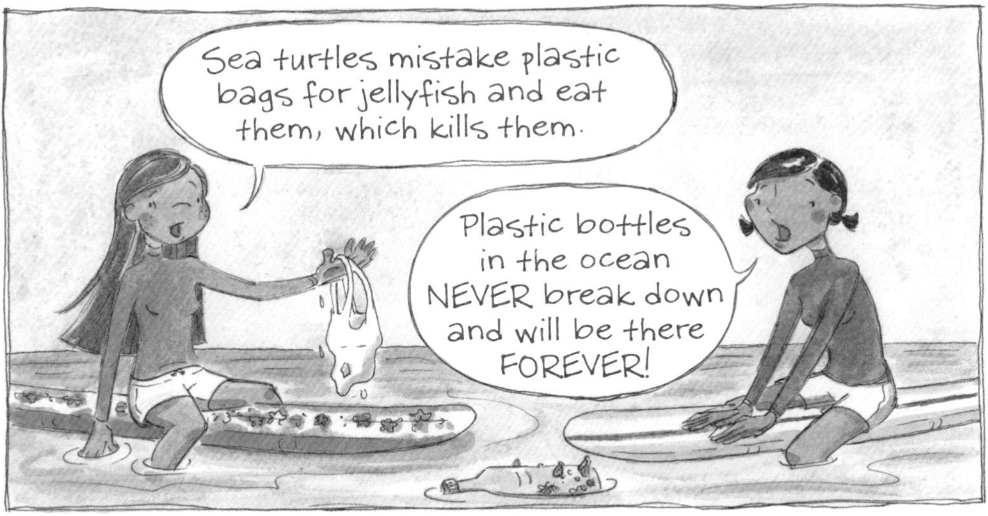
Sea turtles mistake plastic bags for jellyfish and eat them, which kills them.
Plastic bottles in the ocean NEVER break down and will be there FOREVER!

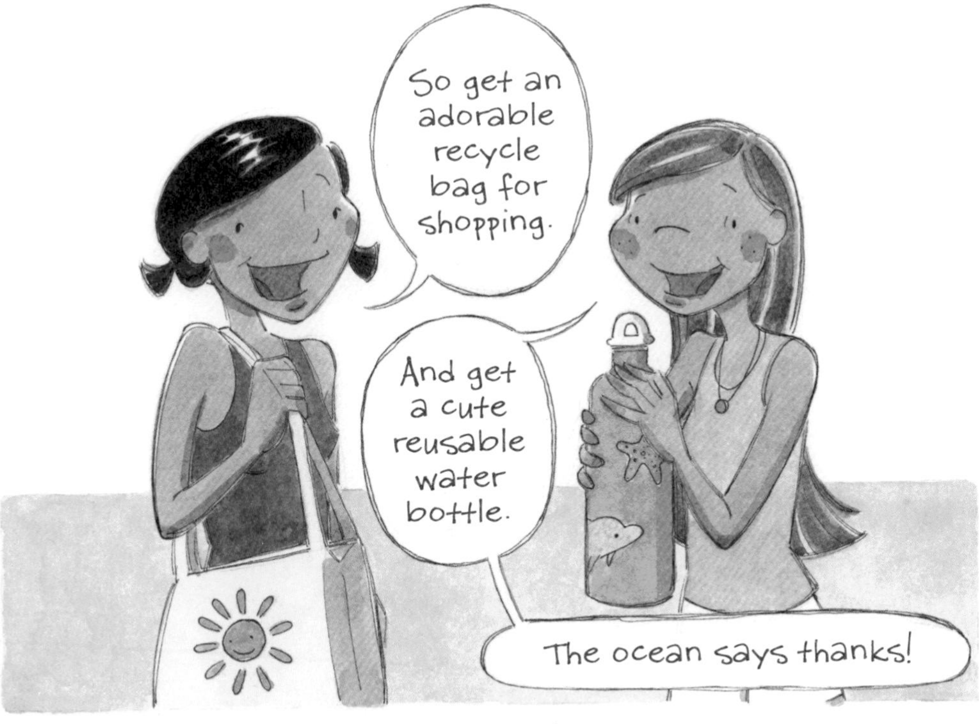
So get an adorable recycle bag for shopping.
And get a cute reusable water bottle.
The ocean says thanks!

3. VOLUNTEER AT A MARINE MAMMAL RESCUE CENTER.

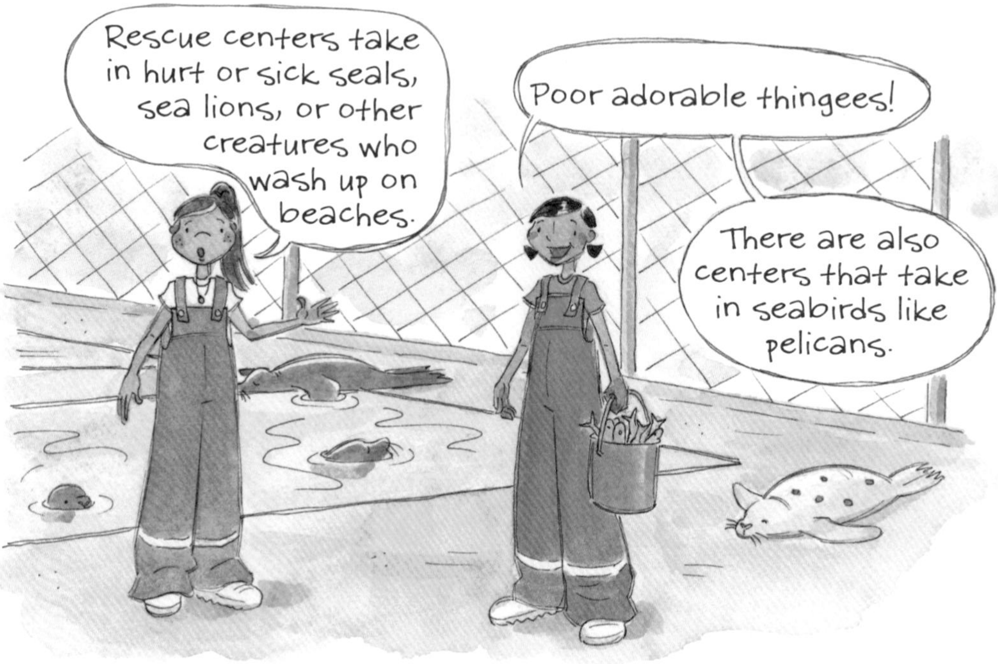
Rescue centers take in hurt or sick seals, sea lions, or other creatures who wash up on beaches.
Poor adorable thingees!
There are also centers that take in seabirds like pelicans.

4. VOLUNTEER AT YOUR LOCAL AQUARIUM.

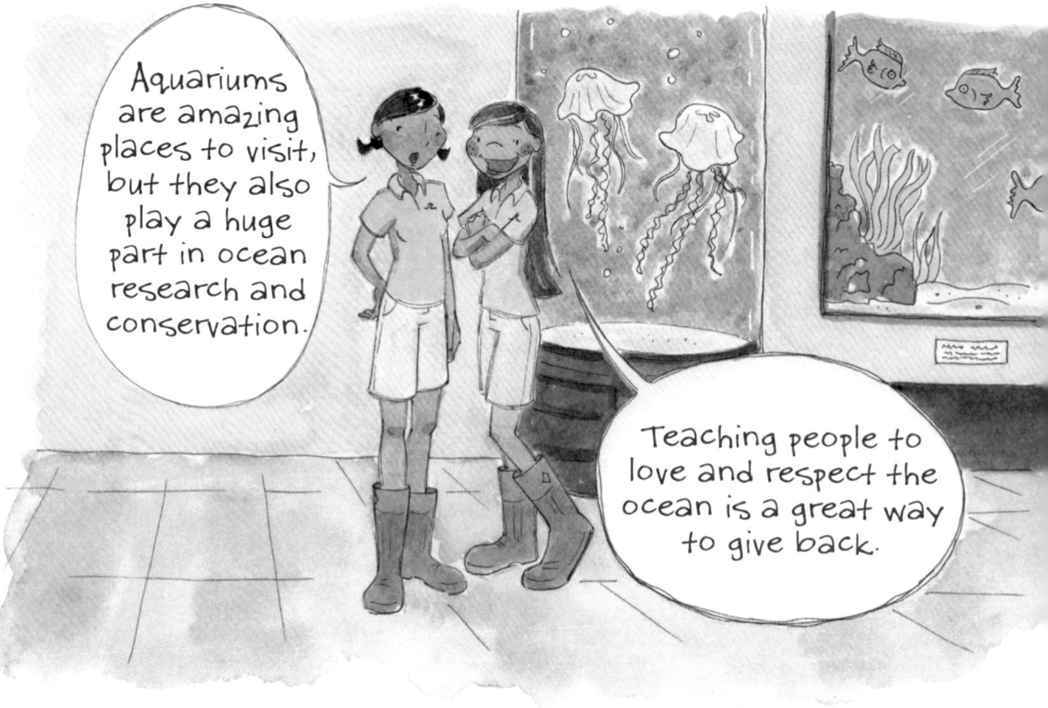
Aquariums are amazing places to visit, but they also play a huge part in ocean research and conservation.
Teaching people to love and respect the ocean is a great way to give back.

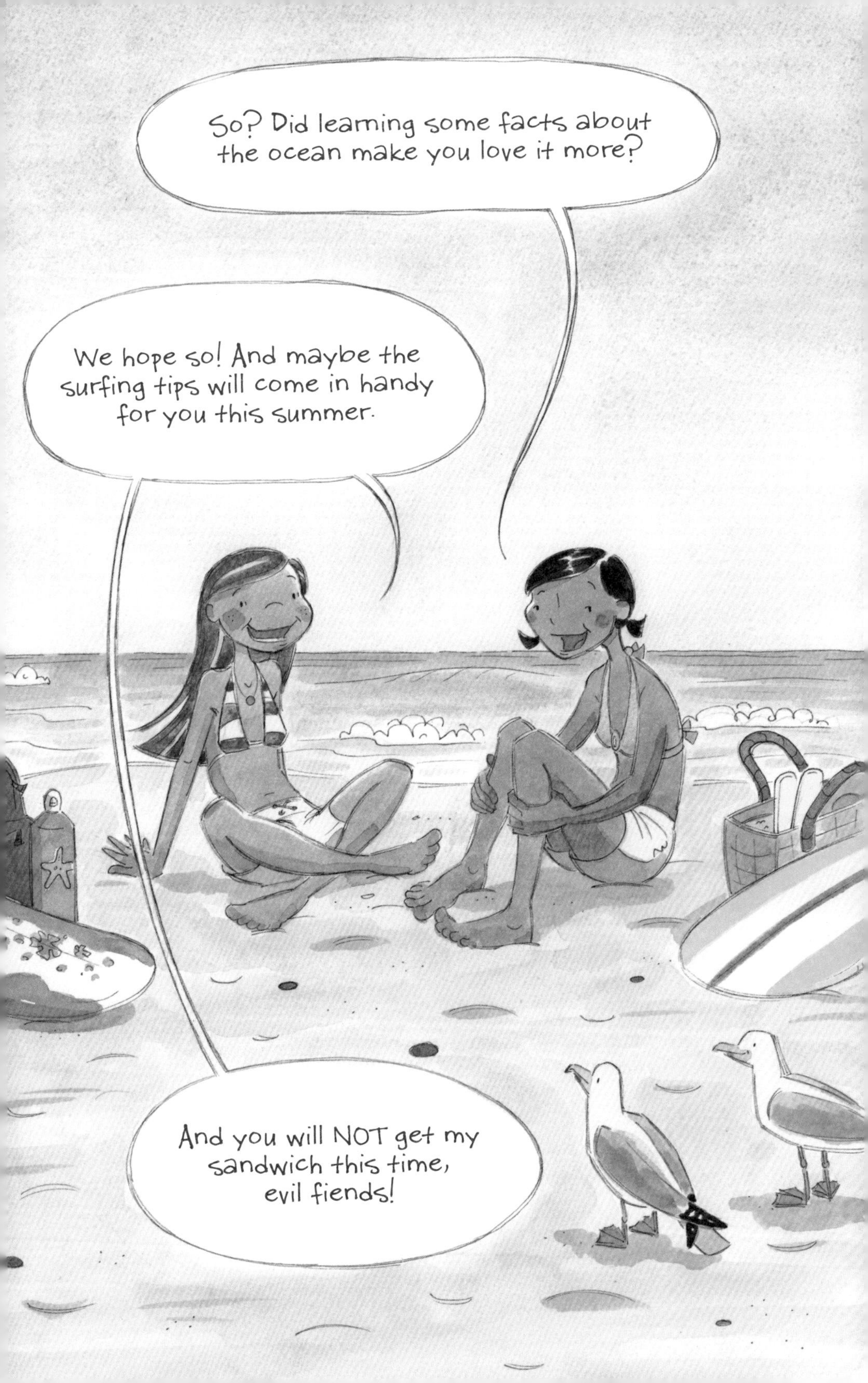
So? Did learning some facts about the ocean make you love it more?
We hope so! And maybe the surfing tips will come in handy for you this summer.
And you will NOT get my sandwich this time, evil fiends!

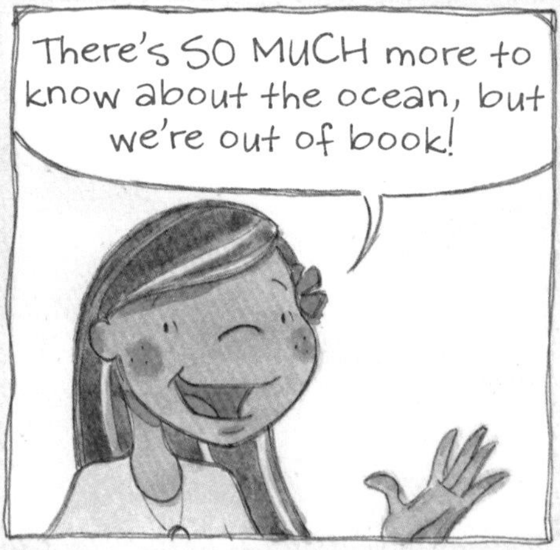
There's SO MUCH more to know about the ocean, but we're out of book!
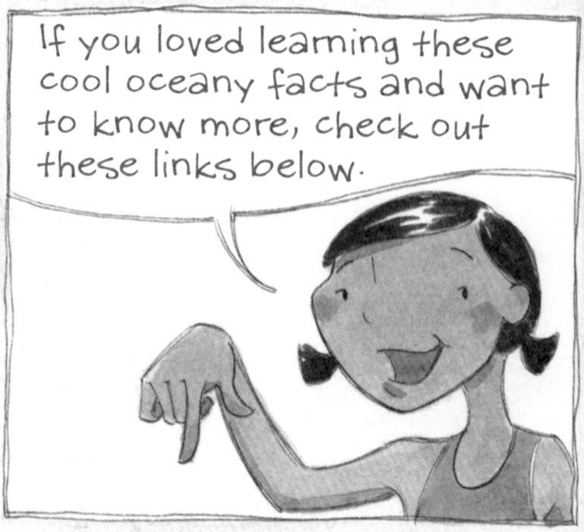
If you loved learning these cool oceany facts and want to know more, check out these links below.

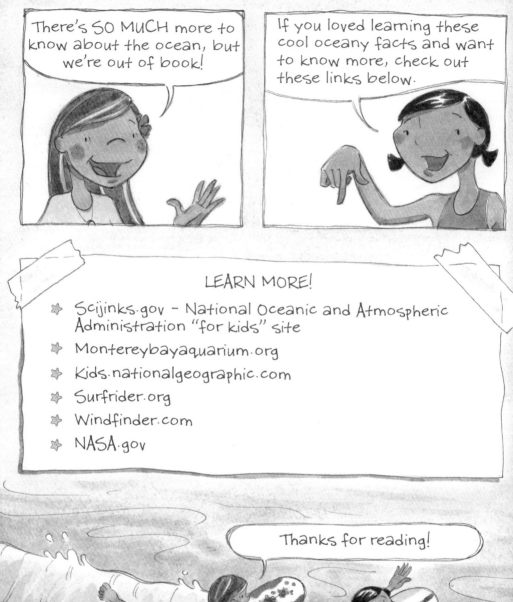

LEARN MORE!

- Scijinks.gov - National Oceanic and Atmospheric Administration "for kids" site
- Montereybayaquarium.org
- Kids.nationalgeographic.com
- Surfrider.org
- Windfinder.com
- NASA.gov

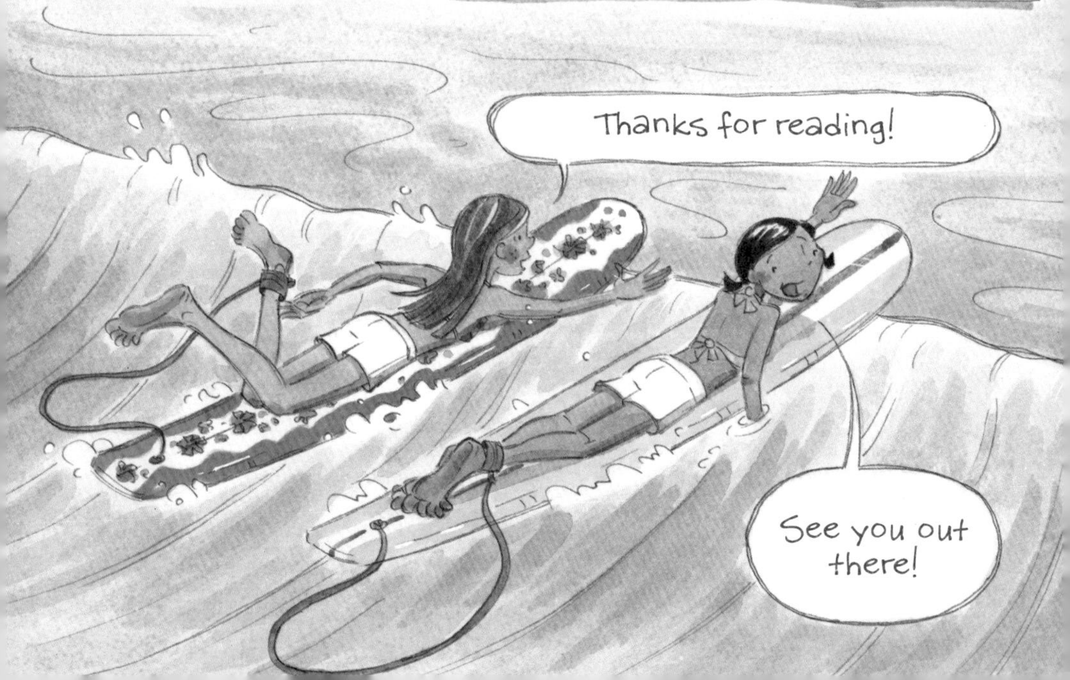
Thanks for reading!
See you out there!